*Eighteenth-Century Travels in
Pennsylvania & New York*

MICHEL-GUILLAUME JEAN DE CRÈVECOEUR

CRÈVECOEUR'S
Eighteenth-Century Travels in Pennsylvania & New York

TRANSLATED & EDITED BY

Percy G. Adams

UNIVERSITY OF KENTUCKY PRESS

Copyright © 1961 by the University of Kentucky Press

Library of Congress Catalog Card No. 61-15625

To My Mother

Preface

THIS TRANSLATION of selections from Jean de Crèvecoeur's *Voyage dans la haute Pensylvanie et dans l'état de New York* will, I hope, supply a need that must have been experienced for a long time by those readers who from Charles Lamb to Ludwig Lewisohn have praised the French-American author of *Letters from an American Farmer* and *Sketches of Eighteenth Century America*. And it should be of great practical help to specialists; for from Moses Coit Tyler to V. L. Parrington to the latest students of eighteenth-century literature, history, and sociology, they have treated Crèvecoeur at length while restricting themselves to his English writings.

The Introduction attempts to bring together all the pertinent facts about Crèvecoeur's *Voyage*. It relies heavily on my five published articles dealing with him as well as on my work with travel literature in general. Yet it and the notes to the text provide much that has heretofore not been published, for example, information about the Indian stories and legends included in the present volume.

A number of specialists in the French language or in the eighteenth century have read parts of the translation and offered suggestions. For their kind help in that respect, I wish to thank Professors J. L. Lievsay and Walter Stiefel, who are my colleagues at the University of Tennessee; Professor Reino Virtanen of the University of Nebraska; William Archer; and, especially, Professor Gilbert Chinard of Princeton, whose books have often rescued and inspired me. Any errors in the translation, however, are entirely my responsibility and not theirs. Percy V. D. Gott of Goshen, New York, very generously took time to clear up one particularly confusing point about Crèvecoeur's geography. Professor Theodore Hornberger, formerly of the Universities of Texas and Minnesota, now at the University of Pennsylvania, first aroused my interest in Crèvecoeur and has long been a friend and adviser to whom I owe much. Because the University of Tennessee Library has afforded invaluable aid by borrowing or buying books that have been necessary for my studies, I thank its staff as well as the staffs of other libraries where I have recently worked for extended periods of time—Duke University, The University of Texas, The Newberry, and the Bibliothèque Nationale. I am grateful also to the administrators of the University of Tennessee Emperor Memorial Fund for the grant which aided in the publication of this volume. And, finally, I thank my wife for smoothing certain sentences, typing certain chapters, and creating the proper atmosphere for scholarly pursuits.

P. G. A.

Knoxville, Tennessee
July, 1961

Contents

Preface	*page* VII
Introduction	XIII
I. *A Trip up the Hudson*	1
II. *Colonel Woodhull of Schunnemunk Valley*	16
III. *A Tour of the Chief Ironworks of New York*	26
IV. *In the Backwoods of Pennsylvania* THE SCHOOLTEACHER FROM CONNECTICUT—A NORTHUMBERLAND COUNTY PIONEER	31
V. *In the Backwoods of Pennsylvania* AT THE HOME OF A POLISH REFUGEE IN LUZERNE COUNTY	35
VI. *Lost on a Bee Hunt in Bedford County*	49
VII. *The Bachelor Farmer of Cherry Valley*	64
VIII. *The Indian Council at Onondaga* THE ARRIVAL	70
IX. *The Indian Council at Onondaga* THE GREAT DEBATE BETWEEN KESKETOMAH AND KOOHASSEN	75

Contents

X. *A Winter among the Mohawks, or, The Story of Cattaw-Wassy*   93

XI. *Niagara in Winter*   97

XII. *Agouehghon, the Coohassa-Onas of Niagara*   101

XIII. *Two Indian Tales*   116

XIV. *Wabemat's Reward, or, Why the First Beaver Was Made*   127

XV. *The Use Made of Salt in America, and, The Mountain Pasture Lands*   146

APPENDIX. *The Content of the Voyage*   159
    A SUMMARY BY CHAPTERS

Index   163

Illustrations

Michel-Guillaume Jean de Crèvecoeur   *frontispiece*

Kesketomah   *facing page* 84

Koohassen   *facing page* 85

The Falls of Niagara   *facing page* 100

Introduction

IN FRENCH, *Eighteenth-Century Travels in Pennsylvania & New York* was called *Le Voyage dans la haute Pensylvanie et dans l'état de New York*. Issued in Paris in 1801, it was the last published work of Michel-Guillaume Jean de Crèvecoeur, whose first book, written in English and later in French, was once the most popular commentary on America, thought of by Europeans as both a guidebook to the New World and a work of art. Although Crèvecoeur was one of those rare personages who write for publication in two languages, he is remembered today only in one, as a chief figure in American literature of the period of the Revolution, the author of *Letters from an American Farmer* and the posthumously published *Sketches of Eighteenth Century America*. This emphasis on the English writings has been accompanied by an astonishing neglect of the three-volume *Voyage*.[1]

The neglect is astonishing because the book is both unique and valuable. As literature it displays a Crèvecoeur more at home while writing in his native French, more sophisticated, more versatile, wandering from realistic analyses of the frontier to dramatic accounts of farmers, from romantic descriptions of Niagara Falls to poetic reproductions of Indian councils and legends. And as history the *Voyage* is in many ways Crèvecoeur's most important, certainly his most pretentious, book: It concentrates on a time later than that treated in the English works; it has a much greater variety of information, one-fourth of it, for example, dealing with the Indian, a subject neglected by the earlier Crèvecoeur; and it attempts—more successfully and more in detail—to analyze motives and trends, in other words, to handle history more in the fashion of the "moderns" of the author's own century—Montesquieu, Hume, Voltaire, and Gibbon. The present translation attempts to adjust the perspective by presenting this new Crèvecoeur, a necessary complement to the well-known American Farmer.

THE AUTHOR OF THE *VOYAGE* AS TRAVELER, FARMER, CONSUL, AND MAN OF LETTERS

Crèvecoeur was born in Caen, Normandy, in 1735.[2] He was educated in a Jesuit school, and after a few months spent with relatives in England, where he learned English and lost a sweetheart by death, he served under Montcalm in Canada as a mapmaker. Dissatisfied with the army and attracted by life in the New World, he asked for a discharge in 1755 and remained behind when his company returned to France. After much wandering in the English colonies, he took out citizen-

[1] Although heretofore unpublished in English it has been put into German as *Reise in Ober-Pensylvanien und im Staate Neu-York . . . mit Anmerkungen begleitet von Dietrich Tiedemann* (Berlin, 1802).

[2] It is not necessary to give many of the details of Crèvecoeur's life, since there are three biographies: Robert de Crèvecoeur, *Saint John de Crèvecoeur, Sa Vie et Ses Ouvrages* (Paris, 1883); Julia Post Mitchell, *St. John de Crèvecoeur* (New York, 1919); and Howard C. Rice, *Le Cultivateur Américain* (Paris, 1933). The problem of Crèvecoeur's name has been quite confusing. On the baptismal record he is called Michel-Jean-Guillaume, but the clerk made a mistake: "Jean," from the patronymic "Saint Jean," should have been in third place. When Crèvecoeur decided to stay in America, he adopted the name of Hector and chose the English form of his last name, Saint John. Genealogists trace the Norman Saint Jeans to a common source with the English Saint Johns, the most illustrious son of whom was Lord Bolingbroke. Crèvecoeur confused the matter even more when he signed his first book "J. Hector St. John"—the "J." for "James"—and when he refused to be consistent in signing his letters, sometimes using "St. Jean," sometimes "St. John," and sometimes "Crèvecoeur" with any combination of other names. See Robert de Crèvecoeur, p. 284, and the letters in the appendix to Miss Mitchell's biography. Note that all three full-length studies of the author, including that by the grandson, employ "Saint John de Crèvecoeur."

Introduction

ship papers in New York in 1765, made a long trip down the Ohio and through the Great Lakes region in 1767, became a farmer in Ulster County, then in Orange County, New York, and in 1769 married Mehitable Tippet, by whom he had three children.

When the Revolution broke out, Crèvecoeur, the successful, peaceful, happy farmer, found himself in an untenable position. His wife's father was Loyalist and his brother-in-law was a De Lancey, one of the best known of New York Loyalist families. But he had friends and neighbors among the opposite faction and, furthermore, felt little personal interest in the events leading up to the war. So he tried to remain neutral. When both sides became suspicious and he could no longer bear the persecution they inflicted on him, he carried out a resolution, made before fighting started, to return to France to settle some family business. There he intended to await the end of the conflict. It was hard to get permission to leave rebel country and go into English-held New York City, and harder still to get permission to sail for England; but after many suspicious letters were exchanged among the rebels on the one hand and among the English on the other, and after he had spent months in an English army prison in New York, he left for Europe in 1780, accompanied by his eight-year-old son, Alexander. In the following year he arranged with Thomas and Lockyer Davis in London for the publication of his *Letters from an American Farmer*, a collection of twelve English essays written, with one exception, before the Revolution began. By the end of 1781 he was in France.

His book, not only because of its literary charm and optimistic picture of America but also because of its very timely publication, made Crèvecoeur immediately famous, both in the British Isles and on the European continent. Editions appeared in Ireland, Holland, and Germany, and a second edition in London. The author's sudden rise to fame brought him influential friends, among them Madame d'Houdetot, the poet Saint-Lambert, and the naturalist Buffon, and an appointment as Consul to New York, Connecticut, and New

Jersey. Before leaving for his new post, in November of 1783, Crèvecoeur spent many months translating, revising, and adding to the original twelve Letters, and a few months after his departure the two-volume *Lettres d'un cultivateur américain* was published in Paris.

In America again, the now famous author and political figure found his home burned, his wife dead, and his daughter and second son in the home of strangers in Boston. He gathered his family about him and set up his headquarters in New York City, where he busied himself in organizing and developing the packet service between France and America. He also continued his interest in botany and began publishing articles on agriculture and medicine. In June of 1785 he went to France on furlough, remaining there for two years while he prepared his second edition of the *Lettres*, which came out in 1787 in three volumes. Three more years as Consul, until July of 1790, and Crèvecoeur left America once more, this time for good. In 1801 appeared his last literary effort, the three-volume *Le Voyage dans la haute Pensylvanie et dans l'état de New York*. Twelve years of comparative obscurity preceded his death in 1813.

Although his last book was never popular and, in fact, was almost unknown, *Letters from an American Farmer* made Crèvecoeur's reputation in the last two decades of the eighteenth century, when he was read and reviewed, attacked or admired throughout Europe.[3] After his death that reputation was forgotten and he was ignored for almost a century. In 1904 an edition of the *Letters* was prepared, and in 1912 the same book was brought out by the Everyman Library with an introduction by Warren Barton Blake. These two editions helped to renew an interest in the author which was further stimulated in 1919 by Julia Post Mitchell's biography. Then, in 1923, in an attic in France a group of essays was discovered which Crèvecoeur

---

[3] According to Bernard Fay, *L'Esprit révolutionnaire en France et aux Etats-Unis à la fin du XVIIIᵉ siècle* (Paris, 1925), p. 177, during the last twenty years of the century "les *Lettres d'un Cultivateur américain* donnaient le ton." This fact is noted by others before Fay; see, for example, Charles H. Sherrill, *French Memories of Eighteenth Century America* (New York, 1915), p. 242.

Introduction

had written in English but had not published, although some of them were translated for the *Lettres* of 1784 and 1787. The publication in 1925 of these newly discovered *Sketches of Eighteenth Century America, or More Letters from an American Farmer*,[4] inspired further studies of Crèvecoeur, the best and most thorough of which is Howard C. Rice's *Le Cultivateur Américain*, a biographical and critical work finished in 1933.

But all this flurry of scholarly and critical activity almost completely ignores Crèvecoeur's most pretentious book. The full-length treatments of the author devote little space to the *Voyage*,[5] and other works do no more than refer to it. The few opinions expressed about its merits vary from high praise on the part of Mitchell, to coolness on the part of Rice, to almost complete dismissal by Blake. Mitchell says that Crèvecoeur's last book is "a better piece of workmanship . . . than the *Letters* in either their French or their English dress;"[6] Rice calls it a "livre à tiroirs," believes that "le livre lui-même n'est pas très réussi," and concludes that Crèvecoeur "semble avoir perdu le talent d'écrire simplement et directement;"[7] and Blake says that "This *Voyage* is a work of slight worth."[8] In spite of certain faults, however, it is not a "work of slight worth." In fact, it contains so many good chapters that one is inclined to blame its failure not so much on any lack of merit as on the fact that it was a book about America published in France at a time when relations between the two countries were strained to the breaking point.

[4] Ed. Gabriel, Bourdin, and Williams (New Haven, 1925). Besides the essays published in that book, four others, edited by the same men, were printed in various periodicals. See the bibliography in *The Literary History of the United States*, ed. Spiller et al (New York, 1948), pp. 461-62, and Rice, pp. 231-54.
[5] Rice did use material from the *Voyage* in a chapter on Crèvecoeur's analysis of the Indian; but the passage he chose (see Rice, p. 129, and the present volume, p. 73) as evidence that Crèvecoeur's matured opinion of the red man was anything but romantic had been quoted before him for the same reason by H. N. Fairchild, *The Noble Savage, A Study in Romantic Naturalism* (New York, 1928), p. 102. The feelings expressed in that passage, however, are often in sharp contrast to those found in Chapters IX, XII, and XIII of the present volume.
[6] P. 294.   [7] P. 103.
[8] *Letters from an American Farmer* (London, 1926), p. 240n.

THE *VOYAGE* AS TRAVEL BOOK

Before the appearance of Crèvecoeur's *Voyage* many Europeans visited America and reported what they saw, what they thought they saw, or what they thought their readers would believe they saw. Prior to the War of Independence, a typical travel book on America described the country along the larger rivers—the St. Lawrence, the Mississippi, the Missouri, the Ohio—and included information, both false and true, on the Indian tribes and on plants and animals. Such were the books by Josselyn, Lahontan, Lawson, and Charlevoix. The last two decades of the eighteenth century produced a new type of travel writer. Though there were still books which dealt only with geography, Indians, and natural history—notably those by Carver, Bartram, and Imlay—the new school was chiefly interested in the more populous eastern settlements; for in the East was the cradle of liberty, and there were the homes of Washington and Jefferson and Franklin. So the representative traveler of the 1780's and 1790's visited Boston and Philadelphia and New York. He wrote of travel conditions, buildings, commerce, government, and of dinners and prominent political figures. To the newer class of writers belonged such men as Chastellux and Brissot de Warville.

When Crèvecoeur prepared his last book for the press, he had both types of travel literature as models. Moreover, there were his own volumes—English and French—of *Letters from an American Farmer,* the great success of which must have helped to determine the form and content of his last publication. Finally, after returning to visit and later to live in France, he came in contact with the incoming tide of European Romanticism, notably the school of landscape poets, of sentimentality, of the Noble Savage. Each of the four literary groups exerted a great influence on the *Voyage,* especially since its nature was that of a fictitious rather than an authentic travel book.

Introduction

Its three volumes total over twelve hundred pages, about three hundred of which are filled with notes. Crèvecoeur, perhaps hoping to avoid trouble with the censors because of his idealization of American democracy, claimed that the book was a translation of English manuscripts found in Copenhagen after a shipwreck. This ancient literary device, so popular in the eighteenth century, enabled the author to pretend that he was only the editor. It also added a touch of mystery and realism, for the "editor" sometimes "lost" a few pages of manuscript or found it impossible to read certain water-soaked sheets. Crèvecoeur may have hoped his expedient would have another value, that of explaining the book's lack of organization.

In a posthumously published manuscript, Crèvecoeur said with regard to his writing, "I can not submit to any method. Method appears to me like the symmetry and regularity of a house. Its external appearance is often sacrificed to the internal convenience."[9] And there is, indeed, little method in any of his books. He apparently did not, or could not, follow any prearranged plan. The nature of his early writings provided an excuse for a lack of continuity of subject matter, since they were groups of essays that were only occasionally connected by either time or place. And even in the *Voyage*, the travel framework of which offered an opportunity for a neat, though mythical, arrangement, the author made few attempts either to observe chronology or preserve his anonymity. It is apparent that he tired of his game of the water-soaked manuscripts and, after the first volume, threw his materials together with a diminishing consideration for logical sequence.

As a result, the author would have been truer to the facts and in keeping with the contemporaneous use of long titles if he had called his *Voyage* "An Account of Several Excursions in the States of Pennsylvania, New York, New Jersey, Delaware, Virginia, and Connecticut, Which Includes a Number of Topics of General Interest and Much Information on the Geography, History, Aborigines, and Flora and Fauna of

[9] *Sketches*, p. 126.

North America." The excursions are not connected by a continuous narrative and not a single opening chapter in any of the three volumes is concerned with the supposed trip. One opening chapter is an analysis of the character of the red man; another is an Indian legend; and the third is a long biography of a European monk, a digression which, though well told, has little to do with America.

The time of the "voyage" is given as about 1790, all of it taking place within two years of that date, when Crèvecoeur was actually in France. The first-person narrator is apparently an American; he is accompanied on his travels by a young German named Herman, who, because of his naïveté and his ignorance of the New World, is a foil to the informed older man. Herman is a good confidant; he listens and asks questions and is amazed at the information given by his companion and by the many people they visit.

In the third chapter of Volume One the travelers decide to attend two Indian councils at Onondaga and Fort Stanwix. They set out sometime in 1789 from Shippenburg, Pennsylvania, a town Crèvecoeur had known well[10] during his early, real wanderings in America. Carlisle, twenty-one miles away, is reached the first day, and the junction of the Juniata and the Susquehanna the second day. Another forty-eight hours bring them to Northumberland. From there to Philippopolis in Luzerne County is a tortuous journey through dense woods and across creeks and rivers. Beyond Philippopolis the two men enter New York and traverse the districts of Tioga, Otsego, Harper's Fields, Cherry Valley, and Schoharie to arrive at Albany. The remainder of the journey is made by water, up the Mohawk River.

Along the route from Shippenburg to Fort Stanwix, the companions often have to spend the night in the open air; but just as often they come upon clearings and newly erected log cabins where they always receive hospitality. Sometimes

[10] "I knew this village in its infancy; I saw the neighboring forests become fertile fields, and the swamps, beautiful prairies. Never have my thoughts returned to this place without arousing in me the most vivid memories." [From a note in the *Voyage*, I, 363-64.]

Introduction

they spend the night at a town. More than once the reader loses track of the place and time, for Crèvecoeur was not careful about either.

For the return trip the companions, with the aid of Governor Clinton, procure Indian guides and go by land back to Lake Otsego. At this point the narrative of the trip is discontinued and we jump to New York City and a time one year later. During the year Herman has spent six months in New England. The friends determine to make another excursion, shorter and easier than the one to Onondaga, and sail up the Hudson to visit several of Crèvecoeur's former friends and to inspect the important ironworks of the state. The volume closes with these visits.

The travels in Volume Two begin in the Juniata Valley in Pennsylvania, where the travelers are resting from a trip to the west of the mountains. From here the men start for Niagara Falls. The details of the tour from Shippenburg to Schenectady being omitted, they go up the Mohawk again, this time to Whitestown, across Lake Oneida in an Indian canoe, and down the river of the same name to Oswego on Lake Ontario, where they take a boat to Fort Niagara. The remainder of the account of this particular trip is devoted to the Falls and the people and country nearby. Then comes a break similar to the one two-thirds of the way through the first volume, and at least one of the travelers is in the bath country of Virginia. The final chapters of the volume report Herman's trip to New Haven and Hartford.

The third volume finds the friends in Wilmington, Delaware, from whence they go to Clermont, to Albany, to Schenectady, up the much-traveled Mohawk to the mouth of the Oriskany, and then across a number of new districts to Tully "County" and a long visit with the Surveyor-General of New York. Finally we accompany them to a mansion on the Passaic River in New Jersey, after which Herman sails for Europe. In the last two volumes, especially, Crèvecoeur made little attempt to keep his travelers going. They act rather as collectors of essays and recorders of long stories that sometimes have little or no relation to each other or to a "voyage." More than once the "editor" is forced to begin a chapter with a note such as this: "The date, as well as several of the first pages of this chapter, were found to be entirely illegible." (II, 275)

The rather arbitrary organization of the *Voyage* relates it to Gilbert Imlay's *Description of the Western Territory of North America*,[11] which had been very popular in England during the nine years after its publication in 1792. The *Description* had not pretended to be a travel book, and the title page lists a number of famous Americans of the day who submitted essays to the author-editor for inclusion in his book. Crèvecoeur apparently wanted to do for France what his predecessor had done for the English-speaking nations. But he was more ambitious. Not only did he include data on all the sections of North America treated by Imlay, but he provided much information on the eastern states, in particular, Pennsylvania, New York, and Connecticut, an area the Englishman had slighted. In fact, he was careful always in the *Voyage* to keep his two fictitious travelers in the East, where he had lived so long and where he knew himself to be on safe ground. Details on other sections of the country—the South and the West—were presented as having been told to Herman and his friend. In his last book, then, the American Farmer was hoping to employ the method so successfully handled by Imlay, to provide a more nearly comprehensive compendium, and, at the same time, to create a more entertaining book by combining Imlay's method with that of the travel literature of the time. But while the *Voyage* is not a record of one extended

[11] The full title of Imlay's book shows the similarity between it and the *Voyage*: *A Topographical Description of the Western Territory of North America: Containing a succinct Account of its Soil, Climate, Natural History, Population, Agriculture, Manners, and Customs, With an Ample Description of the Several Divisions into which that Country is partitioned, and an Accurate Statement of the Various Indian Tribes* (London, 1792). Imlay was the lover of Mary Wollstonecraft—later Godwin. O. F. Emerson, "Notes on Gilbert Imlay, Early American Writer," *PMLA* (June, 1924), pp. 406-39, quotes from Mary Wollstonecraft's *Letters from Sweden, Norway and Denmark* (London, 1796) to show that she was a friend of Crèvecoeur and that Imlay and the American Farmer were acquaintances. Emerson believed that Imlay's *Description* owed much to the earlier *Letters from an American Farmer*.

trip, Crèvecoeur's very real knowledge of America makes it invaluable as history; and his eye for detail, drama, and color causes many parts of it to rank among his best pieces of literature.

THE *VOYAGE* AS HISTORY

Since his revival in 1904 Crèvecoeur has been of great importance to students of American history, for his oft-quoted melting pot theory as found in the essay "What is an American?"; for his pictures of colonial life—farming, religion, recreation, and politics; and for his analyses of the philosophy of the eighteenth-century frontiersman.[12] A reviewer of *Sketches*, writing in 1927, claimed that one of Crèvecoeur's essays, "Thoughts of an American Farmer on Various Rural Subjects," gave "a more adequate idea of the way of life of an eighteenth-century colonist—the daily life—than any other single book it has been my lot to read."[13] V. L. Parrington had great praise for Crèvecoeur the historian; and Michael Kraus, in *A History of American History*,[14] said that William Byrd "was not so careful a student of the frontiersman as was . . . de Crèvecoeur, author of *Letters from an American Farmer*." But those who give Crèvecoeur such a high rating never refer to his last book, though it may be his most valuable contribution to history.

The selections in *Letters*, with one exception, were written before the Revolution and attempted to give an account of the life of the Colonial farmer; *Sketches* tells of the farmer too, but most of its essays and stories are of the war itself, the struggle between Loyalist and Revolutionist; and the *Voyage*

[12] There are many treatments of Crèvecoeur as historian, one of the best being that by Rice in his critical biography. To supplement Mr. Rice's essay and the present very brief discussion, see my article "The Historical Value of Crèvecoeur's *Voyage dans la haute Pensylvanie et dans New York*," *American Literature*, XXV, No. 2 (May, 1953), 150-68.
[13] J. B. Moore, "Rehabilitation of Crèvecoeur," *Sewanee Review*, XXV (April, 1927), 216.
[14] (New York, 1937), p. 77. V. L. Parrington had used almost the same words (see note 15).

pictures a still later phase of American history, the first decade of independence. By that time the frontier had moved to the Great Lakes and the Susquehanna; the farmers of the seaboard area had recovered from the war and were thriving; industry was being built up; and the citizens of a new nation were talking about politics, westward expansion, and a bright future. The new frontier, its problems and hopes, is dramatically presented in the present volume in the stories of visits with recently arrived settlers in the backwoods of Pennsylvania and New York: a schoolteacher from New Haven, Mr. Nadowisky from Poland, and a young bachelor from Jamaica. The prosperous farmers of the coastal area are represented by Colonel Woodhull, Crèvecoeur's old neighbor near Goshen, a busy man of many practical talents, a breeder of fine trotting horses, and master of broad acres in Schunnemunk Valley. Much of the information about manufacturing and trade found in the three-volume French work is not so valuable today because it is in other books of the time, but the more interesting and important chapters on those subjects are represented here by the account of a visit to the principal ironworks of New York state. In his last book Crèvecoeur recorded many imaginary discussions of politics, citizenship, and the promising future of the United States, one of the best of which is that found in a conversation between the fictitious travelers and the ex-Polish physician, Mr. Nadowisky of Luzerne County, Pennsylvania. All of these selections show Crèvecoeur to be more versatile and a better observer than other eighteenth-century visitors to America—Chastellux, Brissot de Warville, Moreau de St. Méry, or even Pehr Kalm. There is great truth in the flattering statement that one educated frontiersman in the *Voyage* made to Herman and his friend after they had read to him from their journal: "If all the Europeans who travel in this country took the trouble to observe things as carefully as you do, Gentlemen, they would treat our efforts and abilities more fairly." (I, 169) At least the fictitious frontiersman's comment agrees with V. L. Parrington's estimate of Crèvecoeur himself, the author of the English *Letters*

Introduction

and *Sketches*, the only Crèvecoeur that Parrington knew. "Perhaps," Parrington said, "no other American before the Revolution was so intimately acquainted with the French and English colonies as a whole, with their near background of frontier and the great wilderness beyond, as this French American."[15]

Although Crèvecoeur's last book is like his earlier ones in that the author is still best at short sketches, graphic pictures, and haunting stories, it succeeds in being more nearly the work of the philosophical historian, the broad observer, the analyst of group movements. The third "Letter" of his first book employs the modern historical approach in that it divides the American colonies into three groups—the seaboard traders, the middle area farmers, and the frontier trappers and hunters—and in that it compares the abilities and studies the accomplishments of immigrants from all the west-European countries. But the *Voyage* goes deeper and further. Here is the best evidence. In that book—long before Frederick J. Turner, thirty years before the sources that Turner used—Crèvecoeur divided the growth of the frontier into the same three periods described by Turner in his famous history-making essay of 1890: "The first generation of settlers uses the axe; the second improves the land; the labors of the third are not sufficient to complete the job." (II, 367)

But the bare statement is not all that the *Voyage* gives us; it provides many examples of each generation, including their biographies, their European or American background, their reasons for settling in a particular place, their formulas for success and for failure. Mr. Nadowisky, almost alone on the shores of the Susquehanna, is one of the "rough-hewers," those who cleared land, burned brush, erected log cabins, and looked forward to good roads, mail service, and neighbors. Mr. Seagrove, the young bachelor from Jamaica, represents the second generation, the "improvers," the group to which Crèvecoeur himself had belonged before the Revolution, those who replaced the first wave after it moved on to new frontiers. The Seagroves had frame houses, land already cleared, or-

[15] *Main Currents in American Thought* (New York, 1930), I, 141.

chards, a hired hand or two, good furniture, infrequent mail service, and perhaps a musical instrument and some books. The third generation, if Colonel Woodhull is a good example, owned broad acres of ploughed fields and many teams of horses and oxen, gathered the harvests from tall corn and from loaded fruit trees, made experiments with plants and animals, visited with friendly neighbors, and read from well-stocked libraries. Taken all together, these farmers give a history of the American frontier that would have been of great use to scholars like Professor Turner and Lucy L. Hazard.

Certain less readable sections of the *Voyage* have been omitted from the present voulme in spite of their authoritative nature, among these being Crèvecoeur's notes on the eastern swamp lands. Before the Revolutionary War he had taken a leading role in the draining of some of the great swamp areas of New York and New Jersey, known as "drowned lands," for which he received some recompense from the government. His part in this undertaking led to a knowledge of the problem and an interest in all the great swamp areas of the East, an interest that is often demonstrated in the *Voyage*. Descriptions of Lord Sterling's five-thousand-acre swamp near Baskind Ridge in New York, of the 192,000-acre Dismal Swamp in Virginia and North Carolina, and of the "drowned lands" of Delaware and New Jersey, are short pieces[16] in which the historian of colonial America would be interested.

Certain other sections are reworkings of material found in Crèvecoeur's earlier, published writings.[17] In general, these are not so detailed or valuable as the originals, but there are at least two exceptions. One, translated for the present volume, is a description of Niagara Falls. In the *Voyage* Crèvecoeur stated that he had been to Niagara twice before the fictitious visit with Herman in the 1790's.[18] It is highly probable that he saw the Falls during his days in the French army and again when he made a western trip with the surveyor, Sir Robert

[16] *Voyage*, I, 389-90, 398-400; III, 325-26.
[17] Compare, for example, *Sketches*, pp. 104-105, 123, with the *Voyage*, I, 389; III, 256.
[18] II, 166, 134, 137, 188.

Introduction xxvii

Hooper, in 1767. It is certain that he did see them at least one time, for he has left—besides the treatment in the *Voyage*—a long, detailed description in English that could only have been the result of actual experience. This visit was made, Crèvecoeur claimed, in July of 1785, and the account was published first in the *Magazine of American History* in 1878 and again, in part, in 1921.[19] Certain short passages from the English version were reproduced in the *Voyage*, such as the descent of the western side by means of Indian ladders and the description of the three rainbows; but the two accounts are far from being alike. The *Voyage* contains a longer and more picturesque description of the bend in the western sheet of water and gives a beautiful picture of the Falls in winter. The English "letter" is more compact and factual, concentrating on the problems encountered by one who wanted to "do" the Falls thoroughly. It also helps to clarify one or two points in the *Voyage*. For instance, Mr. E., who occupies so much space in the book and who is said to be an opulent planter on the New York side of the Falls, turns out to be a Loyalist named Ellsworth, who really lived on the Canadian banks of the Niagara River.

A treatment of the surveying of frontier lands and the chartering of townships, omitted from the present translation, is also a reworking of earlier material. A discussion in the *Lettres*[20] of the problems involved in laying out new districts was concerned primarily with the differences in religion among the settlers. In the *Voyage* Herman and his friend visit with the Surveyor-General of New York, Simon DeWitt,[21] and from him

[19] See the *Magazine of American History*, II, Part II, 604 (October, 1878), and Charles Mason Dow, *Anthology and Bibliography of Niagara Falls* (Albany, 1921), I, 69-74. The English description is said to be a letter from Crèvecoeur to his son Alexander and is dated July, 1785, but there is ample evidence to show that he was in France at that time. Dow said that Crèvecoeur "evidently did the Falls more thoroughly than they are done by many a modern tourist."
[20] *Lettres* (1787), III, 56.
[21] DeWitt was a member of the American Philosophical Society with Crèvecoeur, who could easily have obtained information from him. However, this use of DeWitt's name can probably be ascribed to the same motives, whatever they were, which prompted the author of the *Voyage* to attribute much of his material to outstanding men of America, such as Franklin, Croghan, and Butler.

learn the facts about the naming and surveying of the frontier districts and about DeWitt's masterpiece, a chart fifty feet long and eighteen inches wide of the New York-Pennsylvania boundary line laid out in 1786 by DeWitt and a board of commissioners. The accompanying account of the New England system, adopted by New York in 1785, of laying out new districts displays Crèvecoeur's interest in and knowledge of surveying. Payson Treat and other students of the American land system and the American frontier, such as Shosuke Sato and Frederick L. Paxson, might have profited by this long chapter, which gives information about DeWitt and about surveying that is not in other books of the time.

But in spite of its value to the historian, the *Voyage* is not primarily history, for Crèvecoeur was more than an observer and reporter. He was also a man of literature. Even those of his essays that are most important to the student of eighteenth-century America—and this is true of the earlier works—are primarily literary; they dramatize history, present it vividly as coming from the mouths of invented characters in appropriate settings. And it is for their literary quality that most of the chapters in the present volume have been chosen.

THE *VOYAGE* AS LITERATURE

Crèvecoeur, the author of over two dozen English essays, stories, and even a play, has long been extolled as a writer of fresh, detailed, simple prose, a creator of vivid tableaus, a man of intense feeling and acute observation, a master of short narratives and descriptions. These qualities, in spite of a tendency to repetition and wordiness, in spite of awkward errors in handling the English language that he had adopted, made him a favorite with writers like Hazlitt, Grimm, Lamb, Campbell, and Southey. From the early writings, one remembers in the *Letters* the account of life on the island of Nantucket, the touching analysis of the optimism of immigrant farmers, the Thoreauesque description of a humming

Introduction

bird and of a fight between a black snake and a water snake, the pathetic scene of the caged Negro, and the agonizing distress of the frontiersman who rejected both the British and the Colonist cause. From *Sketches* one recalls the pastoral, Whittier-like description of a snowstorm and its effect on the life of a farmer, the naïve picture of "Ant-Hill Town," and the sad stories of the Revolution, such as "The Wyoming Massacre" and "The American Belisarius." The author of all these pieces was a comparatively untutored writer, a farmer who had little leisure in which to record his thoughts.

Twenty years elapsed between the time of Crèvecoeur's English essays and tales and the time of the *Voyage*, twenty years of activity away from the farm, as a Consul, as a much discussed author, as a friend of famous people like Buffon, Turgot, Mme. d'Houdetot, Saint-Lambert, and Mary Wollstonecraft, and as correspondent of men like Jefferson, Franklin, Madison, Ethan Allen, the Duke de la Rochefoucauld, and the Marquis de Lafayette. The broadened outlook on life that such activities gave him, his associations with well-known writers, and his return to his native French as a medium of expression, were influences that made his last book less naïve, more consciously artistic, less spontaneous, more inclined to conform to the literary fashion of the day. But the book does give evidence that it was written by the American Farmer.

The earlier Crèvecoeur, the practical farmer and the narrator of tales of misery, is seen in such chapters as those that tell of the uses of salt on the farm, that present humble farmers—like Mr. Nadowisky and the ex-schoolteacher—clearing land and making plans, that narrate the melancholy biography of the old Indian Agouehghon and the touching stories of the unhappy Indians told at the council at Onondaga. All of these chapters have been translated for the present book.

The new Crèvecoeur, heretofore a stranger to students of early American literature even more than to the historians, is introduced in the following pages in an exciting adventure story of two travelers lost on a bee hunt in the backwoods of Bedford County, Pennsylvania; in a travelogue of a boat trip up the Hudson; in an account of a visit with Colonel Woodhull; in descriptions of nature like those of the mountain pasturelands, Niagara Falls in winter, and scenes along the Hudson; and particularly in the mass of Indian material that includes both legends and tales and the long, imaginative account of the Council at Onondaga.

In comparing the new Crèvecoeur with the old, one is struck by differences in both tone and subject matter. In spite of his optimism, his idealism, and his strong emotional quality, the author of the *Letters* and the *Sketches*, because of his accurate and minute observation, has been correctly called a realist. The author of the *Voyage* was also a realist, as will be seen in the selections that tell of the feeding of salt to farm animals, give details about the many farms visited, and carefully describe the mechanism of the ironworks. But in his last book Crèvecoeur showed himself to be more of a romanticist.[22] The optimistic tone and the "noble idealizing sentiment" that Moses Coit Tyler and others found in the English works are even more prominently displayed in the *Voyage*. For example, all of the Americans visited by Crèvecoeur's two travelers were successes, although some of them—including the ex-schoolteacher —discussed the hardships of frontier life and of farming in general, and all of them insisted that only the industrious settlers succeeded. Furthermore, Crèvecoeur's farmers were all good citizens of a wonderful new land, almost a Utopia, who praised their freedom, their luck, their country, and who looked to an ideal future. Perhaps the most notable change in tone is in the new emphasis on opulence and size in the farms of America. Whereas the English essays described small farms, like that of Andrew, the Hebridean, the travelers in the *Voyage*, though they visited pioneers along the Susquehanna, spent more of their time with the owners of huge estates at Niagara Falls, at Lake Otsego, on the Passaic River, at New Haven, and in Orange County.

[22] For a more nearly complete discussion of the romantic qualities of the *Voyage*, see Percy G. Adams, "Crèvecoeur—Realist or Romanticist?" *The French American Review* (July-September, 1949), pp. 115-35.

Introduction   xxxi

In the following selections Crèvecoeur's romanticism is probably most apparent in the new types of subject matter, especially in the treatment of nature and in the many chapters of Indian lore. The old Crèvecoeur had been an amateur botanist and a student of animal life; the new—in accordance with the nature school of the day, but more successful than his friend Saint-Lambert and other artificial painters of a "nature de salon"—loved to describe wild panoramas like mountain pasturelands and Niagara in winter. The old Crèvecoeur had avoided the Indians as subject matter; the new, bowing to the demands of the time for information about the Noble Savage, found enough in books and in his own broad experience to fill up over one-fourth of his three-volume work.

From that mass the present volume reproduces only the portions that are original. These include a short account of a winter that Crèvecoeur spent among the Mohawks on the St. Lawrence; a dramatized version of the Jacob-like labors that a young warrior performed to win the approval of his sweetheart's father; the provocative and sentimental story of the Land of Hoppajewot, an Indian Utopia; and, best of all, the legend of the great Manitou and the first beaver. The last two of these stories were presented as actual Indian legends, making use of what have since become the accepted paraphernalia of Indian tales, such as the great Manitou, the animals, and the colorful figures of speech drawn from nature. And they were perhaps based on tales that Crèvecoeur had heard. Nevertheless, they were at least embellished by the author. The story of Hoppajewot, for instance, uses symbolic names —like "the forest of Ninnerwind," meaning "everybody's forest"; and "the island of Allisinape," meaning "the island of man"—and has a moral very much like that of other sections of Crèvecoeur's last book that decry the wicked influence exerted by the white man on the red man.[23] The legend of the first beaver also contains a lesson found frequently in the *Voyage*,[24] that on the evils of cannibalism. Furthermore, this

[23] See, for instance, the speech of Koohassen in Chapter VII of this book.
[24] As in Chapter VIII of this book.

legend is garnished by the addition of a little story taken from Jefferson's *Notes on the State of Virginia*.[25] These embellishments do not detract from the charm of the tales but rather enhance their value and their interest, for Crèvecoeur's taste and ability as a narrator usually guided him well in making choice of materials.

As a narrator of short tales Crèvecoeur had many good qualities. Although he lacked the ability to portray character as well as it is portrayed by the better nineteenth-century short story writers, the tales translated for the present volume do have movement, drama, suspense, character contrast, vivid scenes, ethical instruction, and a pleasing style. The story of Hoppajewot, where red men permitted no firewater, is made more dramatic by the introduction of the churlish, disillusioned Indian warrior who hates what liquor has done to his people but who cannot refuse a drink. It is also unique in that it provides what is perhaps the only touch of humor in all Crèvecoeur's works, a scene in which the white invaders of Hoppajewot are enabled to escape only because one of their number loses his wig in the mêlée and the stupefied red men, unable to understand what has happened, permit them to get away.

The story of the two travelers lost on a bee hunt illustrates a number of Crèvecoeur's best techniques. A reader is spared no detail, no thought, that will help to reproduce the feelings of the travelers when they suddenly realize their horrifying predicament, when they begin to feel the pangs of hunger, when they are saved from suicide by discovering some edible roots, and finally when they hear the sound of a distant cow bell that promises help and food. This story also makes some attempt to depict character, especially by means of contrast. One traveler is older, more reserved, calmer, and more logical; the other is frightened, inclined to blame his companion, and often ready to give up in despair.

The debate between the two warriors at Onondaga is even

[25] See Note 3 of Chapter XIV.

Introduction   xxxiii

a better example of character study and drama, with its vivid contrast between rational old Kesketomah, who wishes to forsake the nomadic life of the hunter for the agricultural life of the white man, and the violent, impetuous, fiery young Koohassen, who vows to have nothing to do with the ways of the hated invaders of his forests and lakes. Furthermore, it illustrates Crèvecoeur's methods of dramatizing history.

Two Indian councils, Herman's unnamed companion reported,[26] were announced in the New York papers, an intertribal meeting of the Six Nations to be held at Onondaga and a council between chiefs of the same tribes and the representatives of the State of New York to be held at Fort Stanwix. No records of the first of these conferences have been uncovered for 1789, the year named,[27] although it was the custom for the Six Nations to convene at Onondaga each year, usually in the autumn.[28] There was, however, a very important council actually held at Fort Stanwix in January of 1789.[29] So Crèvecoeur's account has some factual basis. Nevertheless, there are at least two reasons for doubting that he attended either meeting. First, the *Voyage* names ten important chiefs of the Six Nations,[30] but not one of the ten was at the actual 1789 meeting at Fort Stanwix.[31] And second, there is too evident a parallel between events at Crèvecoeur's council and one held in 1784 at Fort Schuyler, where two famous chiefs, Cornplanter and Red Jacket, tried to influence their people, the former want-

---

[26] I, 35.

[27] The council was held in 1789, according to two statements in the *Voyage* (III, 128, 319); but elsewhere (*Voyage*, I, 378) a council of the Oneida Nation, held at "Skanandoé," was said to have been in 1788.

[28] Lewis H. Morgan, *League of the Ho-de-no-sau-nee or Iroquois* (New York, 1922), I, 62.

[29] *Pennsylvania Archives*, XI, 529-33.

[30] I, 91ff.

[31] See *Pennsylvania Archives*, XI, 531-33, for a complete list of the Indians present. A search among other records reveals that an Indian named Kanadoghary was at a conference at Philadelphia in 1742. [See Cadwallader Colden, *The History of the Five Indian Nations* . . . (New York, 1902), II, 77.] At Crèvecoeur's 1789 council, forty-seven years later, there was a very old and blind Indian named Kanajoharry. However, the name was a common one and, according to Colden (II, 218), was used as a tribal name to designate the upper Mohawk castle.

ing to adopt civilization and live in peace, the latter desiring to spurn civilization and wage war on the whites.[32] Lafayette attended the 1784 meeting and made a speech to the Indians. With him was Crèvecoeur's friend and immediate superior, Barbé-Marbois, who went along as "Minister of France,"[33] and who, no doubt, told Crèvecoeur of his adventure and of Cornplanter and the fiery Red Jacket. At Crèvecoeur's council the spotlight was taken by two Indians, Kesketomah and Koohassen, who, like Cornplanter and Red Jacket, argued for and against civilization.

One of the most pleasing qualities of Crèvecoeur's last book is his new style. It is here perhaps that he is most different from the author of *Letters from an American Farmer*. There is little need to point out that the later style, a French style, better trained and more sophisticated, was not marred by the mechanical faults of the English *Letters* and *Sketches*, that is, the confused spelling, naïve mistakes in diction, and errors in syntax. Such faults did much for the "charming simplicity" of the earlier works, a simplicity which, if it is lacking in the *Voyage*, is at least partly compensated for in the later work by the better arrangement of thoughts, the smoother sentences, and the same clearness and vividness of expression that the American Farmer had been noted for.

The most striking difference between the new style and the old is the *Voyage's* very frequent use of figures of speech. Especially is the metaphorical language of the Indians beautifully reproduced in the Indian tales and the speeches at the council. Crèvecoeur's Indians never became sick but were struck by the great arrow of Agan Matchee Manitou; they never died but fell victim to Matchee Manitou's great black serpent. Young warriors had big hearts and burning breaths and swam like the

---

[32] Thomas L. McKenney and James Hall, *History of the Indian Tribes of North America* . . . (Philadelphia, 1858), I, 185.

[33] *Pennsylvania Archives*, X, 346. For a full account of the part played by the Frenchmen at the Council, see E. Wilson Lyons, *The Man Who Sold Louisiana* (Norman, Oklahoma, 1942), p. 44; *Our Revolutionary Forefathers, The Letters of François, Marquis de Barbé-Marbois, during his residence in the United States as secretary of the French Legation, 1779-85* (New York, 1929), pp. 185 ff.; and Crèvecoeur, *Lettres* (1787), III, 334-42.

Introduction xxxv

tewtag and the maskinonge; but old warriors had blood that was whitened by the snows of winter and the ice of old age. When a brave had a troubled heart, sleep sat perched like a bird on his roof and refused to come down; when he faced danger he did not bend like the reed on the river bank but stood up like the mountain oak; and since he was independent he refused to serve anyone, just as the proud vulture scorned to serve the fugitive ring-dove, or the mountain eagle to serve the cowardly fishing-hawk. And often this metaphorical language is joined with rhythm and alliteration to produce a poetic prose, as in this short plea from the oration of Kesketomah:

> Je le dis donc à qui veut m'entendre; avant que les cèdres du village soient morts de viellesse, et que les érables de la vallée aient cessé de donner du sucre, la race des semeurs de petites graines aura éteint celle des chasseurs de chair, à moins que ces chasseurs ne s'avisent d'en semer aussi. (I, 116)

The style, the subject matter, and the tone of those pieces of the *Voyage* selected for the present translation raise them to the level of Crèvecoeur's best writing and demonstrate the fact that the mature but heretofore unknown author is a worthy development from the American Farmer.

PECULIAR PLAGIARISMS IN THE *VOYAGE*

One characteristic feature of the *Voyage* is the large number of essays in it by writers and speakers identified as prominent Americans. Gilbert Imlay's *Description* had included papers by such men as Benjamin Franklin, Thomas Hutchins, Major Jonathan Heart, and Benjamin Rush, while Crèvecoeur acknowledged that he had made use of Franklin, Heart, and others, such as General Butler, Colonel George Croghan, a certain Senator B***, Bernard Romans, and Frederick Hazen. A study of Crèvecoeur's authorities reveals a number of enigmatic and intriguing facts.

Travel writers as a group have always been great plagiarists, and those of post-Revolution America were particularly so. Jonathan Carver's *Travels*, for example, was the standard source for French and English visitors to America who wanted to include in their books information on the Indians. Even those writers who actually went among the red men—and they were few—checked their findings with Carver's. What the plagiarists did not know, however, was that Carver's *Travels* itself was not original, having depended very much upon such earlier writers as James Adair, the Baron Lahontan, and Pierre de Charlevoix.[34] After Carver, other popular sources for materials on America were John Lawson, William Bartram, M. le Marquis de Chastellux, Imlay, and Crèvecoeur.[35] But the American Farmer was not only a source for other writers; he must be counted also among the plagiarists, especially in those sections of the *Voyage* that concern the Indians.

Although Crèvecoeur had been among the Indians of North America in the fifties and sixties of the eighteenth century, his early writings contain practically no information about them. The French *Lettres* had included some studies of the red man not found in the English originals—undoubtedly because the author upon his return to Europe was influenced by the popular demand for facts about the Noble Savage—but the *Voyage* attempted to treat the subject thoroughly. Many of its chapters on Indians, as in Imlay, were attributed to Americans who might be expected to know much about the subject. But, in spite of Crèvecoeur's apparent honesty in naming his sources, it is these chapters that contain most of his plagiarisms.

Chapter One of the first volume of the *Voyage* is said to

[34] See E. G. Bourne, "The Travels of Jonathan Carver," *American Historical Review*, XI (January, 1906), 287-302, for a study of Carver's plagiarisms. Many such studies of Chateaubriand have been made, for example, by Gilbert Chinard, "Notes sur le Voyage de Chateaubriand en Amérique," *University of California Publications in Modern Philology*, IV, no. 2 (November 10, 1915), 266 ff. The same article discusses Imlay's unacknowledged borrowings.

[35] Crèvecoeur knew Imlay's book; Chastellux, *Voyages dans l'Amérique septentrionale, dans les années 1780, 1781, & 1782* (Paris, 1787), 2 vols.; *The Travels of William Bartram* (New York, 1928), first published in 1791; but not Lawson, *A New Voyage to Carolina* (London, 1709).

Introduction   xxxvii

be taken from a conversation with the famous Indian interpreter and scout, Colonel George Croghan. Chapter Two, on Indian antiquities, claims to be the report of another conversation, this time with Benjamin Franklin. Chapter Eight of the second volume, more material on Indian antiquities, is a paper which, the author asserted, was given him by a Senator B*** of Georgia. An account of Bouquet's expedition into the Ohio country in 1764-65 and the narrative of a trip among the Indians of Georgia and Florida—both in the third volume—are said to be from Frederick Hazen, aide-de-camp to Colonel Bouquet. An Indian legend in Volume Two is ascribed to the interpreter and trader O'Harrah, and more information is credited to General Butler and Bernard Romans. That leaves as presumably original material on Indians only the great number of notes at the end of each volume, five chapters on the council of the Iroquois nations said to have been held at Onondaga in 1789, and some stories and legends obtained on a visit to Niagara Falls. A study of Crèvecoeur's information on the Indians shows that he used two methods in handling his sources, one of which is unique: first, facts supposed to be original are sometimes not facts and sometimes not original; second, facts said to be from one source are usually from another.

The best known of Crèvecoeur's authorities is Benjamin Franklin. Two of the three passages attributed to him were taken from other prominent writers on America, and the third, though it came from Franklin, was obtained under conditions different from those stated in the *Voyage*. An analysis by Franklin of the cold northwest winter winds is to be found in Carver's *Travels;* a discussion of the Gulf Stream, said to have been given Crèvecoeur in a conversation with Franklin, is a translation, often word for word, of a part of the latter's paper read before the American Philosophical Society on December 2, 1785, when Crèvecoeur was in France; and a long speech by Franklin which Crèvecoeur claimed to have heard in 1787 at Franklin and Marshall College—at a time when he was

xxxviii   *Introduction*

somewhere on the Atlantic and Franklin was eating lunch with George Washington in Philadelphia—is made up of excerpts from Imlay's *Description*.[36] Rather obviously Crèvecoeur was hoping to profit by employing the name of his former friend and correspondent, the American most highly regarded in France.

The speech which was supposed to have been made at Franklin and Marshall College described the Indian antiquities of the Ohio Country. In order to treat the same subject for another part of North America, Crèvecoeur called on Senator B*** of Georgia to list and describe the ancient mounds of the southern part of what is now the United States. It has been assumed that the senator was John Brown, congressman from Kentucky, from whom Crèvecoeur had once received an account of the burial mounds near Nashville. But, like Franklin's supposed speech, Mr. B***'s paper is Crèvecoeur's own rewriting of facts taken from a book, this time *The Travels of William Bartram*.[37]

Another "authority" who, it was claimed, provided many pages for the *Voyage* was Frederick Hazen, called aide-de-camp to Colonel—later General—Bouquet. Mr. Hazen, whom the travelers met on a visit to Senator Vining of Delaware, gave them a written, eyewitness account of the famous expedition of 1764-65 and told them the story of a trip he had taken through the Florida and lower Mississippi territories. But Bouquet never had an aide named Hazen, and Hazen's "eyewitness" account is a shortened version—with a few additions and changes—of Dr. William Smith's *Historical Account of Bouquet's Expedition Against the Ohio Indians in 1764*. Furthermore, the story of Hazen's southern travels is a one-chapter summary of Bartram's *Travels*, the same book that

[36] For a complete discussion of Crèvecoeur's misuse of Franklin, see Percy G. Adams, "Crèvecoeur and Franklin," *Pennsylvania History*, XIV, no. 4 (October, 1947), 273-80. The passages taken from Imlay were, on the whole, not written by Imlay but by contributors to his book, such as Hutchins, Heart, and Filson.

[37] A full treatment of the attempt to cover up the rewriting of Bartram is given in Percy G. Adams, "Notes on Crèvecoeur," *American Literature*, XX, no. 3 (November, 1948), 327-33.

Introduction

furnished the facts of the essay said to have been contributed by Senator B***.[38]

Of the three men, Hazen, Senator B***, and Franklin, two were purely fictitious, and the other was dead by 1801, the time of the publication of the *Voyage*. It seems as if Crèvecoeur was attempting to cover his tracks by using names of people who he thought could not defend themselves. Such a conclusion will hold also in the case of Colonel George Croghan, whose name is signed to the first chapter of the *Voyage*, and who died in 1782. However, it is harder to show that Crèvecoeur did not actually get that chapter from the source named, although it contains nothing that is not to be found in several books of the time, notably Carver's very popular *Travels*, or that might not have been known to a great number of people, among them Crèvecoeur himself.

As for the trader Adrien O'Harrah, who was said to have contributed the Indian tale—included in the present volume as "Wabemat's Reward"—there is no evidence that such a man existed, but there was an Indian agent in the South named James O'Hara, of whom Crèvecoeur may have been thinking. The story, at least in part, is almost surely Crèvecoeur's creation.

General Richard Butler and Bernard Romans, two other Americans from whom Crèvecoeur claimed to have borrowed, were, like Franklin and Croghan, dead when the *Voyage* was published. Romans is cited as the source of facts about the Choctaw Indians, but all the facts are to be found in Bartram.[39] Butler's name is signed to the most unsympathetic of all Crèvecoeur's discussions of the red man.[40] Part of this chapter—the theory about the supposed sexual impotence of the American

[38] For the evidence, see Adams, "Notes on Crèvecoeur." Hazen's story of his trip in the South is recounted in *Voyage*, III, 58 ff. Besides these chapters on the Indians and topography of the South that Crèvecoeur rewrote for the *Voyage*, using Bartram's *Travels*, there are four quotations from the same book, all of them descriptions of plant or animal life in Florida. Each time, however, Crèvecoeur claimed that he was quoting John Bartram (e.g., *Voyage*, II, 314), whom he had perhaps known in America, and of whom he had given an account in Letter XI of *Letters from an American Farmer*.
[39] Compare the *Voyage*, III, 329, and Bartram, p. 399.
[40] *Voyage*, III, 113 ff.

Indian—may have come directly from Crèvecoeur's friend Buffon, who was the theory's most famous supporter, or it may have come by way of Thomas Jefferson's well-known refutation of the theory in *Notes on the State of Virginia*, a book used in the *Voyage* at least twice without acknowledgment.[41] Other information on Indians, usually that found among the notes to the three volumes, was taken, again without acknowledgment, from Carver, Bartram, and John Long.[42]

Although Crèvecoeur's plagiarisms are most apparent in his chapters on the Indians, he frequently employed well-known books for other kinds of information. For example, while visiting Mr. E. at Niagara Falls, Herman and his companion hear their host tell at length of a trip said to have been made by two Russians up the Mississippi and through the northern Middle West. Although Crèvecoeur had actually been in that territory, the tale of the Russians' tour contains nothing of a specific nature that cannot be found in Carver's *Travels*, the book that supplied the *Voyage* with nearly all its facts about the topography of the western lands—its descriptions of Lake Pepin, the St. Pierre River, the Falls of St. Anthony, and the Great Lakes except Ontario[43]—and with many of its facts about natural history, including its long descriptions of the whippoorwill and the firefly.[44]

The evidence, then, points to the conclusion that in the *Voyage*—following the custom of his day—Crèvecoeur borrowed without saying so from William Bartram, Gilbert Imlay, William Smith, Thomas Jefferson, Jonathan Carver, and probably other writers, such as John Long. It shows also that

[41] Compare Butler's account with Jefferson's (Richmond, 1853), pp. 62-63, and the *Voyage*, I, 318 ff., with the *Notes*, pp. 99 ff. See also, in the present volume, Chapter XIV, note 3.

[42] Compare, for example, *Voyage*, II, 400, with Carver (Philadelphia, 1796), p. 28; *Voyage*, II, 381, with Bartram, p. 313; and *Voyage*, I, 23-24, with Long, *Travels of an Indian Interpreter and Trader*, in *Early Western Travels, 1748-1836*, ed. R. G. Thwaites (Cleveland, 1904), II, 125.

[43] Compare the *Voyage*, I, 411, 358, 359, 412-13, with Carver, pp. 34-35, 47, 43-44, 85.

[44] Compare the *Voyage*, III, 349-350, and II, 396-97, with Carver, pp. 310-11, 325-26.

Introduction

the "authorities" he so frequently quoted perhaps supplied no material whatsoever for the *Voyage* but were employed simply to cover up his plagiarisms or relate narratives of pretended excursions in the West or South. And finally, of all the information about the North American Indian found in the *Voyage*, only the Indian tales and the account of the council at Onondaga seem to be original. The quality of these pieces, however, more than compensates for the unacknowledged borrowing that Crèvecoeur did.

THE NOTES OF THE *VOYAGE*

The *Voyage* contains 264 pages of notes, over one-fifth of the entire work. These notes include a great variety of information on such subjects as the North American Indians—their tribes and nations, their customs and beliefs, their ancient mounds and fortifications, and their language; the geography of North America—rivers, creeks, canals, towns, mountains, lakes, waterfalls, salt licks, the new districts in Pennsylvania and New York, and the Bahamas and Bermuda; the animal life—buffaloes, catamounts, fireflies, beavers, drumming partridges, king birds, crocodiles, fish, eagles, the Hessian Fly; the plant life—fruit trees of several kinds, sugar maples, cranberry bushes, wild trees such as oaks, white cedars, weeping elms, and water ash; the history of North America—the colleges, the societies, the governments of certain states, and anecdotes about some of the states; well-known people of America—Washington, Franklin, Pontiac, Sir William Johnson, Oliver Evans, Corlear the trader, Colonel George Croghan; and the farming and industry of North America—hemp raising, potassium, ginseng, iron, wines and brandies.

As with much of his Indian material, some of Crèvecoeur's notes were taken from books of the time. He admitted his borrowings from Chastellux and William Bartram, although he thought he was using John Bartram. Other notes, as we have seen, were taken from Carver[45] and Jefferson. However, the great majority of them are his own, and most of those are of value to the specialist in early American history.

ON THE PROBLEMS OF TRANSLATING AND SELECTING

In making this translation of part of the original three volumes, the translator found that the question of style was of paramount importance. In order to put Crèvecoeur's French into English, it was necessary first to make a study of the style and form of the English works of the American Farmer so that his own expressions and mannerisms as found in those books might be reproduced whenever the occasion demanded, as in the chapter on the mountain pasture lands and the feeding of salt to farm animals. For a part of this chapter Crèvecoeur elaborated on a passage from one of his then unpublished English essays, about the antics of cattle too long deprived of salt.[46] In the same chapter is a description of the feelings of the herdsman at the time of morning twilight in the mountains. The emotions, and sometimes the expressions themselves, are similar to those found in passages of *Letters* and *Sketches*,[47] since sunrise was Crèvecoeur's favorite time of day. But most of the time the new Crèvecoeur forced the translator to work without models, as in the Indian tales and the description of Niagara.

Throughout the translation the chief technical difficulty resided in Crèvecoeur's long, often involved sentences. His punctuation of those sentences is clear and consistent, but his eighteenth-century fondness for the colon and semicolon is a characteristic that the translator did not reproduce. The only other liberty taken with the original was the occasional rearrangement of ideas in a long sentence, or the dividing of one

---

[45] Such as the one on fireflies (II, 396-97), which W. B. Blake selected and translated for the notes of his 1912 Everyman edition of *Letters from an American Farmer*, p. 241, because it "deserves perpetuation."
[46] Compare p. 3, Chapter XV, with *Sketches*, p. 112.
[47] Compare pp. 14-15, Chapter XV, with *Letters*, p. 33.

Introduction

sentence into two, in order to keep the numerous modifiers separated, a problem not so pressing in French, with its two genders for inanimate objects and abstract ideas.

The greatest problem of all, however, was ultimately that of determining which chapters of the *Voyage* should be translated. In general, those not selected demonstrate certain of the admitted faults of Crèvecoeur's last book.

Among these shortcomings is a strong tendency to repetition. On their visits with the frontiersmen and with the older families in the more settled areas, the two travelers were often forced to listen to biographies they had already heard in varying versions from other people. No doubt the histories of many early colonists in America were much alike, but the reader prefers fewer samples than Crèvecoeur chose to give. One of the objects of the present translation is to provide a representative selection from among the accounts of the numerous visits, thereby doing away with the monotony of the original.

Other faults of the *Voyage*, as we have seen, are its lack of organization and its unacknowledged dependence on other writers. Such faults are enough to mar the value and spoil the effect of most books. However, since Crèvecoeur, as shown by his English publications, was a writer of short sketches and narratives, an essayist and a teller of tales, his *Voyage* is far from being a total loss. For, in spite of its attempts at continuity, Crèvecoeur's last book is another volume of essays and tales. As a result, one can extract from its forty-five chapters those that are not original, eliminate others that are repetitious, and discover that he has a book about eighteenth-century America that is well worth reading.

There are, of course, some parts of the French work which were left untranslated for reasons other than their repetitiousness or lack of originality. One of the best chapters, the description of a Gothic castle in Germany, was not included, in spite of its excellence, because it had nothing to do with "Travels" in America. Another section parted with reluctantly, a New England farmer's account of the beauty and effects of a northern blizzard, was too much like an essay in

Sketches. All of the third volume was passed over because it is of interest to the specialist only and is both monotonous and repetitious. But for the chapters chosen no apology needs to be offered. Crèvecoeur's *Eighteenth-Century Travels in Pennsylvania and New York* should sit comfortably, or perhaps move freely, beside his *Letters from an American Farmer* and his *Sketches of Eighteenth Century America,* and like them enhance the reputation of the man whom William Hazlitt once called the "illustrious obscure."

Chapter I

A Trip up the Hudson

Everything having been put in readiness, we took passage on a beautiful sloop of ninety tons bound for the town of Poughkeepsie. The captain of the little ship agreed to put us ashore at New Windsor, a village on the west bank of the river.

There were several reasons why we preferred this sloop to others going up the river. We were particularly attracted by the elegance of its construction, the size of its cabin, and above all by the hope that the conversation of Captain Dean, who had just returned from a voyage to China in this same ship, would be of great interest to us. We were not disappointed. He told us that if the Chinese customs-house at Canton had exacted a duty proportionate to the size of his boat he would have made a profitable voyage. "You are, I believe," I told him, "the first navigator who has dared to cross such a large body of water in such a small vessel."

"That's true," he replied, "but I didn't lose a cent on the trip."

The day was beautiful, the wind and the tide favorable, when we left the dock, doubled the great battery located on the west point of the city, and entered the river, which is more than two miles wide at that place. On the right, its waters bathed the shores of the island on which the city of New York is built; on our left, those of New Jersey. But we were traveling so fast that in less than forty minutes we had lost sight of the Narrows, Staten Island, and the islands of Big Bay; and shortly afterwards, the warehouses and the churches with their steeples, gradually obscured by the vapors on the horizon, disappeared from sight.

What a contrast there was in the aspect of nature on the two banks of this beautiful river! The shore to our right, wooded, pleasant, and fertile, was covered with well-cultivated fields and symmetrically arranged orchards and ornamented with the homes of city merchants, almost all white and elegant, some nearly hidden in thick trees, others placed in the middle of gardens and surrounded by acacias, sycamores, and tulip trees.

The shore to our left, or, properly speaking, that of New Jersey, although rough, arid, and uninhabited, nonetheless merits attentive examination, especially by lovers of botany. On that side, for the space of more than twenty-five miles, the river is held in by a perpendicular wall of rocks more than fifty feet high, whose summit is crowned with tall trees. Enormous piles of rocks that almost seem to have been quarried, so much do they resemble the debris of some ancient castle, occupy, or rather, form, the base of the wall, sloping gently down to the water and partly covered with trees and thick bushes as well as interesting plants. In the intervals that are less barren and unfruitful, the industry of man has already built homes and surrounded them with peach and cherry trees. We passed very close to some of these houses.

Monsieur Herman and I were entertaining ourselves with reflections on the many striking and novel scenes before us, when the captain announced, "You are now in what is called Tappan Sea; but it is really only a part of the river, which is five miles wide here."

"What!" exclaimed my companion, "you mean to say that even though we are so far from the ocean we are still sailing on salt water with all sails set and feel no more motion than if we were on a park canal!"

"It isn't this way in the autumn," the captain explained; "then the winds force us to be more prudent in sailing, and some knowledge of the channel is required."

"What is the purpose of these warehouses," asked Monsieur Herman, "those lifting cranes, and those long jetties that I see on both sides of the river?"

"Those are landings to which highways from the interior of the country come. From them many different products are dispatched to New York; and from New York the produce of Europe and the Indies, so necessary to the inhabitants, is sent back to these same landings. There are many sloops that make the trip regularly. They are means of carrying on a commerce that is increasing with the population. However, it often happens that part of the farmers' wealth goes to pay for these foreign products. And that is why public opinion is so strong for building up local manufactures, and why the government protects and encourages industry with the wisest laws. But I fear that the time is not yet come for America to be a manufacturing nation."

While the captain was entertaining us with these interesting details, we doubled Cape Frederickhook and suddenly discovered a superb chain of mountains that seemed to bar our way, to seal up the river.

"Does the river end there?" asked Monsieur Herman. "I see no opening or passage."

"No. It crosses the mountains, a distance of twenty-one miles, in a channel that is wide, deep, and tortuous. That passage is one of the most interesting phenomena to be seen on this continent; and what is more marvelous yet, the tide comes up the river more than one hundred and thirty-five miles beyond the mountains. That passage," he continued, "must have been there even before the river itself; for if, like the Shenandoah, the Potomac, the Great Kanawha, and the Tennessee, these waters had cut their own channel across the Highlands, we would see rocks, islands, and debris, the evidences of that ancient convulsion. And there are no such evidences. From here to the city the river is perfectly clear. . . . But wait, we are nearing some magic places; you will really see something now."

"What a wonderful view!" exclaimed Monsieur Herman. "How green and fresh it is, from the water level to the highest summits! I do not see a single rock that is bare; everything is covered with the most beautiful trees. Would not this view confirm the opinion of those who think that this continent has more recently risen from the bed of the sea than Europe and Asia?"

While the comments of my companion were entertaining us on the trip across Haverstraw Bay, we rounded without knowing it a long peninsula called Verplanck's Point that formed the foreground of this magnificent picture, and found ourselves suddenly in the middle of a superb canal more than a mile wide, enclosed by the almost perpendicular walls of some very high hills—Thunder-Berg and Anthony's Nose—whose bases, the captain told us, extended more than one hundred feet under the water. The tops of the hills were crowned with cedars that looked, at that distance, like dwarf trees. Turning our eyes toward the stern of the vessel, we saw that everything had closed in; no longer could we see the bay of Haverstraw out of which we had come. Directing our attention ahead of us, we saw a long succession of jutting points and elevated promontories, covered with pines, hemlocks, and cedars, whose forms and appearances were more or less drawn out and softened by the various shades caused by distance and optical illusions. The end of the canal toward which we were making our way appeared also to be entirely closed in.

We were advancing with all sails set when Monsieur Herman, after some minutes of silence, cried out, "How beautiful and imposing all this is! What grandeur, what majesty nature imprints on its creations! How hard it would be here for the coldest imagination to be sterile or silent! The fantastic shapes of the rocks that form the shores, their bizarre roughness, the elevation of the trees, the colossal height of the hills in the middle of which our vessel seems like a mere dot, the invigorating freshness of the air we are breathing, the murmur of the little waves that die against the bank, the multitude of birds that are enlivening the scene and ploughing up the surface of the water—everything here evokes pleasure, astonishment, and wonder. . . . This is in reality," he continued, "only a dream, for the progress of the vessel is so rapid that it is impossible to enjoy fully the general effect of these mighty images. Scarcely are the eyes fixed on certain striking objects when immediately the change in our position gives them a new aspect; their succession is so rapid and fleeting that we do not have time to grasp the images as they appear. In order to enjoy this spectacle completely, which alone is worth a trip across the ocean, it would be necessary to take several days for the journey up the river, stopping from time to time to look again at those scenes that merit being more attentively considered."

No sooner had we passed the second peninsula than the river, turning to the west, opened to our view a new scene, whose objects were less imposing but softer, more picturesque, more varied. The mountains, less rough in appearance here, were resting on bases accessible to the boat, where one could pause with pleasure to breathe fresh air in the shade of the beautiful trees that cover them.

When the wind and the noise of the vessel's wash permitted, we could hear on all sides of us the sound of waterfalls and cascades whose echoes were diffused abroad or softened to a murmur at the whim of the breezes, but we could not make out the course of their waters because of the thickness of the woods.

"Those are big streams," the captain explained, "that come out of the sides of distant hills and reach the river only after having fallen from the tops of tall rocks and after having surmounted many obstacles. Some of them, extremely picturesque, would be worthy of the brush of an artist. As modest as a maiden who carefully hides her charms under the shadow of her veil, it is only in the mysterious darkness of the woods and, especially, in the mountains that nature unfolds without reserve her beauties and her treasures, and there she displays them every minute. Thus, when I go on a walking trip it is almost always in the mountains.

"In times to come," he continued, "when agriculture, commerce, and industry have accumulated wealth in our coastal towns, and when our population has increased ten-fold, luxury and love of beauty will come here to build fine country seats, direct and guide these lovely waters, take possession of all the most charming sites, and convert these deserts, today so wild, into wholesome, cheerful, delightful dwelling places. Here the wealthy, the idle, and the invalid will come to seek repose, fresh air, and health. Nature has done everything, arranged everything, so that one day these places can be made into charming retreats for the hot summer months: it has favored them with nearness to a river that abounds in sea fish, with fertile valleys, with cool, protecting hills, with steady breezes produced by the ebb and flow of the tides, with abundant, clear water; and finally, the enjoyment of all these advantages is enhanced by proximity to the city.

"Never do I go up or down this river," he continued, "that my imagination does not involuntarily roam over these delightful places, so numerous and so varied. Here, in the shade of the beautiful oaks that stand on the banks of this roaring stream, my mind's eye places a large and comfortable house. There, on the south slope of a hill, protected by neighboring heights from the cold north winds, I envisage a little farm on which human ingenuity has united the useful with the agreeable. On the steep sides of one of these rocks, whose bases are bathed by the waters of the river, I envisage a pavilion from which the sportsmen can throw their deceptive hooks and amuse themselves by fishing. On the smooth summit of some eminence, I imagine a terrace where one can stand and admire the sunrises and sunsets of summer, the breaking up of the ice in early spring, or the maneuvering of the boats that go up and down this beautiful river. My imagination even travels up to the highest and most inaccessible peaks of these mountains, on which some productive power has planted cedars; there, it forgets for awhile the turmoil, the misfortunes, the tedium of life, for the cedar tree is the tree of meditation. The Aeolian sound made by the breeze as it blows across the sharp leaves of that tree, a sound in which the soul even more than the ear recognizes harmonious tones; the cedar's amazing durability, and especially that of the granite out of whose crevices it grows; its great height; the pure air that one breathes there —everything stimulates the mind. One treads with involuntary respect on these indestructible witnesses of the upheavals and the changes that the surface of the globe has undergone and that it will continue to undergo during centuries yet to come. Such are the ideas with which my imagination sometimes entertains itself as I make my way up or down this superb and tortuous strait, tacking through its diverse meanderings. Can future generations preserve these beautiful cedars, these gigantic pines, these venerable hemlocks, these oaks, more than a century old, that balance themselves on all the hills, their tops swaying in the wind, and grow even at the water's edge? Human ingenuity could never replace them.

"This is the country of echoes, their favorite habitation. In other places they stutter; here they express themselves distinctly. Nowhere are they so numerous, or so ready to respond. The different intonations of their voices resemble the conversation of people placed on hills at varying distances and heights. Some of them sound like whispers; others are stronger and their accents more clearly pronounced. Some reply immediately; others only after a certain interval, as if they were pausing to think before speaking. Sometimes several talk together. It is particularly when one laughs that the confusion of their responses makes the illusion complete. When ships in their maneuverings approach the banks, it is impossible not to believe that one hears the voices of people sitting behind the big rocks. The echoes from the tops of the mountains give such distinct replies that the eye, guided by the ear, thinks that it can single out the tree behind which they lurk. Of all the possible deceptions this last has always impressed me most. Some time ago, while we were hugging the west bank, one of my passengers was astounded to discover that the echo from a nearby point was not a whisper that came from the person next to him.

"These hamadryads understand all languages and will repeat

with pleasure the songs of travelers on the passing boats. If someone plays the flute or the clarinet, they immediately take up the same instruments; then there is a regular concert, conducted with precision and measure; especially sweet to hear are the simple harmonies, their repetitions softened by the undulations of the breeze and the vague uncertainty of distance. Animated with pleasure because of their own concert, they seem to put into their playing much taste and charm. But in order that the enjoyment of this novel entertainment be more lasting, the ship must be at anchor in a favorable spot. I know two or three such spots near the west bank where one can enjoy these heavenly, invisible symphonies without knowing where the sounds come from, and often they come from as far as a mile away.

"Every time I try to count the number of echoes I am not able to get above eight, not because I do not hear many more than that but because my perception is not quick enough and they repeat themselves too rapidly. The task is even more difficult when I use my speaking trumpet. By using it, I once counted seventeen echoes. Then a great number of hamadryads who at other times never open their mouths make themselves heard, their final sounds being entirely beyond my hearing. Picture my astonishment, when in the middle of my experiments I note that those echoes which are too far away to hear my own voice, repeat what the first listeners tell them, and they in their turn pass it on to others still farther away. So that with increasing distance each echo becomes another me to whom her neighbors reply. I still remember the phrase, divided into four syllables, that I distinctly heard repeated seventeen times: 'Hail! Fair hamadryads!'[1] Would it not be possible, I wonder, during the calm of a fine day, to determine the distance to which sounds from a speaking trumpet might travel, echo by echo, in a manner clear enough to make an impression on the ear?"

---

[1] In the original, Crèvecoeur rendered the captain's call in English; but even if the three words are turned into French, one cannot get four syllables ("quatre syllabes").

As he said these last words, the captain shouted, "Hail! Passengers!" But the wind and the sound of the ship's wake did not permit us to hear more than the nearest echoes.

However, even then, the hills, the slopes of the mountains, the hollows, the points and surfaces of the crags, the tops of the trees and bushes, all seemed inhabited, full of invisible or hidden beings, who greeted us, repeating "Hail! Passengers!" So distinct were their voices, so well determined the places that we supposed them to inhabit, that not one of us was able to understand how it was possible not to see them.

"The time and height of the tides," the captain informed us, "the strength and direction of the wind, the bearing of the mountains from the ship, the position of the promontories, the varying sizes of the coves and bays, the season of the year, the hour of the day—all these are the causes that infinitely modify the number, the effect, and the varied mixture of the echoes. Like the birds, they are more numerous and gay when the trees and bushes are covered with leaves than during the nakedness of fall and winter.

"What would a man think," he continued, "a Hollander, for example, reared in a flat country where such a phenomenon is unknown, if he were placed in the middle of this great solitude and heard for the first time these hamadryads repeat distinctly everything he said? And as if some slight touch were still lacking in the variety and magnificence of this superb tableau, as soon as the sea bass leaves the ocean and comes up the Hudson the fish hawk arrives to make his home in the mountains. After having risen into the air to a great height in order better to distinguish his prey under the water, he dives like lightning, plunges into the river, and soon reappears, holding in his claws that huge fish, whose weight and convulsive movements force him to fly slowly and with difficulty. But near him lives a formidable enemy, the bald eagle, who likes fish without being able to catch it and who because of the scarcity of game in that season is forced to leave the mountains. As soon as he sees that the fish hawk has arrived at his flight level, this eagle, monarch of the birds, leaves his own higher level and pursues at full speed until the fisherman, convinced of his inferiority, abandons his prey. Then the bold antagonist, his wings folded, drops like a shot and with inconceivable dexterity seizes the fish before it hits the river. Sovereign arbiter of great, as well as of small, events, the might of the strongest rules the world always, high in the air as well as on the earth and under the water.[2]

"In these mountains the sea breezes meet with and engage the winds from the interior. It often happens, especially during the summer, that their strength being the same, each rules in his own territory. Then the vessels that come from New York or Albany are obliged, if the tide is against them, to anchor as they draw near the mountains. The interval between the two winds is consequently a variable zone: across it gales blow sharply during the summer; and in the autumn violent squalls escape from the valleys of the interior and fall on the river, where they would cause accidents if experience did not teach the sailors to foresee them. Moreover, the ships can be sure of a great depth of water at this point in the Hudson; they can maneuver, tack, and obey the currents and eddies, even to the point where their bowsprits touch the branches of the trees on the bank."

We were scudding along in the middle of the fourth channel, an extremely imposing one because of its length and the somber majesty of the mountains that border it, when we saw on the west side a very high waterfall (Buttermilk Fall), whose water was as white as milk, at the foot of which a huge building had

[2] In the 1787 edition of his *Lettres* (II, 89-90), Crèvecoeur has another version of the fight between the fish hawk and the bald eagle. François Barbé-Marbois, secretary of the French legation and Crèvecoeur's friend, told of a similar fight on Long Island Sound in the letters presumably written in the 1780's but which he edited and rearranged and never published. Cf. *Our Revolutionary Forefathers, The Letters of François, Marquis de Barbé-Marbois, 1779-1785*, trans. Eugene Parker Chase (New York, 1929), pp. 158-59. The bald eagle's robbing of the fish hawk was, in fact, an intriguing phenomenon for eighteenth-century visitors in America. Other travelers who described it were the Marquis de Chastellux, John Lawson, Dr. John Brickell, and Samuel Jenner, these last two stealing their versions from Lawson. See Percy G. Adams, "The Real Author of *William Byrd's Natural History of Virginia*," *American Literature*, XXVIII, No. 2 (May, 1956), 217.

in Pennsylvania & New York 11

been erected at the very edge of the river. "If this is not one of the most beautiful flour mills in the state," our captain told us, "it is certainly one of the most advantageously located and one of the most profitable. The granite base it rests on is three hundred feet long and forty to sixty feet wide. That is all the ground the owner could get; but a fall forty-five feet high is invaluable for such an industry, and so is this location on the bank of such a large river, whose waters bring grain and staves for casks and carry flour to the city. You will be amazed at the slight amount of water that the wheels of this mill require. The weight and velocity of the water as it falls make up for the quantity. The size of the building, the number of the wheels, the quality of the bolters, the ingenious use made of cylinders to simplify the movements and decrease friction, as well as the fine quality of the flour that comes from the mill, have attracted the attention of experts. Ships from the interior loaded with wheat and those that come from New York to take away the flour anchor at the very door of the mill, where there is always forty feet of water. What a shame that the mountains hide this spot from the sun for part of the day! This fine establishment is reported to have cost over eighteen thousand dollars."

The wind and tide having failed us some miles above the mill, we cast anchor in five fathoms of water in a beautiful cove surrounded by silver poplars and hemlocks venerable with their long moss. At the back of the cove we heard the noise of a fall, which was, we were told, Pooploskill. It was six o'clock, and for some time the sun had been down behind the mountains on the west bank of the river. We were occupied in examining the lovely and abundant cascade, of which some day artists will make a great use, when a sound like that of a violent explosion suddenly struck our ears and stunned our senses.

The echoes that had formerly diverted us were only feeble noises compared with those that we now heard, the rumblings and crashes being repeated with such violence and force that it is impossible to describe the phenomenon. They surrounded us on all sides. We listened long, until the sounds insensibly died away in the distance.

"That is the cannon for retreat," the captain explained.

"I believed myself to be fifteen hundred leagues from Europe," Monsieur Herman said, "in a country of peace and tranquillity, and then I hear a cannon!"

"We are only three miles from West Point,"[3] the captain replied. "Haven't you ever heard of the fortifications that our first congress caused to be built there during the War of Independence? Never was a site better chosen for the purpose! The river makes a large bend there, and the peninsula that forces ships to make a detour is very long; the steep face of the banks and the favorable position of nearby heights caused congress to resolve to close the passage at that point. So the heights were covered with batteries and formidable redoubts, whose fire crossed at several places on the river. Tomorrow, as we go by, you will have a chance to see what remains of these great works; we will all but touch the rock to which was attached the east end of the chain that closed the river. Each link of the chain weighed more than four hundred pounds. Among the causes that have assured liberty and independence to the states, these impregnable fortifications should perhaps be given much credit."

The blackness of night having little by little obscured the magnificent objects along the river, the captain invited us to go down into the ship's cabin. It was furnished in the Chinese fashion and lighted by Chinese candles stuck in glass containers. There we could study the map made during the war and under the direction of General Washington. It showed us the peninsulas and the promontories, the capes, the contours, and the most easily defended parts of that celebrated passageway, which the great man considered to be the key to that part of the continent. The captain then talked to us of the country beyond the nearby mountains, which he had crossed in one direction

[3] See, for a rather complete contemporaneous description of West Point, Chastellux, I, 70.

in Pennsylvania & New York 13

as far as the Connecticut line and in the other as far as New Jersey.

"If I were a farmer," he told us, "and I intend some day to be one, I would prefer a home here to living in Fishkill, Duchess, or Columbia County. Everything here is fine for farming: fertile valleys, clear streams, convenient irrigation, abundance of beautiful woodland, and nearness to ironworks. Some foreign officers, discharged after the peace of 1763, settled here and established farms that for a long time were the objects of praise and admiration. To their love of work and knowledge of farming, they added refinement, gentle manners, and varied talents. Their friends often came from the city to pay long visits, and their homes for a long time presented the most fascinating picture of enlightened industry, pleasant affluence, and happiness. Unfortunately the War of Independence brought ruin to some of them."

The moon, which we had been awaiting with impatience, finally appeared over the mountains; then, gathered again on deck, we saw a thousand strange, new images. They were no longer optical illusions, gradations of the perspective, nor that variety of well-known objects that during the day sparkled in the sunlight, but illusions, more extraordinary and bizarre, to which we could give no name. What seemed most amusing to me was that each man, struck by the beauty of those scenes that appealed to his own imagination, blamed his neighbor for not seeing the same things. What a sight it was, this black void more or less deep, this mixture of light more or less brilliant, more or less weak, surrounded as we were by the waters of the river, by the forts, by the mountains, that the veils of night seemed to bring close to us! It was not astonishing that in the midst of a scene so imposing and so novel our imaginations should borrow from the singularity and the grandeur of so many objects some of the characteristics and some of the charm of their extravagance!

It was midnight, and we were still on deck, occupied in contemplating the majesty of nature, the works of a power that we could never understand, displayed in the heavens, on the earth, and under the waters. The profound calm, the solemn silence of that beautiful Chaldean night were interrupted only rarely and feebly by the rustle of the leaves, by the long, slow undulations of the waves as they lapped the river banks or broke into wrinkles on the cable of our ship, and by the distant murmur of that immense volume of water as it passed down the long and tortuous strait.

We were again amusing ourselves with the echoes, which repeated a number of songs and poems for us, when our ears were struck by a most extraordinary sound, as if some giant atop one of the mountains had thrown a rock into the river.

"Those are sturgeons," the captain said, "that fall back into the river after having jumped to a great height. I have never known the reason for such a peculiar exercise."

The next day, we weighed anchor as soon as the tide permitted, and the captain having decreased sail very much, we had time to study carefully the remains of the immense works of West Point, or, rather, what we could see of them while the ship was maneuvering about. Most of the stone redoubts and the batteries, both those set on the tops of rocks as well as those at the water level, seemed to us well preserved, although in part hidden under the thick foliage of bushes and shrubs; for everything here that the foot of man treads but rarely is soon covered with underbrush.

"This huge amphitheater of defenses," the captain informed us, "required the constant labor of several thousand men for two long years. Of all the buildings put up, there remains only the great warehouse which was used as an arsenal; in it have been stored the heavy artillery from the fortifications and the artillery taken at the capitulation of Saratoga. The ends of the chain that closed the river were defended, as you see, by these two formidable looking redoubts that are so perfectly preserved. It is easy to see that no ship would have been able to approach this place without exposing itself for more than two miles to the devastating crossfire from the banks and the nearby heights."

in Pennsylvania & New York

Finally, after having sailed slowly by these evidences of so much effort and perseverance, we entered the last of the channels, a roomy one, the most imposing of the entire strait. It runs into two tall mountains, which, though nearly perpendicular, are partly covered with trees. From this channel we were able for the first time to see the countryside and habitations on the west bank of the river. Here, between New Windsor and Fishkill, at the entrance of the narrow part, the river is nearly three miles wide.

CHAPTER II

Colonel Woodhull of Schunnemunk Valley

As he had promised, the Captain landed us at the first village soon after coming out of the channel; but as it offered us nothing of interest, being only a wharf where several roads from the interior end, we set out immediately. We had gone but a few miles in the direction of Bethlehem when we met Mr. John Allison, a rich landowner of this district with whom I had crossed the ocean four years before. He invited us to lunch, after showing us his fine flour mill, in which he yearly converts twenty-five to thirty thousand bushels of wheat into flour. His undertakings would be much more successful, he told us, if he were not subject to a lack of water during the summer heat, and if some means could be found of destroying the Hessian Fly, an insect which for several years had caused great damage in the neighboring districts and which had never been heard of before the arrival of the German troops in New York.[1]

Guided by the milestones, we continued on our way to Blooming Green, where we had to leave the main road in order to head into the mountains; but we had just crossed the bridge on Murderer's Creek when we discovered another mill, which aroused the insatiable curiosity of Monsieur Herman.

in Pennsylvania & New York 17

Luckily the proprietor, Mr. J. Thorn, was there and very politely invited us to come in, offering to show us all the parts. He began with the ground floor, where there were four pairs of millstones; from there he took us up through several stories filled with huge fans and with a new kind of bolters for cleaning; and finally he led us to the fourth floor, where the flour was cooled for fifteen days before being sifted and put in large barrels. This last floor ran the whole length and breadth of the building, that is, ninety-four feet by forty feet. He then took us to see his dam.

"Nature and human labor," he told us, "have provided me with a waterfall eighteen feet high. Because of it, my wheels receive their moving force from above and consequently need much less water. Here is my cooper's shed, where I make three to four thousand barrels every year."

"How much wheat do you make into flour?" asked my companion.

"Forty to fifty thousand bushels."

"Where do you get the wheat?"

"From the counties of Sussex, Orange, and Ulster, as well as from upper New Jersey and Pennsylvania."

"How much does it cost you a bushel?"

"The cost on the European market is our thermometer. In general, eight to ten shillings."

"What is the purpose of that big wall built on the other side of the wheels, and which seems to support part of the masonry of your fine mill?"

"It is to shelter the wheels from frost."

"How much has all that cost you?"

"Fourteen thousand piastres (73,500 livres), counting the dam and the piece of ground."

At last we reached the mountains, almost all of which had been farmed for a long time, and after three hours of walking

[1] Later the two travelers return for a two-day visit with Mr. Allison (I, 290 ff.), see his new brick house, and hear about his exports to Europe, his fine collection of old wines, and his expectations with regard to the future greatness of the United States.

we discovered the beautiful valley of Schunnemunk.[2] "Everything that you see here," I said to Monsieur Herman, "belongs to my friend Jesse Woodhull, these meadows, this great orchard, those fields as far as the eye can reach. Would you believe it? It is he who cut down the first tree for this huge estate, and this good man is not yet fifty years old. I think I see his tall figure on that slope where the three plows are working. Let us go over there."

After we had been received as if hospitality itself had taken us by the hand, my companion, astonished to see that each team was composed of two pairs of oxen and two horses, asked Colonel Woodhull the reason for it. "The land is so firmly packed in this valley," he replied, "that our plowing requires a very great force; often, in fact, the breaking is done with four pairs. The soil of the neighboring districts is quite different, the plowing there being done with only three horses."

"Why do these oxen walk so lightly and those I saw in Connecticut so heavily?"

"The ones you see here are not oxen."

Monsieur Herman was astonished at this information, and since he appeared not to understand, the Colonel added, "No, Monsieur, these are not oxen, but animals of a new species for which our language, rich as it is, does not yet have a name. These are heifers on which, in their youth, I performed a very simple and harmless operation that deprived them of their sex. I have made of them animals of a kind much more agile, although as suitable for work and hard labor as the males, but they are a little less docile. Every year I perform the same operation on a certain number of young mares, which makes them much superior to my other horses, both in strength and health, and especially in sureness of step."

"Where did you get that new and unusual idea? Who is the anatomist that performs the operation?"

[2] Crèvecoeur spelled this word "Skonomonk," which, according to Percy V. D. Gott, Goshen, New York, is one of many early spellings for a mountain "extending southwesterly from a point back of Cornwall to a point in the Town of Monroe near the village of that name." The valley which Crèvecoeur called "Skonomonk" is apparently that known now as "Smith's Clove."

in Pennsylvania & New York

"I got it out of my own head," he said. "I did it myself for the first time fifteen years ago. The results were happy and have been so ever since."

"Are you not afraid of doing harm to the multiplying of the two species?"

"No, because here we never kill our calves, and we have a great number of horses."

"We have come," I told him, "to spend a few days with you and then, armed with your instructions, to visit the great forges at Sterling, Ringwood, and Charlottenburg. Would you lend us some horses for that?"

"Very willingly. But I insist that you stay with me a week; then I will accompany you wherever you want to go. If you like hunting and fishing, there is plenty of that here to entertain you."

The next day, after we returned from an inspection of his meadows and fields, he brought several of his geldings out of the stable. "I hunt deer only on horseback," he told us, "and here are my mounts. They are tireless and never stumble. They have other good qualities as well, such as a lively trot, even though they are never shod."

"Where do these good qualities come from?"

"From their training. Three times a week during summer I have lead weights attached to their front feet. They are taught first to walk with these weights on, then to trot. Six months of that exercise is sufficient to keep their hind feet from ever reaching their front feet, no matter how fast they trot or how long they are kept at it."

"How much land do you cultivate?"

"Seven hundred forty-eight acres. That is too much, I know, for one man can scarcely oversee such a big undertaking. But the machinery is in operation; I would not be able to do otherwise. Besides, I have nine children, and if all of them wanted to be farmers like their father, you see that the 1,500 acres that I own here would not be enough to make each of them a good plantation. I have attended to that by a considerable purchase which I have just made in the new county of Otsego."

"Since there are almost no stumps in your field," Monsieur Herman said to him, "this great clearing must have been begun before your time."

"No. I myself cut down the first tree thirty-one years ago; I was then eighteen. I was not here by myself, as you might guess. What a frightful scene the bottom of that valley presented then! The bountiful wealth of nature was buried under the most forbidding debris, trees uprooted and trees partly buried under the ground. These beautiful meadows, these grasslands, today so smooth and green, were only a marsh filled with willows, the ends of whose branches took root again to form new trunks, with trailing black brambles, with thorny vines whose countless shoots intertwined with the bushes and made them impenetrable, and with water ash and water maple trees of a great height. Future generations certainly owe us much gratitude. But could they ever understand what weariness and misery, what disgust and vexation accompanied those painful beginnings?"

[There follows (pp. 268-72) the narrative of how in his youth Colonel Woodhull gave up in despair and left his property for the sea, only to return in a few months cured of the despondency and discouragement caused by the great labors necessary to clear the land for farming.]

"Back in New York after five months absence, I left for Long Island the day following my arrival, in order to throw myself in the arms of my parents, whose just anger I feared. What was my surprise and joy when I learned that my father was out here, and when my mother told me what he had said when he received my letter! 'The discouragement which has seized our young man,' he had said, 'does not surprise me. He is not the first who in similar circumstances was overcome with it. But instead of going aboard a ship and running away from his native land, why did he not come and talk to me? Didn't he know that I was his father and his friend, and you his mother? I know only two ways of making him disgusted with life on the sea. I am going to hire six good workmen, who, with the four already at Schunnemunk will do a great deal of work during his absence. On his return, astonished, delighted with our progress, he will blush at his folly and be conscious of the price of the lesson I wanted to give him. Won't that be worth more than any other kind of reprimand? Soon he will forget the past, and so shall I. As for the second way, I shall speak of that only when he gets back.'

"That was one of the most beautiful moments of my life. Some days afterward I arrived here and found this good father, who told me, as he embraced me tenderly, his eyes bathed with tears, 'Well, Jesse! isn't this a better country than Surinam? It's true that you will not become a rich and voluptuous colonist, a millionaire, but a farmer, a laborer, healthy and with the comforts of life, who is not ashamed to handle the axe and hold the plow.'

" 'Oh, father!' I answered him, 'this climate, this country seems to me today like an earthly paradise when I compare it with the one I have just left. If you will forgive me, I shall devote myself without stint to the hardest work, until I have carried out your plans and made them mine!'

" 'Since you left,' he replied, 'I have had a field of twenty-seven acres cleared, fenced in, and sowed with wheat; grubbed up and burned a great number of stumps; destroyed two beaver dams; and erected a saw mill in order to get ready to build a decent and comfortable house, as well as a barn big enough for the harvests which you will some day have. Haven't I done well during the five months you were gone?

" 'I have another present to give you, Jesse,' he continued, 'a wife, the kind one ought to have, wise, healthy, hard working, and understanding. You know her, S. B. of the district of Cornwall. Embrace me. If you have brought back from Surinam neither sugar nor indigo, you have acquired something during your voyage that is worth much more, a thousand times more valuable to a young man like you; that is—experience. For life is like the ice of winter on which one learns to walk, to stand upright, only after being picked up from the first falls; and then too you will be able to understand your father better.'

" 'I have made a big mistake,' I told him; 'and if you will forgive me, it will be my last.'

" 'Yes, I am sure of it,' he said; 'embrace me! Let's forget everything.'

"Happy are the children to whom nature has given fathers, or, better still, friends like mine! They owe to them more than life. I am sorry to say that he is dead, but his memory, which I bless every day after offering my prayers to the Supreme Being, will be with me as long as I live. My good mother is still living, at St. George, on the island of Nassau.

"The next day, axe in hand, I was leaving for the woods, when he stopped me and said, 'Jesse, leave off. Go see the woman I have chosen for you, and win her love. I shall stay here until the beginning of winter.'

"I married her six months later, that dear and precious woman. And since then, she has completed my happiness. She has made me the father of nine children and is justly famous for her ability in household affairs, a very important talent here.

"In order to crown my happiness, a dear brother, a professor at the college in New Haven, came to spend the holidays of that same year with me. I owe to him several important improvements in farming. In the neighborhood of his town he has a little plantation on which, by dint of care, perseverence, and knowledge, he has brought together all the useful and pleasing things that are grown in these States. It can be said that his garden and farm are an epitome of farming for this continent. Once a year he gives a big dinner for his president and colleagues, for which he has a Greek name that I have forgotten. The linen on his table comes from cotton that he grows; his napkins are bordered by blue lines dyed with indigo, two or three ounces of which he makes every year. I can't tell you of the meats, the vegetables, and the fruits furnished by his poultry yard and his garden. Maple sugar, sesame oil, peach brandy, maple syrup and maple vinegar, cherry cider, cherry mead, cherry wine, preserves, a kind of tea from this country (Labrador tea), coffee even—everything comes from his fields, his garden, or his hothouse, yes, everything, even to his wax-candle. But what would astonish you most is the punch to which he treats his guests. The acid for that liquor comes from his garden too. It was I who, while going through the woods a few years ago, discovered this charming bush. It produces berries, big as a pigeon egg and of the most beautiful carnation color, that are filled with a transparent juice of the same color which our doctors have found to be as good as that of citrons from Jamaica or the Bahamas; this juice is exactly like that of the bog cranberry. It is rather unusual for a shrub and a tree to bear the same fruit, with no difference other than size."

The next day, not finding the Colonel in his parlor, we were not long in discovering that he was occupied in repairing the plow-share of one of his plows. "It is not for the sake of economy," he told us, "that I sometimes beat on my anvil, but in order to gain time, which is our whole fortune here. Time is more rapid than the water in my river. How often have I lost whole days of labor while waiting for the neighboring blacksmith to do a half-hour's work!"

"Why would time be more rapid here than anywhere else?" asked Monsieur Herman.

"Because we don't have any spring, and because summer gives way to winter so fast that often it is hard for us to get seeds in the ground before hay-making time is on us. From another point of view, the length of our winters oblige us to put in a big supply of hay. The work required to provide it sometimes lasts six weeks, for every year I mow nearly a hundred acres; and during that time our plows remain idle. You can indeed see that we have no time to lose, and that if our winters were not so long our harvests would be much greater.

"Then too, as sheriff of the county, I must spend several days at Goshen every time the upper and lower courts come there to hold their sessions; and as colonel of the militia for the same county, I am often obliged to leave my fields because of the four big yearly drills and the frequent inspections. All these extra duties, joined to the urgent care that is required by such a big undertaking and a household of thirty-five people, whom it is necessary to feed and clothe, contribute to make the time more rapid and precious for me than for most others."

"But," Monsieur Herman continued his questioning, "why is there a militia in a country which enjoys such great peace? Don't you have any regular troops?"

"We have none except those absolutely necessary to protect our frontiers and guard our new colonies established beyond the Ohio. There is not a single soldier in our towns. Furthermore, the Constitution requires that all citizens between the ages of eighteen and twenty-five be enrolled, armed, and ready to march. The peace and tranquillity of the towns and of the countrysides being a question only of safeguarding the laws, in case of need the magistrates call in detachments of the militia; by whom can these laws be better maintained, protected from all attack, than by the citizens themselves?"

That evening, having noticed that the candles which lighted up the parlor were green, my companion asked the Colonel the reason for it. "That is because they are not made with tallow," he replied, "but with vegetable wax produced from bushes that are very common in this district. They entirely cover the plateau on top of Schunnemunk Mountain. Nothing is more simple nor more easy than to get as many as one wants of them. Don't you notice how fragrant and sweet its smoke is? This wax has already been successfully whitened. In a few more years we shall have several new branches of industry and commerce that will be perfected. Already some of it is being sent with our beeswax to the Spanish and Portuguese islands, where farming requires the use of candlelight, even though the sun is shining.

"The same promptitude, the same care and foresight that preside over the work in our fields preside also over the management of our household. Here every year are spun enough cotton, flax, and wool to take care of the house and clothe the entire family. The various materials that are made of it are woven under my roof; those that have to be dyed undergo that operation here also. My wife is our chief dyer. We ordinarily dye eight to twelve hundred ells each year. It is the same with soap. Each family makes all it needs for the year, out of fat and vegetable wax. That operation is easier and quicker still than the making of sugar from maple trees.

"I owe to nature three or four hundred of those very useful trees, which I have carefully fenced in, and around which I have cleared away all other plant life in order to increase the strength and quantity of their sap. This fine orchard has become our little Jamaica and annually in the month of April furnishes me all the sugar, syrup, and vinegar that we need. Each tree gives three or four pounds. But in order not to exhaust them, I have divided them into three groups, only one group being bled a year. Since I cleared away everything that squeezed and stifled them, and since the sun now covers them with its beneficent rays, I notice that their sap is becoming richer and more abundant every year. In a few years, I hope that each one of them will give me five pounds of sugar. Already our country is beginning to refine it. Some I have just received from New York seems as fine and clear to me as that of Jamaica or Antigua. As for the vinegar, I know none better nor stronger."

Finally, preceded by the head of that good family, we left Schunnemunk for Sterling, from which we soon began to hear the sound of the great hammers, and where we arrived early.

CHAPTER III

A Tour of the Chief Ironworks of New York

SCARCELY had we put our horses in the stable when the proprietor, Mr. Townsend,[1] came out and welcomed us with all the politeness of a man accustomed to the frequent sight of strangers and travelers. In fact, his hospitality has for a long time been so well known that travelers going across the mountains on their way from the interior of New York always arrange things so that they may stay with him. When he learned that the purpose of our trip was to make a careful examination of his different works, he offered to show us all their details.

First, he led us to the great furnace where the ore was melted and then converted into blocks weighing sixty to a hundred pounds. It was located a short distance from the main dike, which, because of the favorable position of the rocks, had provided him with a huge supply of water at little cost. From a small stream he had made a little lake fifteen thousand acres in size, which he had stocked with fish, and on which he kept a handsome boat. The furnace fire was blown by two great bellows forty-eight by seven feet in size, made entirely of wood, without any iron or leather. The wind that they produced was so strong and loud that it seemed like a tempest.

"That furnace," he told us, "when nothing happens to it, produces yearly two thousand to twenty-four hundred tons of iron, three-fourths of which is converted into bars while the rest is melted into bullets, cannon, etc., for use in trade. These mountains furnish me not only with wood for charcoal but also with several kinds of minerals of an excellent quality, known by various names."

From there we went to see the forge. Here six great hammers were kept busy forging anchors and bars of iron, as well as several parts used in shipbuilding. Lower down, on the same stream, was the foundry with its reverberatory furnace. He pointed out to us several ingenious machines, with various uses, the models for which had been sent him, and which he had cast by using a kind of metal recently discovered in these mountains which, after two meltings, acquired the lightness and almost the color of tin.

"I can," he told us, "make from it the lightest and most delicate of things. What a pity that you didn't come eight or ten days sooner! I would have shown you two interesting products. First, three new kinds of plows, the principal parts of which I cast, but which are, however, no heavier than the old kind. Each of them is provided with a kind of graduated indicator that shows with the utmost precision how hard the team is pulling and consequently the resistance, that is, the tenacity of the soil. Second, a portable mill, designed to separate the grain from the chaff. That invention is only the outgrowth of another, by means of which all the ears of grain in a field are easily removed without the necessity of cutting the stalks at the foot and making bundles of them, as the old custom was. All those things have gone to Mount Vernon. For," he continued, "although General Washington, with talents no less distinguished, discharges his duties as president of the Union, to which he was called by the unanimous voice of affection and gratitude, and although the seat of the government is a hundred miles from his beautiful estate, he supervises his huge farming

---

[1] The first of three generations of Peter Townsends who operated the Sterling Ironworks not far from Crèvecoeur's old home. Here was made the great chain which blocked the Hudson at West Point during the Revolution. A condensed account of Crèvecoeur's visit with Mr. Townsend is found in James M. Swank's *History of the Manufacture of Iron in All Ages* (Philadelphia, 1892), pp. 140-41.

industry and directs the operation of it with a judgment and an attention worthy of much praise. Every week, like a merchant, he receives from there the details, the running account of his affairs. With the help of a giant map that he has let me see, he keeps up with all his fields, knows what their yield is, and decides what should be planted on each one. Never have order, planning, and economy of time been carried to such an extreme. It was the same way during the war. Congress and the public were not a little astonished when, on his returning to private life, he first rendered the accounts of his command, among which were those of the particular expense of services given secretly for seven years, written entirely in his hand and amounting to more than twelve or fourteen thousand guineas. During that long interval, as well as during the time that he has been head of the general government, this illustrious Agricola has never stopped being one of the most enlightened farmers in the United States. Before the Revolution he owned forty plows, and in 1772 he gathered nearly ten thousand bushels of wheat."

From the foundry we went to see the ovens in which the iron was converted into steel. "It is not so good yet as that of Sweden," Mr. Townsend said to us, "but we come close to them. After a few more years of experience, we should reach perfection. The iron that comes from under my hammers has for a long time enjoyed a good reputation and sells for a price of twenty-eight to thirty pounds per ton."

He continued, "Do you see this big beautiful meadow, surrounded by the two branches of the river? I call it my masterpiece. It hasn't been ten years since this low spot was the drainage ditch for the mountains. I tried to have it cleared with axes, but the thickets and bushes with which it was covered offered so much resistance that that instrument was useless. I didn't know how to get the job done until the idea came to me of putting three hundred goats to pasture there and leaving them until the beginning of winter. Urged on by hunger, they quickly killed the bushes by stripping them of their bark. The following summer a general fire completed the job. I sowed my land in clover and timothy, and the next year that impenetrable mass of branches and thorns was replaced, to my great joy, by an abundant harvest of hay. That island has since become one of the best grasslands in the district. Several other farmers have done the same thing."

After spending two days examining the various works, admiring the ingenuity with which the flow of water had been directed, as well as the order and arrangement of the piles of wood used in supplying the charcoal that such a great enterprise needs, we left Mr. Townsend and the same day arrived at Ringwood, whose owner, Mr. Erskine, we knew had spent three years in Europe visiting the principal forges of Scotland, Sweden, and Germany. Although smaller, the works of this place did not seem less interesting to us. The structure and arrangement of the different machines designed to simplify operations made these works still more perfect than those we had seen at Sterling. Such a huge machine for making the iron into plates and then splitting it into bars seemed to Monsieur Herman a masterpiece of simplicity; but what made it still more singular was that the flour mill on top of it could be lowered whenever needed or raised as soon as it had finished grinding the grain. All of the parts of this flour mill were made of tin. Not far away was another machine used for boring cannon. Mr. Erskine told us that in an ordinary year he sold five hundred tons of iron in bars and two hundred in steel, without speaking of the cast-iron. But Ringwood, apart from its supply of water and firewood, enjoys an immeasurable advantage, that of being only a short distance from the Hackensack River, which flows into the great bay of New York.

"What resources," Monsieur Herman exclaimed to him, "these mountains offer to the inhabitants of the two states of New York and New Jersey! The great size of the forests that cover them to the top of their highest peaks; the different kinds of minerals that can be found in them with as much ease as abundance; the rich and fertile valleys; the numerous streams that water them, as well as the springs that are found at various heights and which are so useful in irrigating the grasslands and fields! What resources for prosperity and riches! If your descendants take care of these beautiful woods, they will for centuries enjoy the precious advantages of having the charcoal necessary for the manufacture of iron, the means of repairing the buildings and mill-gates, and all that a person of influence needs."

"You are right," said Mr. Erskine. "It is probable that that will happen, since the entire chain of mountains has for a long time been the property of a few people extremely interested in the preservation of the forests. From the boundaries of Connecticut all the way to New Jersey, one may count in these mountains seven furnaces and six giant forges, without speaking of the foundries and several refineries, all of which produce annually some 140,000 hundredweights of forged iron, much steel, and anchors, cannon, and other products. If, from another point of view, I could know how much the harvests yielded and the value of the animals raised in the valleys, I am persuaded that a rich and fertile plain of 882 square miles —that is my estimate of the space occupied by these mountains—would not be so productive."

The next day we went to Charlottenburg, across a very mountainous country. The works there had been built before the Revolution by an English company whom the war had ruined. The furnace had just been broken, and the owner was away. We saw there a huge machine for making nails, much simplified by means of a great number of little hammers that were set in motion by an outside water wheel. Iron pins were made there, as well as several other parts used in shipbuilding. We also saw a machine for making sheet metal and the iron plates used in manufacturing spades and shovels. There, as well as at Sterling and Ringwood, the supply of water was immense. We were told that in the preceding year 46,000 hundredweights of pig iron had been smelted there.

From Charlottenburg, we had intended to pay a visit to Bellvale; but learning that we could see only some big hammers there, we decided to give up that plan in order to go and look at a natural prairie containing nearly 70,000 acres, located in a district only recently placed in cultivation.

CHAPTER IV

In the Backwoods of Pennsylvania

THE SCHOOLTEACHER FROM CONNECTICUT—A
NORTHUMBERLAND COUNTY PIONEER

WE WERE slowly traveling on, keeping on our left one of the arms of the Chiquisquaque[1] Creek which we had already crossed twice, when we saw a house covered with shingles and standing in a rather large clearing. The owner, whom we met a few minutes later, with the most amiable promptness offered us a place of rest for the night. We followed him across a moderately sized field of wheat. After taking care of our horses, this honest settler showed us, with a kind of veneration, the stump of the first pine that he had felled some years before, and called to our attention what he had already done and what remained to be done before he should be comfortable and well-to-do. He looked forward to the time when a certain part of his swamp would be converted into pasture land, a certain hill covered with wheat, or another with clover and then planted with apple and peach trees— and all this with such an air of joy and satisfaction that we involuntarily shared it. It seemed to me that I had never seen hope under such affecting colors; it was like the fullness of a happiness not yet achieved.

"Some years ago," he told us, "the desire of contributing to the success of my family, and of assuring its independence after my death, determined me to leave the town of Fairfield, where I kept a school of Greek and Latin. Content with my lot, I was instructing as best I could the youth who were entrusted to my care when I learned of the death of a relative who had just ended his days in Bengal and who had left me 1900 piastres. Fearful of confiding that sum of money to the hazards of trade, I resolved to use it in buying a certain amount of new land, the only speculation in which we are rarely deceived, if we join with it ingenuity and hard work. Having been told that the government of Pennsylvania had just made this part of the state into a county, I came here; and after inspecting it, I bought for 375 piastres—the price of it has more than doubled because of the troubles in Europe—the 426 acres that I own here. I hired a man from my state, who is still with me. Together we built this house from the trunks of the first trees that we cut down. At Wilkes-Barre I bought provisions for a year, a pair of oxen, two mares big with colts, and the tools I needed for my work. Finally after six months of labor, employed in drying up some acres of swamp-land and in clearing seventeen acres that we sowed in wheat, I went for my family. Since that time, hope has not left me for a single instant. I see in the fertility of the soil and in the price of food a certain recompense offered to whoever wants to merit it by intelligence and hard work. I plant much less than my neighbors, and yet I harvest more than they because I spend more time with it. Since coming here I have not felt the least touch of discouragement, although there have been many obstacles to overcome. Quite different from me, my nearest neighbor, who lives five miles away, is dissatisfied, I know not why, with his situation and with the condition of his land, which is, however, as fertile as mine, and intends to get rid of his poor improvements and move elsewhere. He will not be happy anywhere and will spend his life going from one new place to another, a frame of mind that is quite common among the first settlers.

[1] Crèvecoeur's spelling.

As for me, I have such a great idea of my powers and my courage that often I accomplish much more than I intended to, and that simply because I believed it possible. This feeling is, in fact, a powerful lever when a tree has to be felled or a stump uprooted.

"I have had the foresight to bring with me a great quantity of fruit stones and seeds which I have planted with great care. In a few years all the orchards and fruit trees in the district will come from my nursery. I owe nothing; already I am beginning to sell the surplus of my little harvest to the settlers whose establishments are newer than mine. The only inconvenience that I have is the distance that I find myself from a mill, from a church, and from a blacksmith. Eight shillings per year to encourage the killing of wolves and panthers is the only tax that the government imposes on us, but we pay that much with pleasure and gratitude. Our government is busy opening up some very useful roads. Tomorrow you will travel the one known by the name of Bridle Road, which begins at the sources of Muncy Creek, on the west branch of the Susquehanna, and ends at the sources of Shickshinny Creek, on the east branch. The stumps are still there, it is true, but the bridges have just been finished. As we dry up our swamps, the insects disappear. The laws of Congress are encouraging foreign trade, and a flourishing trade encourages farming. Our country enjoys peace and tranquillity. Up to now heaven has blessed the works of its children, and the seasons have been kind to us. Morning and evening we implore its grace and its instructions, so that we may strive to merit our blessings, not only by our prayers but also by our industry and harmony. I fear only the brevity of time, which, like the water of the stream, flows away and passes with such quickness."

That, gentlemen, is how the schoolmaster of Fairfield has become a citizen of Pennsylvania and a freeholder in the county of Northumberland.

Struck by what he had just heard, Monsieur Herman said to me that evening, "The simple conversation of this good settler from Connecticut has made a most profound impression on my heart. I blush at my own weakness. Just think! This man, transported from the center of a town to the middle of the forest, where there is hardly a path, submits to what is a hard and painful labor when compared with his earlier occupations, and, far from his relatives, his friends, and the help of society, is still cheerful and contented. In the evening, happy for having accomplished the task of the day, he gives thanks to the deity and the next day starts anew with the same courage and cheerfulness. The hope of comfort and independence animates him, encourages him, and takes the place for him of present happiness. He is at the same time a good father, a good husband, and a good farmer; and I, whom fortune has favored, I who have crossed the ocean in order to enjoy the sight that the origin and development of these young societies offer here to the meditation, I have not the strength to overcome a few minutes of disgust and to endure a few inconveniences in travel that just a little experience would cause to disappear! I feel myself suddenly a new man. If ever the obstacles and difficulties along the way or the inconveniences of the lodgings cause a reappearance of that shameful pusillanimity, I shall recall what Mr. W. Doolittle has just told us."

The next day, as our host had said, we traveled along a new road that had just been built and which led from the Muncy on the west branch to the Shickshinny, which falls into the east branch (known as Bridle Road).

CHAPTER V

In the Backwoods of Pennsylvania

AT THE HOME OF A POLISH REFUGEE IN LUZERNE COUNTY

WE WERE pursuing our travels much more contentedly, through very thick, gloomy woods, when the courage of Monsieur Herman was put to new tests by our having to swim across the two branches of Fishing Creek, which were filled with trees and bushes that had been brought down by the spring floods. "How much time and work it will take," he said to me, "before the beds of these rivers are entirely cleared and their banks, today so damp and inaccessible to the traveler, have become laughing prairies like those that lie along the banks of the Elbe between Magdeburg and Cuxhaven! How much labor, how much toil, before these settlers can, on the afternoon of a beautiful summer's day, gaze out on fields covered with the wealth of their harvests, on their orchards loaded with fruit!"

The monotony of that long and painful trip of sixty-seven miles, from the ferry at Meshoppen on the big river,[1] was softened for us not a little by our meeting with a rather large number of families, almost all European, but so recently established that we could hardly find a shelter and something to feed ourselves and our horses. Occupied with splitting rails, with girdling great trees, and with piling up and burning dry bushes, they so far had harvested only a few vegetables.

"Yes!" we were told by a man from Sweden at whose home we had stopped to refresh our horses, "I can die without being uneasy about the future of my children, since I am going to leave them in a country of abundance where labor is amply rewarded. They will not be exposed to the shame of begging, to remorse, nor to the dangers of crime."

"Yes!" another said, "No longer shall I hitch wretched cows to a sorry plow in order to skim the surface of the sandy soil in my private land! Here the oxen and horses plow deep and fertile soil that belongs to me."

"Born in the midst of the avalanches and glaciers of Savoy," said a third, "industrious as I was, I needed nothing to be happy but good laws and good soil. Here I have found all I wanted, and even more, since the government and the god of harvests require only our gratitude and our prayers."

After crossing the Susquehanna we were slowly making our way into Luzerne County when my companion said to me, "Yes, I confess it; I have begun to fulfill the object of my travels only since we met the settler from Fairfield. Since then I have been more interested than before in these cabins of logs and bark, the first dwellings of the colonists, destined to be replaced some day by cheerful homes, just as these rude clearings, through industry and necessity, will be converted into fertile fields. With much less aversion I cross these forests whose soil, heretofore harsh and sterile, will soon provide food for thousands of families, and these humid and impenetrable swamps on which countless herds of animals will some day graze. I am having the opportunity," he continued, "of observing what can truly be called the origin of society. Yes, without doubt, because in these places where, just seven months ago, only the cries of panthers and the howls of wolves were to be heard, we see the plow tracing its first furrows, the fire consuming the bushes and useless grass, and we hear the sound of axes, the songs of happiness, the bustle of labor and life.

1 The Susquehanna.

Yes, without doubt, because we are traveling paths which will some day be great and beautiful highways, and because we are conversing with the first magistrates, who, like the other colonists, are occupied in clearing the surface of their land, in planting their corn, or in sowing their first fields of wheat among trees that have been left standing and among branches, stumps, and roots piled up and burning!"

"To own a piece of land," I said to Monsieur Herman, "to farm it, is here the universal ambition. Furthermore, since the beginning of the colonies, agriculture, although still in its infancy, has been the favorite occupation of both classes of society and the foundation for the prosperity of these states. However, the colonists do not all succeed. Here, as elsewhere, success does not crown all undertakings. Here, as elsewhere, man is exposed to danger from accidents, bad weather, and the caprices of fate. The settlers do not all bring with them the necessary disposition, nor the habits, nor the intelligence that this new way of life requires. They do not all have the same amount of strength, of courage, of judgment, and they are not all equally happy. Illness, insects, negligence, and laziness often destroy their hopes. If, when the time comes that the land must be paid for, the settler is not able to supply the necessary sum of money, the law gives back the land to its original owner, after recompensing the purchaser for any improvements he has made. And even among those who owe nothing, how many times is it not found to be true that some grow lazy when they find out that with just two days of work they can live for the rest of the week! Examples like these are found much more often among the foreign born colonists than among the settlers from the northern states, whose way of life, intelligence, and industry are so often worthy of great praise."

In the meantime we were traveling on toward the salt lick farms in the district around Philippopolis and west of Mount Ararat, when on the evening of the third day after crossing the great river, as we were making our way through a large swamp —which I have since found out is the source for one of the branches of the Wyolusing—we heard a clock striking. Encouraged by this sound, so unusual in such a sparsely populated country, we continued on our way more gaily and soon arrived at a field of corn, a young orchard, and a house, a newly built house, it is true, but one with four little wooden windows.

"All this," said Monsieur Herman, "gives signs of being a good place to stop. Let us rejoice and forget the fatigues of this long day's journey."

We still had some little distance to go when a man with a distinguished looking form and countenance appeared and said to us, "Welcome, gentlemen; get down and come in. You have either powerful motives or a great deal of courage to dare a trip through a country still so thinly populated. Have you not strayed from your road?"

"One is not off his road," replied my companion, "when he has the good luck to meet a colonist such as you seem to be, and the good luck to be invited to spend the night under such a fine roof."

"Ah! Gentlemen, don't praise the hospitality of the woods more than it deserves. If you knew how great my pleasure is and how real the need of hearing news from informed travelers, you would realize that it is I who thank you for a good turn."

"You underrate what you want to give us."

"Well! Think of it as reciprocity, and I shall be satisfied."

"How many years have you been living here?" I asked him.

"Seven," he replied. "Tomorrow I shall let you see that I haven't wasted my time. When a person wants immediate results, it costs something; but money that is wisely spent in clearing land and drying up swamps returns more than a hundred percent. My ambition is some day to have great meadows and pasturelands on which to raise and feed many cattle and horses. I have great respect for the plow, but I take even more to the scythe, because that kind of farming requires fewer hands. Ten years ago this country was scarcely known and was frequented only by hunters; the land was hardly worth six silver sous an acre. What a difference today! It is the same everywhere. The 110-acre lots that the Penn family sold on the other side of the Alleghenies for twenty-five piastres are now worth more than ninety; and we haven't been enjoying the benefit of municipal laws for more than three years!"

"Is this a healthy country?" asked Monsieur Herman.

"Except for a kind of fever that comes at certain times of the year," he replied. "But it is caused by the ignorance of the settlers rather than by the climate. After getting hot from their labor, they lie down in the shade of a tree; perspiration stops and they grow cold. I brought with me out here a simple and sure remedy, which has already been of great benefit to many of these colonists."

"You talk like a man who understands medicine."

"I practiced it a little in Europe."

"What! Are you a European?"

"Alas! yes. I am from Poland, and Poland is no more. You have heard of our confederations, of the first division of our lands—which took away five million subjects from the king of that unfortunate country—and of the general dismemberment made by the Northern Powers.[2] Since that time the wails of my unfortunate compatriots have resounded through the world in vain. What a deplorable event! Russia having seized the province where I was born, I was forced to go as a surgeon into the hospitals and dress the wounds of those who had ravaged my land and then enslaved it. Angered by this shameful servitude, I formed the plan of breaking my bonds or perishing. Everything in this world, as you must know, depends on chance. I owe my escape to chance—to my lucky arrival at Copenhagen and to the good fortune of being of assistance to a captain of a ship ready to leave for Lisbon. He had hardly discharged his cargo there when he took on another for New York, where we arrived after forty-seven days. And in less than four months, from the village of Orsa on the Dnieper River, I found myself landed on this continent. What is it then that controls the fate and fortune of men? Some days after my arrival, because of my knowledge of the German language, I made the friendship of Doctor Ebeling, the minister of the Luthern church at New

[2] The "first division" was made by Russia, Austria, and Germany in 1772; the "general dismemberment" occurred in 1795.

York, who recommended me to his colleague, the Reverend Mulhausen, at German Flats, on the Mohawk River. This worthy and respectable churchman welcomed me as if I had been one of his countrymen; and when I had finished telling him of my misfortunes, he became even more friendly and interested. After making it known in his neighborhood that I was a surgeon, he volunteered to give me advice and direct my first steps in this new land.

"Oh! when compared with the slavery I had just left, how sweet and delicious seemed this new independence and this thoughtfulness, which I was quick to enjoy! It was for me like a second birth. Of all the moments of the day, the time of waking was most filled with charms for me, because then, since my dreams often took me back to Poland, to find myself an inhabitant of North America and a citizen of this new state was a new and exquisite joy. At last, feeling for the first time a happy existence, I swore to forget the past and to concern myself only with pleasing hopes for the future.

"If my imagination was vividly struck at the sight of the beautiful rivers, the great lakes, and the mighty waterfalls of this country, how much also were my heart and mind aroused by a close examination of the bases on which these new societies were founded! The mildness and the justice of the laws; the ease with which one can acquire land; the civil importance that goes with that possession; the ample recompense assured by work and skill; the harmony and the great number of children that are found in almost every family; in short, the general happiness! At the sight of this moving spectacle, I began to conceive a better impression of human nature and to love my fellow men. After I had practiced medicine for a few years in the land of the Mohawks, the Reverend Mulhausen gave me his daughter in marriage and made me a present of the 750 acres which I own here. It is to him that I owe the greatest, as well as the most precious, of blessings, the best of wives. There she is, that angel of goodness and sweetness, to whom I owe everything—the children she has given me, the land that I am clearing, and the happiness, as well as the order, the comfort, and the neatness of my little dwelling.

"Furthermore, it is the long and interesting conversations of her revered father," he continued, "that have given me the advantage of learning the history of these states during the period of their colonial infancy, the details regarding the new social compact which has held them together since their separation from the mother country, the boundaries that separate them from the three neighboring nations, and the code of civil laws on which rest the freedom of the individual and the freedom of religion. What a contrast between the absurd and barbaric feudal customs known in Poland for so many centuries and the system, adopted by these states, which protects both life and property! What a contrast between the religious oppression which has been the source of nearly all the ills that have inundated my fatherland and the constant protection that this government accords all religions equally, a protection that is not the result of tolerance, but of justice, since it is founded not on opinion but on natural law.

"One day my revered father-in-law said to me, 'For a long time I have been at once a minister of the gospel, a physician, and a farmer. I dare appeal to the divine inspector of hearts, as well as to my neighbors; they will judge whether or not I have done everything that is in my power to fulfill the duties of those three positions in life. I took charge of the clearing of four hundred acres of land that the government had donated to the church of this district at the time we were given a map of incorporation, and since then I have been asked to set aside two-thirds of that land for the support of a free school. I have grown old while following the beautiful and interesting career which you are about to enter. But the fruits of this old age are neither sad nor bitter, unlike the experience of those who pursue goals less honorable and less useful. The store of knowledge I have acquired is a little treasure which I wish to bequeath to you as to one who is charged with contributing to the happiness of my daughter. In this way I shall have a part in your success. My desire is only the natural result of the friendship and affection which I feel toward the man whom I have esteemed enough to make my son-in-law.

" 'They are deceived,' my father-in-law continued, 'who expect to become rich at farming; it does not make people rich in these northern states. The seasons pass too quickly, the winters are too long, and help is still too costly. But for those who work hard, it brings comfort and abundance. In order to succeed in the woods, one must have some money to start with, so that he will not be crushed by the yearly interest on borrowed funds; he must also have some knowledge of this new way of life. Since the job of farming is like a bundle composed of several parts, everything that pertains to work, to supervision, and to planning must be equally the object of your daily attention. It is indispensable to know the nature and quality of soils in order to plant in them only the seeds that suit them best, and to have some of the skill of the veterinarian, although the animals who roam at liberty and eat enough salt are rarely sick.

" 'The first of all those virtues that are so useful to a colonist, after the love of work, is a soft and conciliatory spirit, which is absolutely necessary for getting along with one's neighbors; for you will not be isolated forever. The peace of a neighborhood is a constant source of prosperity. You will see what wonders a spirit of brotherly harmony can perform among men who are destined to help each other in the great and painful task of clearing the land. I know of no obstacles that a union of wills and efforts cannot cause to disappear. Everything becomes easier and more beautiful; and in a few short years the most dismal forests, the driest deserts, will be covered with flowers, with fruits, with harvests.

" 'After having felled the first tree on your plantation, pray to heaven that you will be given health, the mother of strength, the aid to perseverance and courage. Yes, that is necessary, even more than one thinks, to bear the solitude of the forest, to strip from the surface of the soil those giants at the foot of

in Pennsylvania & New York 43

which man seems so weak, to clear the land and burn everything that encumbers it, to dry up the swamps, to plant and enclose fruit trees, to open up roads, to build houses and barns. If ever you begin to have feelings of disgust, the forerunners of discouragement, think of the wife I have given you and of the children she will give you. If that powerful incentive does not call you back to activity and devotion, you are not destined to become a good and true colonist.

" 'Have a care,' he continued, 'for the illusions of the imagination, which, too often, make distant objects seem more beautiful than they are; for nothing is more seductive than the project of setting up an establishment in some new place. Don't do as so many farmers I have known. Cut down only the trees that are in your way; for the cold of your long winters, the building and repairing of your barns and sheds, the upkeep of your fences, all require a huge amount of wood. The second generation will regret bitterly that the first destroyed so many trees, something that has already happened in several districts of New Jersey and Connecticut, where, for lack of wood, the value of the land has diminished considerably.

" 'And even if one considers the forests only as an ornament, as a magnificent robe with which nature in its kindness has covered this continent, are they not beautiful and majestic? How can one keep from venerating these gigantic pines, which no amount of human skill and cultivation can ever replace? Those oaks, whose origin is much more ancient than that of our greatest cities? This respect for the forests and the beautiful trees is so natural that, in spite of the labor and the expense necessary to clear, enclose, and cultivate the fields, in spite of the distressing habit of looking at the trees only as enemies, as 'intruders' who occupy the soil one needs, a landowner, after some years of possession, is instinctively more moved, more flattered, on going through his woods than in crossing his fields. Once cleared and submitted to the plow, these fields seem to him to be only his own work; nothing grows there except what he has sowed or planted. In his forests, on the other hand, everything carries the mark of grandeur and endurance, a sentiment with which men, even the most ignorant, are involuntarily struck.

" 'The colonist,' he went on, 'who has surmounted the first difficulties of his establishment, and who owes nothing, is happier and richer than he thinks. He is as free as he can be in a social state; his fortune is better assured than in any other situation; he has only a few outside connections; the source of his independence is within himself, if he has known how to summon peace and moderate his desires; his joys, so long solicited by labor and active industry, are keen and pure; and finally, the laws which in other places favor some and oppress others are here designed to favor no one.

" 'Do you wish to increase your happiness? Contribute to that of your neighbors. Assist them in their illness; give them advice that will keep them in health. That is what I have been doing for a great many years. Do you want to become a distinguished and respected colonist? Teach your neighbors by your example and by your discourse the love of work, of industry, of order, of justice, as well as the worship of a God who repays virtue and punishes crime. If ever your talents and the public esteem make of you a representative in the federal government, never forget that the strength of the federated states was born out of their union, that the greatness, the prosperity of this new country are founded only on that unity. All the laws destined to cement it will be obtained by your vote and your support, as well as those laws whose end will be to encourage the clearing of land and the perfecting of the art of agriculture. It is our national taste, a sure guarantor of religion and customs, which has raised us so rapidly from the feebleness of infancy to the vigor of adolescence; and that it is which, in less than a half century, will lead us to the strength of manhood.

" 'As a son loves his parents, you must love your new country. Bend all your efforts to propagate the system of public education that has been practiced so long in the northern states, the most useful perhaps that modern times have discovered. The light of a good education spread through all classes of society strengthens the happiness of family life and assures the tranquillity and glory of the nation. Honor a government that reason has founded on the eternal bases of justice and libery. During peace, consecrate your talents and your example; during war, your courage and your blood, if they are necessary. At this price only can a good citizen pay his debts to his country. Scorn those orators who, in order to curry favor with the public, blame without ceasing the form and the laws of government, as if what comes from man can be perfect. To want to go beyond the bounds of human reason ought to be looked upon as foolishness, and these fanatics, as the enemies of the public peace.

" 'Like you I saw the light of day in a country where for centuries men were bound to the soil; like you, after overcoming a thousand obstacles, I landed on the shores of this new world, towards which penury, despair, intolerance, and misfortune lead the debris of the old, as the waves of the sea carry the debris of the tempest to the nearby land. Just as a plant, blighted by the shade of trees, spreads out and grows as soon as it has been transplanted to a place where it can enjoy the dew of the sky and the rays of the sun, so the happy seeds that I had received from nature, long stifled by misery and ignorance, sprouted soon after my arrival in this country and produced fruit. I remember it well. The day after my naturalization, full of joy and hope at the sight of a country, of a city, where work, industry, and useful talents were so amply rewarded, and where there was so much space, I forgot that I was a Salzburger and thought of myself only as a member of the new family of the United States.'

"That, Gentlemen, is what this venerable man, this worthy minister of the gospel, has so often told me."

The next day, struck by the size and the beauty of his barn, I asked him why it was such a handsome structure when his house was built only of squared logs.

"My father-in-law," he told me, "exacted a promise that I would not consider a better house until after the ninth harvest.

If all the new settlers acted as prudently, misfortunes would occur less frequently among them. Most of them build too much above their means. The pines and oaks of which my barn is constructed I hauled across the snow to a sawmill belonging to one of my neighbors, and although it is very big, it cost me much less than you would perhaps imagine; I paid out only three hundred piastres.

"Here is an orchard," he continued, "whose trees came from Schoharie. I planted it on the south slope of this little hill so that it could be more easily irrigated by the waters of the stream you just crossed. That's what gives it the air of freshness you noticed. But I shall not enjoy that advantage very long; this creek diminishes in size as the number of clearings in the neighborhood grows larger. I know some people who, because they did not see that the source of their streams was in the marshes, built mills that have today become useless. If this stream ever dries up, it will be an irreparable loss; for it is hard to understand, without having seen it, the effect that irrigation has on young shoots and on the growth of trees, particularly in the month of August. This orchard will be covered with blooms and fruit long before those of my neighbors."

"But why," asked Monsieur Herman, "are your roads still so bad?"

"That is the result of the great territorial dispute between this state and Connecticut. Happily for us it is now ended. Since then everything has been changed. The government has made this section of the country into a county and has subdivided it into districts, according to the custom. In order that the influence of the law can extend to all these places, it has just opened up a road that runs from the Susquehanna to the line of demarcation. We are told that the road from New York will be extended across the counties of Tioga, Otsego, and Albany. Already we have nearly three hundred free-holding families in this part of the state, as well as several flour and saw mills, two churches, and some schools. Next year, bridges will be built across the principal creeks. And, gentlemen, I was almost alone here only a few years ago!

"There have been several reasons for this progress: the navigation of the Susquehanna as far as Northumberland, the great quantity of lowlands, the encouragement that Congress has given to the cultivation of hemp, and the introduction of two branches of industry that were previously unknown in these districts. The first of these is the production of potash; the second, the extraction of maple sugar. It is the philanthropic society of the Quakers to whom we owe the advantage of having the latter. What would you say if I assured you that within the space of two years there had been sold perhaps 5,000 hundredweights of maple sugar at the Exchange in Philadelphia? What a benefit of nature! This benefit is to be found from the plains of Kentucky, at the thirty-fifth latitude, to Canada, at the forty-seventh."

On our return from the fields, his wife led us into what she smilingly called her parlor. On the table was placed one of the most pleasing meals that we had seen since our departure from Carlisle.

"What luxury for new colonists!" my companion observed.

"Why do you call it that," she replied, "when it is only the enjoyment of the fruits of our labor? The tea comes from China, it is true; but we pay for it with ginseng from our woods. The shad, the ham, the beef, the honeycombs, the preserves, and the sugar, everything is our own. My husband owns one-eighteenth of a seine on the big river, which brings him nearly two hundred of these fish every year; and we know how to use smoke in preserving beef and ham."

During this conversation, Mr. Nadowisky, who noticed that we frequently turned our eyes to a little oil painting on which could be seen the following three words written in big Anglo-Saxon letters, PROPERTY, PROTECTION, JUSTICE, said to us, "Gentlemen, those names that you see are the names of three charitable spirits whose aid I had uselessly implored in my native land; here, placed by the side of the laws, and under their tutelary aegis, they have received from me a peculiar kind of worship, that of gratitude."

On leaving this splendid family, Monsieur Herman took the

hand of the head of the household and said, "After living for a long time in the midst of the old social institutions, and after experiencing degradation and misfortune, how happy you should be for having escaped and for having become a member of a society founded on such different principals! How this striking contrast should contribute to making your sojourn in the forest less sad and dismal, and in easing the painful task which you have imposed on yourself! Never shall I forget what I have seen and heard in this home of prosperity, happiness, and blessing."

CHAPTER VI

Lost on a Bee Hunt in Bedford County

EARLY the next morning, according to our plan, we lightheartedly set out to hunt for bee trees, provided with a tinder box, flint and steel, and various other necessary articles, the weight and bulk of which prevented us from carrying guns. Nothing could have been more exact than the information which Mr. —— gave us before we left; with it we should even have been able to cross the Alleghenies safely. In less than half an hour we found ourselves on the edge of a wide and deep ravine, which appeared to serve as a drainage for the torrents occasioned by the melting of the snows. In all our travels we had never seen such a striking scene; it was the picture of destruction and havoc. On one side there were pools of stagnant water filled with reptiles and with the heads of isolated rocks against which the flood waters had broken with great violence. On the other side there were accumulations of mud, sand, and gravel; some heaps of interwoven trees, built up like dikes, which, judging by the great masses of leaves and dry dirt, appeared to have resisted the violence of the waters; and finally, some stumps and branches so piled against the banks that one could not approach them.

Knowing how difficult it would be for such novices as ourselves to cross over these obstacles, we were astonished that Mr.

—— had not told us about them. We decided to follow the banks of the gully until we should find a place not so deep and easier to cross. Such a place we found after traveling two or three miles farther. But too preoccupied and distracted, we went straight on after our crossing and failed to ascend the ravine as far as our next marker. Fatal carelessness! We had gone into the woods I know not how far when Monsieur Herman, stopping suddenly, cried out, "Our trees! Where are they? We have lost our way! We are ruined!"

Like a light that reveals to the traveler's eye the precipice to whose edge darkness has led him, these words, suddenly opening my eyes, caused me to perceive the danger into which our carelessness had led us.

"Let us go back the way we came," I told him. "Since we have been keeping the moss on the trees to our left, we have been going west; if we keep it to our right, we will find ourselves again at the ravine, whose course should be north and south." But not having, like the Indians, the ability to trace our steps by the displacement of the leaves, besides being anxious and uneasy, we were deceived in our hopes. Night surprised us before we could find anything that would set our fears at rest. In the woods, as on the sea and elsewhere, one error leads to another; the greater the distance that one travels in trying to find a lost road, the farther one gets from it. That is what happened to us.

Although seven months have gone by since that unhappy adventure, I still recall those frightful images that appeared when day left us in the woods. Time, with its file and its sponge, will never efface from my mind the painful memory of the moment when I saw the face of death behind the horrors of despair and hunger. Night having come, I was occupied in the search for dry wood to light a fire, when Monsieur Herman, who was a little distance away, cried out, "What are we going to do? What will become of us?"

"What's the matter? What has happened?" I asked him.

"I have lost the flint and steel, probably in the fall I took crossing the ravine. Would it be possible to find them in these woods?"

"That isn't very likely," I answered him; "Moreover, one could scarcely see now to make the search."

It is indeed true, as I have often heard it said, that misfortune never comes alone! "Give me the tinder box," I told him, "I am going to try to light it with the first stones that we find." But our attempts were fruitless.

"What!" my companion exclaimed to me sadly; "must we be exposed to the fury of wolves and panthers for the lack of a single piece of flint when there are so many pieces of it lying useless on the earth! Of all the possible combinations of misfortune, this one appears to me to be the most fatal. Of what, I wonder, does good fortune in life consist? Elsewhere the kind of rock we so much need is used lavishly in the building of roads; here one alone would console us, would bring back confidence and courage, by producing fire and light."

"Let us not give ourselves up to despair," I told him, "because of one night passed without fire at the foot of a tree. We are lost if we do so. Give me your shoes. I am going to place them, and mine, some distance away from us. Be sure that, with the help of this feeble ruse, we shall pass the night tranquilly, and tomorrow we shall get out of this maze."

Weakened as we were by hunger and fatigue and bowed down under the weight of mournful and gloomy reflections and presentments, how the hours of that night seemed to drag out! Our eyes soon accustomed themselves to the darkness. The more or less faraway cries of the wolves, the shrill voice of the nighthawks and the owls, repeated over and over by the nocturnal echoes of the forest, the noise, the slightest suspicion of movement, the sighs even of the breezes, gave birth to a thousand conjectures in the agitated mind of my companion. His imagination, exercising all its power in the creation of the most sinister forebodings, drove away sleep from his tired eyes. Whence comes this effect of darkness on the spirits of most men?

After having for a long time occupied myself with recalling what little I knew of the geography of that part of the mountains, the course of the ravine, and the direction of the route we had taken since crossing it, I resolved that at daybreak I would climb to the top of a tall tree and watch the sun come up. I was telling Monsieur Herman of my intention, when, in an angry tone, he said to me, "You led me into this awful predicament, telling me about bee hunting."

"Well," I replied, "and am I not here also? Is bitter feeling now going to replace friendship and confidence? That's the way men are: circumstances alone decide their feelings for each other."

That eternal night finally rolled away, and as soon as day appeared I carried out my plan. Then, marking the point on the horizon where I had seen the sun rise, and persuaded that our route should be to the northeast, we set out in that direction. We should truly have found our way back to the ravine if we had not been forced to cross several valleys filled with high bushes, in the middle of which we again lost ourselves. How is one to guide himself through these forests, when each new object so closely resembles one that has just been left behind? What is one to use for the signs so necessary in traveling through these lonely and unknown woods? Is one to depend upon study or upon inspiration? How do the Indians manage so well? I spoke to my companion of what I knew concerning the inconceivable sagacity of the animals, who never get lost in the woods. "That is what causes me to blush with shame," he said, "when I think that two cows with their instinct are better equipped to get out of the predicament we are in than two men, with their reason and their judgment."

We kept on walking, or, rather, we wandered about all day, without perceiving the slightest sign that would suggest the presence of some nearby plantation or the ravine for which we sought; nor could we find a single fruit, a single berry with which to appease the hunger that was gnawing at our intestines. How many times in the course of that long day did we give ear to the slightest sound without hearing any-

in Pennsylvania & New York 53

thing but the lugubrious accents of the forest birds and vague, indistinct murmurs which, in a more happy time, would have sounded to us like the voice of Nature! How many times did we call out without hearing any response except those faraway echoes which made us shiver more than once because we believed them to be the answering voice of a man! Why does time, which ordinarily passes like the shadow of the sun, without its progress being noticeable, permit our moments of happiness to roll away so fast and prolong, on the contrary, our moments of unhappiness, as if to make us feel more vividly all the bitterness? Tormented by hunger, irritation, and despair, we ended the second and the cruellest night that I have ever known. And filled with sad forebodings we began the third day of that ill-fated excursion into the woods.

We no longer spoke. Absorbed, plunged into the depths of consternation and weakness, we were walking slowly towards what we believed to be the northwest, when Monsier Herman suddenly cried out, "We are not far from a settlement! We are saved! Here are some holes recently dug which can only be the work of hogs."

"Alas! Would to Heaven it were so," I said. "This is only the work of one of the flocks of wild turkeys that fill these woods. Still, if we had our guns, one of these beautiful birds could sustain us for a long time, since nature has not placed here a single sort of fruit with which man can nourish himself. Never have forests been so sterile."

As if dark despair and the burning and excruciating pains of hunger were not enough to fill to the brim our cup of woe, towards the middle of this day a mad rage took possession of us. If we opened our mouths, it was only to overwhelm each other with abuses and biting reproaches concerning the trip. If by chance our eyes met, although dim and weak, they were still able to become enflamed with anger and hatred. These passions, which, until that time, we had never known, manifested themselves without warning and with great violence, as if some wicked genius had suddenly breathed them into our hearts. But no, the germs that nature had hidden there were undoubtedly waiting to develop themselves during just such sad circumstances as those to which we had been reduced. Ah! if, in these terrible moments of madness we had been carrying guns or had possessed the strength to seize each other, frantic as we were, one of us would have killed the other.

These tempests, which I recall now only with shame and fright, changed toward evening into the calm of extreme weakness and depression. We sat down underneath a tree, and immediately we were seized with a burning of the bowels which, at each instant, made us desire something to drink. Thus, to the torments, to the perpetual irritations of extreme hunger, was joined the devouring fever of thirst, the most insupportable of the needs to which man can be subjected. Happily, the changing of the wind having brought us the noise of a nearby waterfall, we followed the sound, and leaning from time to time against the trees for support, we finally found ourselves at nightfall on the border of a river, which I have since learned was one of the branches of the Aliquippa. There we quenched our burning thirst.

Monsieur Herman spent almost all that third night in the most frightful delirium. He cursed the day he was born, his trip across the ocean, and, above all, his companion, whose last agonies he hoped would come before his own so he might have the pleasure of watching them. But although this transport of fever and despair appeared to have given him new strength, I feared that he could not survive another paroxysm like that we had experienced at sunset. The great quantity of water that I had drunk produced a contrary effect upon me. It calmed the fever and the acute pains, but it deluged my face and body with a cold sweat; my faculties were duller, more enfeebled, than those of my unfortunate companion. Perhaps, though I was as unhappy, I suffered less. My eyes closed, and the last impression which today I can recall is that of the state of resignation into which I had fallen and the consciousness of the rapid decline of life. I regretted, however, that I was dying alone, abandoned at the foot of a tree. The idea of being devoured after death by carnivorous animals aroused in me the most profound horror.

Nevertheless, nature still had an eye to our preservation; the cessation of thought was with us the beginning of drowsiness. We seem to have slept for some hours, and, in spite of all our sinister forebodings, we saw the light of the fourth day. But, like a funeral torch, it served only to augment the horror of our predicament by permitting us to see the doors of the tomb which we were approaching.

Our eyes, covered with the film of death, in place of real objects saw only fantastic images, like us, agitated and trembling. Sometimes the shadows that surrounded us would suddenly be dispersed by shafts of flickering, short-lived light. Sometimes they offered us phantoms which, after fluttering towards us, skimming over the surface of the ground and grazing the tops of bushes, came finally to rest in the trees above. Often our eyes, almost out, saw everything through a translucent haze, unable any longer to distinguish anything. Such were the images produced by two imaginations nearly hidden in the shadows of death.

"It is sometimes when the cup of misfortune is full," I could yet say to my companion, while leading the way to the bank of the river, "that suddenly consolation, a gleam of hope, arrives. Have you never observed at sea those comforting intermissions during the most frightful storms? Here we are, arrived at the last possible stage of misfortune, still hoping!"

"How do you pronounce that word?" he asked me with the tone and gesture of wrath. "Despair and death have dissipated my last, lingering illusions. Since you are so inclined, keep on hoping. As for me, I am going to throw myself into that river, at the bottom of which peace and quiet sleep await me. Who would want to endure longer these biting pains, when from the middle of hell to a place of rest there is a distance of only twenty feet?"

"Let us try one more day," I said to him, "if that is possible. Let us drink more water, and if there comes to us no favorable sign, this evening we will drown ourselves together."

"Why should anyone suffer as I do?" he replied. "This evening is a hundred leagues away. . . . Well! since you have become my enemy by trying to persuade me to live a few more hours, kill your dog and give me my share that I may eat my fill. If you are so inhuman as to refuse me this, be generous enough to let me die on the instant."

The thought of killing that animal, a thought excused by the knowledge that a need so pressing had never yet existed, recalled me suddenly to hope and to life.

Far from heeding my affections and pity at the sight of the dog, as weak and languishing as ourselves, I was seized by a feeling far more violent than anger, a feeling of madness. I shivered. My trembling hands eagerly sought the knife that they had dropped among the leaves, while my companion, given new life by the hope of gratifying his hunger, accused me of slowness and overwhelmed me with new reproaches. As I reached for my submissive victim, an impulse from that invisible power who presides over our destinies guided my eyes to the stalk of a groundnut plant.

"We are saved!" I cried. "We are saved! The soil on which we spent the night, and where we expected to die, conceals that which will give us life again, for wherever there is one of these plants there will be a thousand of them. And all the time we were in ignorance!"

"Merciful God! Blessed God!" he cried out in his turn. "Are you not deceiving me?"

Immediately I offered him the first of the roots which I had just pulled up. But we were both so weak that it cost us much sweat and labor before we could obtain enough for our needs. Ah! if we had only possessed the means of lighting a fire, what a wonderful meal we could have had!

But how can I describe the effect that was produced on our spirits by the certainty of being able to provide enough food? How is it possible to depict this exquisite, new feeling, this unutterable rapture, which suddenly restored our depleted vigor, got hold of our withered spirits, and recalled the delicious and divine consolation of hope? And how can I render in words those feelings which, though hard to describe, I felt nevertheless so vividly: that sudden transition from extreme need to the possession of nourishment gathered by the light of a feeble ray of hope; the change from a desperate condition to a state of tranquillity; the passage finally from the banks of the gloomy Cocytus to the land of the living?

The passions which nearly caused the death of my poor dog were doubtless the same as those which, engendered by days of unsuccessful hunting, brought about the beginning of cannibalism; for the distance is not so great as one might think, between killing one's dog and killing one's friend. Like us, after having so long fought against hunger and irritated to the point of madness, lacking a dog, the strongest will kill the weakest. What a sad and deplorable result of an organization submitted to the rule of necessity! But then, that same necessity has never been able to cause the most ferocious and the most carnivorous of animals to fight their own kind in order to eat their carcasses. The second stage of cannibalism must have come as the aftermath to war, with the starving conquerors eating the vanquished people, a situation that still exists among the nations in the interior of North America, among the tribes of Brazil, and everywhere that Captain Cook landed.

Cannibalism ceased, however, when man learned to tame and raise animals. But how many centuries must have come before that happy discovery was made! Without this benefit of nature, where would we be today? And I, myself! Have I not approached cannibalism? Yes, without doubt, when I started to feed myself on the flesh of a being I loved, when I almost killed a companion who during so many years had been my faithful servant, even saving my life in a river, a friend whose experience, sagacity, and affection have so often struck me with respect and admiration. Ah! poor Ontario! What a happiness for you, and even more so for me, that you can never know that I reached the point of lifting my fratricidal hand against you! But even if you did know it, you would either not be able to believe it or you would forgive me.

However, having become more calm after satisfying our pressing needs and after enjoying some hours of a beneficent sleep, we again occupied ourselves with the search for groundnuts, of which we wanted to make an abundant provision, when I thought I heard the faint tinkle of one of those bells that the colonists fasten to the neck of the strongest animal in their herds. My ears . . . what am I saying! . . . my whole soul was recalled from its torpor by the mere thought of that consoling sound; I placed myself to leeward of the tree by whose trunk I had been standing when I thought I heard the bell. How long and cruel were those minutes that slipped by, tormenting me with doubt, with anxiety, and with the fear of being deceived! I was going to tell my companion, when that sound so much longed for came again, and so distinctly that my eyes suddenly filled with tears, my heart swelled and palpitated; I could scarcely say to him, "Yes! It is the ringing of a bell. I am sure of it. We shall not perish in these somber, uncultivated solitudes. The Alleghenies will not be our tomb. . . . Listen to that comforting and delightful sound! May the breeze that carried it to us be a thousand times blessed! . . . Yes! It is Heaven who sends hope to our aid; it is she who calls us. . . Get up. . . Obey her!"

But still much affected, trembling, our eyes fixed, our ears turned to the wind, it was only after having several times heard the bell that, reviving little by little, recalled slowly to life, we were able to find strength to move toward it. The sound became more and more distinct as we advanced, until about five o'clock we at last came upon the saving herd of animals grazing in a bog meadow.

"Let us give thanks," I said to Monsieur Herman, "for this unexpected favor, for our restoration to life, to society, and to our friends, not only by our feelings but also by expressing aloud our most heartfelt gratitude." And on the instant we fell to our knees underneath a tree, in order to address to Heaven the words that our agitated hearts inspired in us but which our feeble lips could scarcely pronounce.

The herd of animals, to whose wisdom and instinct we owe our return to a settlement, was composed of forty-two head, among which we counted eight cows. "I see those eight good ladies," my companion said to me," but how can we get milk from them?"

"With patience and gentleness," I answered. In fact, after several attempts, we were able to milk three of them into our hats. How exquisite this nectar sent from heaven seemed to us! It was the restoring balm of life, and I did not fail to give some of it to that humble and faithful servant which I had almost sacrificed during my delirium of hunger.

While we were waiting with impatience for the homeward trip of the herd, Monsieur Herman, recalling all that he had said to me in the access of despair and rage, begged me to forget it. "Those reproaches," I said to him, "those abuses, were the result of the deplorable condition to which we were reduced. Alas! That was only the least of our misfortunes. We have surmounted them all, however. Let us talk of the time when we shall get out of these woods and see again the light of the sun, the cultivated fields, the people who will become our friends because of our misfortunes; for how could man hate his own kind unless his passion or his interest dictated it? Let us free our hearts—blighted so long—to the sentiments of joy and tenderness, to the sweet emotions of friendship and kindness. Let the sad and painful thoughts be forever effaced from our memory and consigned to the deepest well of forgetfulness."

The bell-carrying ox finally stopped grazing and set out, as well as I could judge, in the direction of the northeast. We were slowly following the herd of guides, when Monsieur Herman, who could walk only with pain, said to me, "The night is coming on, as you see. I am not yet reassured. I am afraid that these animals are lost and will not be able to find their home."

"Do not worry," I said; "put your trust in the infallibility of the instinct that guides them. That unalterable light seems to be much more trustworthy in everything that is useful to them than is our pompous reason. I know some examples of sagacity and foresight among the animals raised in the forest that would bring honor to any man, no matter how proud he might be of his intelligence. How different are they from animals kept constantly within enclosed fields."

And finally, our eager, restless eyes, continually peering in the direction toward which the herd was moving, beheld a clearing. They suddenly filled with tears. We were seized by a sensation so extraordinary, a suffocation so violent, that, almost succumbing, we sat down at the foot of a tree. The sweat streamed down our faces; our hearts beat violently as in the first moments of fright. We were both in a condition of weakness so extreme that we could foresee neither its length nor its end. But our ecstasy finally becoming calmer, we rejoined the herd of animals.

"O memorable day!" I said to myself, "the day of my second birth! It shall never be erased from my memory! If ever misfortune, unhappiness, or sorrow assails me, I shall allay its pangs by thinking of the awful misery that is now about to end."

If the sudden passage from the darkness of the woods to the light of a clearing is always a striking contrast for those who have been long in the forest, how much more of a contrast was it for us who were emerging from the shadows of the tomb! But the horizon expanded little by little; already we could distinguish a field, some apple trees, some cherry trees. "I see these very interesting objects," said Monsieur Herman, "but where is the house?"

"A little patience," I replied. "The home of the family which has cleared this land is not far away." And in a few minutes we caught sight of a column of smoke rising perpendicularly, for the wind had fallen with the sun.

He who, swept away by the strength of the current, is saved at the instant when the waves are about to engulf him, or the sailor who, uncertain of his latitude, in the middle of a fog discovers his landfall, does not experience a greater, more profound joy than we did at the sight of that smoke, which was to us the lighthouse of salvation. At last we reached the house. And none too soon! The state of weakness and trembling to which we had arrived would not have permitted us to go another two miles.

"You will have much less milk today than you had yesterday," I announced to the lady of the house, who at the sound of the bell had come forth accompanied by her two daughters. "Dying of hunger for four days, we had the good fortune to find your cows, three of whom we milked. Then, with our strength renewed, we were able to follow them here in order to beg your hospitality."

"Sirs, even my enemies would have the right to my hospitality if they had gone through what you seem to have experienced," she replied. "Give me your arm, and come into the house."

Never were words pronounced more clearly, nor listened to with more attention and gratitude. The first service that generous woman rendered us was to perfume with maple sugar the beds which were destined for us; the second, to bring us a bowl of broth made from allagriches,[1] from which she permitted us to eat only a little at a time. When we reproached her with some bitterness for the small portions, the sweetness of her voice, which was that of humanity and reason, repressed our desires and silenced our tongues. What nutritive power is contained in that dish! I have often wondered since why it is not better known. However, I have heard of several doctors who prescribed its use for convalescents. The good woman assigned one of her daughters to remain with us until her strength-restoring diet guided us insensibly to sleep. . . What did I say? . . . to the most profound repose, the most balsamic rest that ever nature in the plenitude of its kindness saw fit to accord the shipwrecked mariner. The sun had climbed to its meridian on the following day before our eyes again opened.

By that time the master of the plantation had returned from a trip to the village of Bedford, where he had gone on business.

[1] Of all the dishes made from Indian corn the one known by this name is the most nourishing and the most useful to travelers. When the ears are just ripe, the Indians dry them and give them a light washing to take off the husks. After removing the grains they grind them in a mortar and add to them an equal quantity of maple sugar. This is the panacea which they use when they find nothing on searching the forests. Prepared as a broth nothing is more pleasant to the taste, nor more refreshing. When crushed these grains look much like rice. It was under this name that Penn's earliest companions sent some of them back to England. [Crèvecoeur's note, II, 391-92.]

He brought us a beautiful salmon trout and permitted us to eat our fill, giving us also several glasses of currant wine that had aged five years in his cellar, a wine that is found more commonly among the good colonists of Pennsylvania than among those of other states. What an event that meal was for us! What a contrast between the sweet and ravishing thoughts that now revived our spirits and those which on the previous day had caused us so much torture! We now enjoyed the most delicious calm and immobility.

After thanking the master of the house with all the effusion of our hearts for his wife's kindness, we told him our long, sad story. "It is not unusual," he explained, "for people who do not know the direction the streams take, or the way the mountains run, or the method of retracing their path by the displacement of the leaves, to get lost in this territory and almost die of hunger. You are not the first who have had this unhappy experience. I am thankful that it is my herd of cows to which we are indebted, you for your salvation and I for the pleasure of having you under my roof. I shall guide you back to my neighbor's house when you are entirely recovered; he lives only seven miles from here. And in the meantime, be assured that we will take care of you as if you were our relatives or our friends."

"May Providence permit us," Monsieur Herman told him, "to show you some day that you did not give refuge to a pair of ingrates. Could you be even kinder and send one of your people to our friend's house? He is no doubt much disturbed on our account and perhaps even considers us dead."

"Write him a letter," our host answered, "and I shall see that he gets it right away."

In fact, the very next day this good old soldier arrived early to see us; he was still quite overcome with pleasure and astonishment, and could not understand how we had wandered as far as the banks of the Aliquippa. He and his people had looked for us, he said, through the forest, both on the right and the left of the way we should have taken. They had been

in Pennsylvania & New York 63

as far as the foothills and had finally abandoned the search on the third day.

How pleasant it is to recall so many kindnesses, rendered with so much promptness and good will! No, never shall I forget what I owe to the saintly hospitality of the Forbes family, who live in Bedford County in the Allegheny Mountains.

Finally, after four days of rest, we were permitted to take mild exercise and go for walks; then, accompanied by our host, we set out for his plantation.

CHAPTER VII

The Bachelor Farmer of Cherry Valley

ALTHOUGH we had only fourteen miles to go before reaching the plantation that Mr. Wilson had told us about, we did not arrive there until four o'clock in the afternoon. Not since our departure from Onondaga had we found a country so heavily wooded or marshes so difficult to cross. Our horses were exhausted and Monsieur Herman almost discouraged, when we at last discovered a very tastefully built house. The entire front was decorated with a piazza supported, according to custom, by columns of white cedar. The windows, provided with outside shutters, were painted a pleasing color. Everything about it declared an extraordinary taste, to which our eyes had not been accustomed since our leaving Pennsylvania. "At last," said my companion, "here is a sanctuary which promises good beds for us and a good stable for our horses. . . To whom does this beautiful house belong?" he asked a man who was passing by.

"To a Jamaican," was the reply, "a man who works hard, but apparently for no reason, because he has neither wife nor children."

"What!" Monsieur Herman exclaimed to me, "to come from that rich and splendid Jamaica in order to establish himself in these dark and gloomy forests of New York! To prefer the raising of grain and hay, under a climate which for three months

in Pennsylvania & New York 65

of the year brings snow and ice, to the culture of sugar and cotton, under a climate that is like eternal spring! Such an idea seems strange to me."

Impelled by a desire to learn the reasons for his move, as well as by our need for rest, we stopped at the door to beg his hospitality for the night. "You don't need to ask for that," he told us; "how would one travel in these forests if the doors of the houses were not open to travelers? In inviting you to come in, I only give back what I have often received."

His house was roomy, neat, and comfortably arranged. I even saw some beautiful mahogany furniture. But I saw neither women nor children. He immediately gave orders for the care of our horses and then brought us refreshments, which we needed very much. As soon as our meal was served, he asked us, according to the custom, who we were, where we were from, and where we were going. We answered his questions in a manner that seemed to please him so much that we felt ourselves justified in asking in our turn for the reasons which had caused him to leave Jamaica.

"Slavery and the climate," he told us. "I was born of a father who, unhappily, was carried off in the middle of his life by one of those epidemic diseases to which our island is so often exposed. He owned some Negroes, and although he was more their friend than their master, he always regretted being forced to command their will and make their arms work for him. He often talked to me about it. Those sparks of humanitarianism which lighted up my boyhood did not die out; but since the government of the island does not permit emancipation of slaves except under conditions very difficult to arrive at, I was not able to follow the inclinations of my heart.

" 'What,' I have asked a hundred times, 'is the origin of this unholy and sacrilegious trade?'

" 'Strength and need,' the answer has been.

" 'But why should a man born at the equator be condemned to work all his life for one who saw the light of day at the fiftieth degree of latitude? Would it be that latitude from which come strength and preeminence?'

" 'That is true,' was the answer, 'but the Europeans are not the first who have gone to seek slaves in Africa. Centuries ago, the Moors, as well as several other nations, carried on this commerce; Negro slavery dates from the most ancient time.'

" 'What a horrible situation!' I replied. 'Isn't it possible that some day the majority will at last subdue the minority? Then the avengers of so many years of oppression will soil the earth with new deeds of violence, and their vengeance will erase neither the horror nor the memory of the crimes that their oppressors committed.'

"If the inhabitants of those islands had been of my opinion, sugar would soon have risen in price in Europe. Or perhaps it would have become cheaper, because instead of arousing wars in Africa, instead of corrupting the miserable, guilty chiefs, the Jamaicans would have agreed with the thinking man of all Europe and joined their efforts to those of that ever celebrated and respectable company which conceived the sublime project of obtaining funds and buying lands on the coast of Africa, there to establish colonies of free Negroes, whose industry and example would have encouraged the black princes to lead their subjects in the raising of sugar cane.

"Humanity will not cease regretting that a motive so praiseworthy and noble was not able to keep war out of the colonies on the Sierra Leone River and the island of Bolama. In those places, men, who said that they were armed in the name of liberty, have destroyed, have completely extinguished everything that the most ardent desire, the purest zeal, for that same liberty had conceived and realized. When man wants to do evil, all the means of accomplishing it are at his disposal; he is often embarrassed only by the number of choices. But if he wants to do good, everything, even nature, is opposed to his plans! Is it any wonder that good is so rare on the earth, whose surface sometimes seems to have been poisoned by man's presence?[1]

---

[1] Without doubt, this statement is entirely too dogmatic. The evil here on earth is admittedly more abundant than the good, but to assure that nature (and to what blasphemous ideas would such a conclusion lead us!) is opposed to and resists the good that men sometimes wish to do, that is to exaggerate, it is to go beyond the bounds of virtue's permissible and natural indignation. [Crèvecoeur's note, II, 165.]

in Pennsylvania & New York 67

"The wasting climate of that island has been the second motive that caused me to leave it. What is life without health? A burden, a continual source of regrets, especially for a man of my age; for I am only thirty-five. Would you believe it! I have spent a dozen years in suffering, in stagnating, in longing for an end to such a sorrowful existence. I have had to contend with the heat of a sun whose rays are almost vertical, about which a person living in a climate like this can form only a very imperfect idea. If, on the one hand, its extreme heat produces a cheerful nature, animated and fecund to the extreme, on the other, it allows only a fleet instant between the time of the fullness of life and the time of destruction, whose accumulated debris often gathers around him, stifling his productive power. Danger lies not alone in the work; rest and inactivity are equally disastrous. Sobriety and temperance are not, as here, guarantees of health. In certain seasons, pestilential vapors rise out of our swamps, infect the atmosphere, poison the air that we breathe. Life there is only the flower of a day, a fugitive dream. And, as if the intemperance of the climate were not enough to shorten that life, the violence of the passions drives it still more quickly to ruin and destruction.

"I came to New York to seek health. I have found it. But for fear of losing this inestimable gift a second time, I took out naturalization papers; and after looking over several districts, I bought the six hundred and fifty acres that I hold here. I found what I was looking for: a little lake of about one hundred and fifty acres in surface, whose waters flow into the Queen Charlotte—for I passionately love to fish—and an elevated spot from which I shall some day have a beautiful view and where I breathe fresh, pure air. Here I enjoy every minute of my life, far from the hurry and tumult of the cities, free from the danger of bankruptcy, of fires, and of those destructive hurricanes that cover the earth with ruins and fill hearts with terror and sorrow. Elsewhere, one would like to free himself from the weight of time; here, I would like to find a way to prolong it.

"To lay out a new piece of land—become dearer by the labor

that is required in felling the useless trees with which it is encumbered, in planting useful and pleasing ones, and in damming up and guiding the waters wherever they might be needed—to cultivate, to sow a fresh and fertile soil—these occupations, so new to me, have brought me pleasures of which I formerly had not the slightest knowledge. Healthy, vigorous, active, I am busy from morning till evening. I have an ample collection of choice books, the reading of which in my moments of leisure entertains and instructs me. Six months ago the Director General of the post established across this district a mail line that would connect with the one in Ontario. In order to let him know my appreciation for a benefit that, judging by the size of our population, is so premature, I offered him the use of my house and my services. The more I read the newspapers and the accounts of all that is going on in the old world, the more I commend myself for the project of settling in this place.

"I have neither wife nor children. Sometimes, however, I regret being alone and working only for myself; but to give life to beings condemned to encounter all the evils that once flew out of Pandora's box, to be necessarily exposed to all the plagues that ceaselessly desolate the inhabitants of the earth, that vast arena of robbery, murder, and unhappiness, it is as if, during the storm and the tempest, one were to send his dearest friends out to sea in a frail bark. A thoughtful reading of history, the pages of which are stained with blood or sullied with crime and wickedness, long ago made a deep impression on my mind. No, the earth is not inhabited by men, as I thought in my youth, but by tigers. It is impossible to understand what the intentions of the creative power were when, after calling us forth from nothingness, it made our hearts the seat of the passions which necessarily must be so fatal to us and which condemned us during the short duration of our life to undergo all the suffering, pain, and anguish to which we could possibly be susceptible. No, never would I reproach myself for having introduced new victims into this theatre of tears and misery, where crime and dishonesty prevail. No, never would I expose myself to the heart-rending and harrowing sorrows that a good father must feel as he watches the child of his tenderness languish, suffer, and die in his arms without being able to help him. The pleasures of the exquisite and sublime sentiment of fatherly love are bought with too many risks and dangers. I prefer to make the voyage of life alone rather than in the company of loved ones whom I would perhaps have the misfortune of surviving.

"In order to avoid these sad reflections, I study Buffon, that foremost painter of nature. I have made some interesting experiments on the transpiration of leaves and on the growth of trees. I have a friend, however; for according to the laws of life one must love at least those among men who are good and loving. My friend is by inclination a turner and a cabinet-maker. He has made the beautiful furniture that you see here, using wood that has been sent to me from Jamaica. I am alone no more than it is good and useful to be. I complain only of the great rapidity with which time passes. The friendship that I have made with the Wilson family fills up and improves my moments of leisure, that is to say, the holidays and Sundays."

The next day we left this young misanthrope, who, while apparently enjoying all the most attractive things that life has to offer—health, energy, affluence—had however conceived some very dismal and very distressing ideas about human nature. Perhaps he had looked at only the reverse side of the picture.

CHAPTER VIII

The Indian Council at Onondaga

THE ARRIVAL

O N OUR arrival at Onondaga the first two people whom we met, and who invited us to smoke the opoygan,[1] were Siategan, an old chief of the Chippeway nation, and Yoyowassy, a sachem of the Ottawas, both of whom I had formerly known at Montreal. They told us that because of the ravages of smallpox the number of their people had decreased so much in recent years that they had decided to unite the remnants of their tribes with the old Oneida stock.

Fortunately, since the council fire was not to be lighted for a few days, we were able to spend some time caring for and feeding our horses, quite a difficult thing to do in an Indian village, and my companion was able to accustom himself gradually to the appearance, the habits, and the way of life of the Indians.

Indeed, how novel must this view of human nature appear to one who, four months before, had been living in one of the capital cities of Europe! "Is that all that nature and the ages have done for them?" he asked me.

"Yes," I replied. "What was man centuries ago when he lived in a state of nature? When we consider the brutishness, the debasement of his tardy and unhappy infancy, we are unable to understand how a being so weak has been able to survive all the reverses and disasters that he has experienced during so many centuries of ignorance and misery, nor by what happy luck he was finally able to learn how to light a fire, to forge iron, to domesticate the animals, to cultivate the earth, and to lift himself by his own abilities to an understanding of the arts and sciences.

"What was the human race before those memorable times? The earth was then inhabited only by wandering hordes, divided into tribes like those one sees today on the shores of the Dutch East Indies, New Zealand, and the lands that Magellan discovered. That primitive organization, by destroying the idea of common interest, has been for all times an inexhaustible source of quarrels, of hates, of revenges, and of wars more implacable than those of tigers. However, the conquerors in these wars ate the conquered, as they sometimes do today, and the tiger, no matter how hungry, never ate his own kind. What a distance there is between the man of nature and the man of civilization, between the first ages of the world, so often praised by the poets, and the present state of Europe!

"Such today you see these Indians," I continued, "and such, with only slight differences, were their ancestors at the time this continent was discovered. They have kept with stubbornness the same habits, the same opinions, and still prefer hunting to farming, the wandering life to the sedentary life, a blind indifference to a wise foresight. Nothing has been able to open their eyes, neither the example of the whites, nor the rapid decrease of their number, nor even the annihilation of so many of their nations, some of which have disappeared only within recent years."

"What can be the cause of their inconceivable blindness?" Monsieur Herman asked me. "Would their intelligence be inferior to that of the Europeans, who, like them, were formerly hunters and wanderers? Why has the energy of nature done nothing for these Indians when it has created the great lakes

[1] The Chippeway word for "Pipe of friendship." See Long, p. 306.

and rivers of this continent, covered it with magnificent forests, and filled it with animals and birds of a marvelous instinct? When all the beings that nature has endowed with this sublime faculty have developed it to the last degree of perfection to which they are capable in the short time they have, why, on the contrary, has she given man the preeminence of reason and then left him with nothing but his hands, uncouth, ferocious, cannibalistic, unsociable? Would that primitive state be then the one for which we Europeans were formerly intended?"

"That is very possible," I replied. "Are not this continent, New Guinea, the Dutch East Indies, New Zealand, and so many other countries discovered by our modern navigators—are not they all still inhabited by hordes who for thousands of years have been sunk in the brutishness of this primitive state? What difference does it make to the creative power whether we live under birch bark or gilded marble? When we occupy the place that she has set aside for us in the scale of being, her plan is fulfilled, no matter whether we are hunters, nomads, or farmers.

"When one considers carefully," I went on, "the long chain of disasters that those first generations had to undergo before reaching the stage of harpooning fish, lighting fires, and conquering the bear, the wolf, and the deer, one is astonished that they were able to survive the dangers and misfortunes of that long, slow period of infancy. What superiority of strength, intelligence, and resources those animals must have had when compared with the weak, foolish, naked human beings! Well clothed, well armed, crafty, clever, they exercised an empire which, during such a long time, might have been fatal to the first societies that providence placed in the forests. How has man been able to raise himself from those sad and painful beginnings to the place of power and preeminence that is held today by the nations of Europe and Asia? That is what is hard to understand."

"There have, however, been some great writers," replied Monsieur Herman, "who have written beautiful discourses to prove that civilization is not a gain but a sad departure from the primitive and sublime imprint that we received from the Creator. I myself had been persuaded by them."

"What those writers have said," I answered, "was inspired only by a spirit of criticism and originality. They preconceived the savage being, whom they did not know, in order to satirize their contemporaries. If, like me, they had accompanied these Indians in their devastating wars; if their eyes had witnessed the tortures that these Indians inflict on their prisoners, as well as their deadly fastings, the product of the blindest lack of foresight; if, finally, they had been present at those cannibalistic orgies, at those scenes of drunkenness that make one shiver to think about them, very certainly they would go elsewhere than among the men of nature to seek for the original of their lying portraits."

When we had stopped entertaining ourselves with these reflections, and had put some questions to our hosts Siategan and Yoyowassy, we left them in order to pay a visit to old Kesketomah, my former traveling companion, whose dwelling I knew to be one of the best in the village.

"I come, my brother," I said to him, "from the land of Onas[2] in order to be present at the council fire. My long trip has tired me and I should like to rest under your roof. Would you have two bearskins to lend me? For, as you see, I have brought with me a friend who comes from the land of the rising sun."

"I do have, Kayo,"[3] he said to me. "I am very grateful to you for your confidence. My fire is lighted; my pot is full. Smoke my opoygan. And you also, Cherryhum Sagat,[4] since you are my brother's friend, rest your bones here."

We spent part of the day in talking of the general news of the nation, of the beginnings of agriculture which some of the chiefs had undertaken, of the aversion which the young people seemed to retain for this new way of life, of the folly of the

---

[2] Crèvecoeur later explains (I, 379) that "Onas" was the name given to William Penn by the Indians and that "the land of Onas" was Pennsylvania.
[3] Friend.
[4] A European; a man from the land of the rising sun. Long, p. 254, lists this as an Iroquoian expression.

Cayugas, of the ways of making them open their eyes to the danger of selling their hunting lands to the government of New York. He also gave me news of my adoptive family, of whom I was astonished to see no representative, and in the evening we attended the dances of the young people. The next day, after having dined at the lodge of Tocksikanehiow-l'Anier[5] on salmon that he had caught the day before, we were invited to take our evening meal with the old and revered sachem Chedabooktoo, of the village of Ossewingo, who, having learned, I know not how, that we had brought along our flutes, requested us to give him a little concert. I still recall the deep attention with which we were heard, by him as well as by the numerous company which he had invited, and the effect produced on their countenances, up to that time expressionless, by the tender and melancholy passages, especially by the harmonies in thirds and fifths. Finally, the council fire having been lighted, we went there with our venerable host; and as he knew the English language better than did any other of the sachems whom I knew, we seated ourselves at his side in order that he might interpret for us what we did not understand.

[5] Crèvecoeur explains (I, 379) that this was the name formerly given to the Mohawks by the Canadians. But no one, he says, knew why.

CHAPTER IX

The Indian Council at Onondaga

THE GREAT DEBATE BETWEEN KESKETOMAH AND KOOHASSEN

SEVENTY-EIGHT people—chiefs, elders, and warriors—were gathered, according to the custom, around a fire lighted in the middle of a large hall, whose walls were made of neatly squared logs joined at the corners by means of dove-tails. All of them, their heads bent forward, their eyes fixed on the ground, were inhaling the smoke from their pipes and, after a rather long interval, exhaling it slowly out of their nostrils in two uninterrupted columns, an indication of profound meditation on important matters. None of them were painted, and none were decorated with feather headdresses. Their beaver mantles, fallen behind them, left exposed on their great chests and robust arms the different figures of animals, insects, or fish that had been tattooed on them in their youth. Here a painter would have been able to draw bodies striking in their beautiful proportions; limbs set in motion by muscles lightly covered over with a kind of fatness unknown among the whites and which, among them, is a sign of vigor, strength, and health; and heads and faces of a kind found only in the heart of the forests of the New World. That gathering of almost naked men, so fierce in war, so implacable in the satisfying of their vengeance, so soft, so peaceful in their villages, offered to the eyes an impressive sight, and to the mind a source for new meditations.

Since the debates of that first meeting—concerned entirely with the questions of the boundaries of their lands, the plan of the Cayugas to sell theirs, and the invasion of some white families—would interest only those who know the geography of that part of the continent as well as the relations between these nations and the neighboring governments, I will refrain from telling of it in order to get to the meeting of the next day, which discussed the question of the adoption of agriculture.

This was the first time that any of the elders had publicly addressed themselves to the young warriors in an attempt to show the indispensable necessity of farming. To my great surprise, our host, the venerable Kesketomah, offered to be the orator in favor of it.

On the second day the assembly was much more numerous and colorful; the chiefs and the warriors were painted; their arms were decorated with silver bracelets; their heads and ears were covered with war feathers; and each had a pearl suspended from his nose. After the opening silence, or rather profound contemplation, and after they had slowly smoked their pipes, Chedabooktoo, of the village of Ossewingo, of the Maskinonge[1] tribe, stood up and spoke:

"The other night as I was smoking by the light of the moon, a voice came and knocked at my ears. I went toward it; I listened. It was Wequash, of our tribe. 'What!' I said to him, 'You are moaning, you are complaining, and you are a man! To whom then are you addressing your cries and moans? Don't you know that the Good Spirit is too far away to see what is happening on the earth, and that the Evil Spirit, who inhabits the snows of night, makes fun of our miseries? I have seen you suffer hunger, thirst, weariness, nakedness, and wounds; why did you not complain then?'

" 'I am not complaining, Chedabooktoo,' he answered. 'I am not thinking of the Good or the Evil Spirit, for I do not know

[1] Sturgeon, according to Crèvecoeur, I, 100.

where either one of them is, nor even if they exist. Some people say they do, others that they do not. Have you ever noticed how the air and the sap escape with noise from a piece of green wood which has been thrown on the fire, how the sap flows from a tree whose bark has been gashed in the spring, how the streams and rivers swell after the rains of autumn? Well! My heart has been struck; it is doing the moaning and not my spirit, which is as strong as yours. Temiskaming has left me, Chedabooktoo. I am alone; my bear skin is cold; my fire is out; the ashes of my fireplace are scattered; and my pot ... I no longer have the heart to fill it. When a warrior hunts or fishes for himself alone, can he be as patient and as clever as when he hunts and fishes to feed his wife? And if I do hunt, who will compliment me on my success and take me by the hand? Ah, Chedabooktoo! Evil descends on us by torrents, like the rains of autumn; good comes drop by drop, like the dew of spring.'

" 'All that has happened, Wequash,' I said to him, 'must disappear; all that is going to happen must also vanish. We are disappearing too, since we have come like the traveler's dug-out that the course of the current overturns, like the waters of the rivers which lose themselves in the great waterfalls. I have heard the white medicine men say that the newborn child has come, that the dead man has gone. 'Where has the child come from? Where is the man going?' I asked them. They told me such queer things that I never want to put them in my memory. 'Everything that is on the earth comes from it,' I told them; 'everything that has come from it will go back.' They made fun of me. I turned my back on them and left them there.

" 'I have not grown old, Wequash, without having often been struck by the great arrow of Agan Matchee Manitoo.[2] Each time I pulled it out and laid it on the ground. In my lifetime I have shed more blood than tears. They ought not to flow, these tears, except from the eyes of our women, and never from yours, which with dry eyelids have more than once beheld misfortune. Live, if you are a man! You will see that

[2] The Evil Spirit. Cf. Carver, pp. 249-50, and Long, p. 269.

tomorrow you will complain less, the day after, still less, and so on, until forgetfulness, the son of old time, comes to heal the wounds in your heart. Do like Keskimenetas, your grandfather, whom I knew during my first moons; avenge yourself on the Evil Spirit; look for another Temiskaming! You know the cure of adoption. Who will say to you that your new wife will not cultivate your corn and stir your pot better than the one who has just gone away?'

" 'Chedabooktoo,' he said to me, 'you are talking like the old man that you are. You have forgotten the time of your youth, when your heart was big and your breath burned. Everything comes, everything passes, as you say; but I who am here, I have not yet gone away; I have not yet heard the sound of my waterfall. You speak to me of another Temiskaming! How are we to forget the one whom we love, and who loved us too? That is not the work of a day. When the ice has broken my canoe, or the fire destroyed my wigwam, I easily build another; but a companion of so many moons, when she is gone... Well! Don't you know that good wives are like ermine, hard to find? And if, among the girls of our tribe, I find none who want to blow on my firebrand,[3] nor listen to my war song, will I remain on my bear skin then like an old man? What will I do? Where will I go?'

" 'Well!' I replied, 'Go and look for one among the other nations; do like Ockwacok, like Matamusket. It turned out well for them. They live in harmony with their wives; their race is multiplying; they are united like trunks of the same tree, like oyster-shells. Does their pot get empty? On the instant, it is filled. Do the ashes begin to cover their fire? Immediately some wood is thrown on it. They are living under a beautiful sun. At the time of the next full moon, go to the fire at Onondaga and you will hear what the wisdom of the chiefs will say to you.' That is what I told him. I have spoken."

After a rather long silence, Yoyogheny, of the village of

---

[3] Crèvecoeur later (I, 381) explains this interesting custom at some length. The Indian brave held a firebrand in front of the girl he wanted to marry; if she blew on it, he was encouraged to continue the courtship.

Lackawack, of the Meegeeses[4] tribe, stood up and spoke.

"As I came back from fishing, I saw Muskanehong at the entrance of her wigwam. She was uttering cries, shedding tears, and striking her chest. 'Why do you grieve so much?' I asked her. Has the Evil Spirit come in the night and broken your doorsill?[5] Has your mind recalled some bad dream? Did you see some stars fall as you were bowing to the full moon? . . . You do not answer me. Why then in such a fashion do you interrupt the peace of the night, which is the time for rest? Is the bright day not long enough for weeping?'

" 'You speak of rest!' she replied. 'There is no more of that for me on earth. My spirit is in the shadows; clouds are darkening the sun of my life; the night wind has driven away my sleep. I have lost Mondajewot,[6] the companion of my days, the friend of my youth. When I followed him into the forest, I did not fear flesh-eating wolves nor catamounts nor fierce panthers. When I paddled across the lakes at the front of his canoe, I felt strong and proud. Like him, without flinching I kept my face to the wind. Never did he say to me, 'come,' that I did not come; never did he say to me, 'go,' that I did not go. His will was always mine; and mine, when I had one, was always his. He who swam like the tewtag and the maskinonge disappeared under the waters as he went down the rapid of Nepinah,[7] and his body has become food for the fish. Who will console me? Who will take my hand when I am old? No

---

[4] Eagle. Long, p. 300, spelled this word "Meegeezes."
[5] Of all accidents, this is the most unfortunate that can happen to them, that piece being considered the symbol of domestic happiness, security, and safety. It is the only part of their little structures to which they seem to attach mystical significance. One can remove the door itself and break it, leaving the sill untouched; then they make another without misgiving; on the other hand, the removal of the sill, even involuntarily, is enough to arouse melancholy thoughts and cause them to want to go elsewhere to raise their wigwam. As they have always refused to answer the questions I asked them about this matter, it is impossible for me to say anything more that is satisfactory. [Crèvecoeur's note, I, 382.]
[6] One of Crèvecoeur's symbolic words. It is apparently made up of the French "mon" and the Chippeway suffix "dajewot," meaning "world," or "country." Cf. Long, p. 296. In other words, Muskanehong's husband meant all the world to her.
[7] Probably Crèvecoeur's coinage from the Algonquin-Chippeway word "nepee," meaning "water." Cf. Long, p. 253.

one, because I am alone on the earth. Oh! if only I had offered the Evil Spirit a roll of tobacco on the roof of my wigwam, he would perhaps have kept the canoe of Mondajewot from overturning and I would not have broken the stillness of the night nor aroused your anger.'

" 'You could have offered Matchee Manitoo all of the tobacco of your harvest,' I told her, 'and the canoe of Mondajewot would have overturned just the same. Don't you know that Matchee Manitoo is deaf and insensible? that it is he who sends us the hurricanes and hailstorms, the snows and freezes? that it is he who swells the rivers and lets loose the floods? that the thunder is the sound of his voice? the lightning, the sparks from his eyes? that he is no more interested in the success of our hunts, of our wars, in our condition on earth, than he is in the migratory birds, or even the fish that the current hurls over the falls to the rocks below? Your loss is great, Muskanehong. You are a woman; weep. Your tears and the passing of time will heal your wound. Time either cures us or kills us. In time, the floods roll by; in time, the storms break and the sun shines through. Time is like a long trail; whoever follows it, this trail, will soon find forgetfulness lying on the ground or seated at the foot of a tree. Muskanehong, is there not in our village, or somewhere else, a white man for you to adopt?'

" 'Yes, she replied, 'but can wolves and foxes go hunting together? What good are white men in the woods? As soon as the clouds hide the sun, they lose their way and no longer know where they came from nor where they are going; if snow falls, they stop right there; if they come to a river, they must have a raft to get across; if hunger overtakes them, they don't know what to say to him, nor how to turn him back.'

" 'Muskanehong,' I said to her, 'among us, just as among them, there are some good ones and some bad ones. Look at the trees in the forest; are they all of the same height? No. Are the stalks of corn of the same strength and greenness? No. It is the same way among men. I know some white men who, like us, are brave warriors and fine hunters, and who are as good as we in the woods. Among our people are there not many who sell all they own in order to get firewater? Would you not prefer to light your fire yourself than have as husband one of those fools, who would be able to keep neither your wigwam nor your canoe in good order? Whatever we do, Muskanehong, everywhere we meet with more evil than good, more brambles and thorns than flowering bushes.'

" 'Why is that?' she asked me.

" 'When you put your head out of the door during a very dark night, what do you see?'

" 'Nothing,' she answered.

" 'Well! Your question and my answer are like that dark night,' I told her. 'Perhaps if men were less unhappy, they would get too thick on the earth; and for lack of game and fish, the strongest would eat the weakest, as is sometimes done now. Go to Onondaga at the time of the next full moon, and your heart and mind will hear what the wisdom of the chiefs will say to you.' That is what I told her. I have spoken."

Siasconset, of the village of Pentagoet, of the Outagamy[8] tribe, stood up and spoke.

"As I was coming back from the wigwam of Naponset, I met Kahawabash, who is my relative, although an Ottawa by birth. Instead of holding his head high, as warriors do, he was walking slowly and had covered himself with his mantle. 'What are you doing in our village?' I asked him. 'You have the appearance of an old man or a sick man. Have you already come back from your far distant hunts?'

" 'I no longer hunt,' he answered. 'I fish when I am hungry. I have opened the door of my wigwam to the night birds and forsaken the village of Togarahanock.'

" 'Why have you done that?' I asked him.

" 'My heart bleeds like the deer struck by the hunter's arrow; my eyes burn, because sleep sits perched on top of my roof and does not want to come down; I am tired, and yet I do nothing; I am no longer either hot or cold; Matchee Manitoo has sent his great black serpent into the village and killed my

[8] The Algonquin word for "fox." Cf. Long, p. 243.

wife, Nezalanga, nearly all my children, and most of our people. I have come to warm myself at your fire and take the advice of your wisdom.'

" 'Wisdom is dumb,' I said to him, 'when unhappiness speaks. I knew your wife well; was she not of the Pakatakan family?'

" 'Yes,' he answered me.

" 'Well! Why have you not gone to warm yourself at their fire? The mother, the father, the brothers, and the sisters of Nezalanga, they would have taken you by the hand. The hand of a relative is softer than that of a stranger, or even that of a friend.'

" 'There is no longer on earth a single drop of the blood of the Pakatakans. The mergum-megat[9] of the white man, like the fire that comes out of the clouds and eats up the forests, has destroyed almost the entire village while I was hunting the beaver in the land up above.[10] On my return I found only the bones of our people, for their dead bodies had been eaten by wolves and flies. Not a fire was burning, not a door was closed; nothing was living except the dogs. The animals are less unhappy than we, Siasconset. If, as it is said, the Good Spirit is the father of men, why does he not come down among us in order to drive away misfortune? Why does he not hurl the war tomahawk to the bottom of the lake? Why does he not with his burning breath melt the snows of winter? It is said that he has given us speech in order to raise us above the wolves, the bears, and the beavers, and yet we are more unhappy than these wild beasts. Does there not then exist anything on earth or above the clouds to protect us in our weakness?'

" 'You make me tremble,' I told him. 'Your wife, your relatives, your friends, almost all your village destroyed by the greatest of arrows! Kahawabash, when we learn of new misfortunes, or that some great unhappiness has come to us, our spirits are overwhelmed, our hearts bruised, like canoes gripped by the ice of winter, like the roots of the cedar in the cleft of the rock. We do not speak; we think only of that. The next day, at hunting or at fishing, we think of it a little less.

[9] Smallpox.   [10] Canada.

Without our knowing it, the first impressions grow dim and disappear, as do the figures drawn by our children in the sand of the river bank, in proportion as the waves reach them. That is the way it will be with your loss, Kahawabash. It is a great loss and hard to forget, I know. And I, to whom you have come for advice because you believed me less unhappy, do you not know that I had three brave boys, Tienah, Tiogo, Nobscusset? Well! The Evil Spirit has struck them; they are no longer here to keep my pot full and to carry Siasconset's tomahawk to war. You are young, and I . . . I have seen many moons. Stay under my bark roof until the great council fire is lighted. There you will see elders and chiefs who, like you, have experienced great losses, and who have repaired them by adoption. But do not shed tears in front of them; they would scorn you and would say nothing to you.'

" 'Here is what he said to me. 'Siasconset! Have you not often heard the plaintive cries of the bear whose mate has been killed? Have you not often seen tears flow from the eyes of the beaver who has lost his wife or children?[11] Well! Am I beneath the bear or the beaver? No. I am a man, as good a hunter, as good a warrior as your chiefs. But how is the arrow to be kept from falling when the bowstring snaps? or the trunk of the oak or the stalk of the reed from bending when the storm bursts? When the body is wounded, Siasconset, it sheds blood; when the heart is broken, it sheds tears. That is what I shall tell your elders; I shall see what they say to me about that.'

" 'Well!' I said to him, 'Kahawabash, shed your tears under my roof, since your Good Spirit wishes it and it will please the Evil one; then your eyes will be dry when you are at the fire of Onondaga.'

" 'What is to be done,' he replied, 'when one person wants what another does not want?'

" 'What is to be done?' I said. 'Think of your life as a crossing from Toronto to Niagara. What difficulties do we not experience in doubling the capes, in leaving the bays which the

---

[11] Crèvecoeur (I, 111) refers the reader to two notes—one on the cries of bears, taken from William Bartram; the other on the tears of the beaver.

winds have forced us to enter? What chances we take in such frail canoes as those we have! It is necessary, however, to take time and events as they come, since we cannot choose them. We must eat, love our wives and children, respect our tribe and our nation; rejoice at good when it happens to us; bear up under evil with courage and patience; hunt and fish when we are hungry; rest and smoke when we are tired; expect to encounter misfortune from the day of our birth; rejoice when it does not come; and think of ourselves as birds that are perched for the night on the branch of a tree and which at daybreak fly away and disappear forever.' That is what I told him. I have spoken."

Aquidnunck, of the village of Adquakanunck, of the Skenonton[12] tribe, stood up and spoke.

"As I was smoking near my fire, Tienaderhah, of the Larneck[13] tribe, opened my door and came to sit by my side. 'What are you doing here so late?' I asked her.

" 'I am come to speak of my sorrows,' she said, 'and to seek your advice.'

" 'What has happened?'

" 'The wind of misfortune, like the burning breath of the dog-days, has dried up my tree of life and carried away its shade and leaves. My little Tigheny has left for the West. I want to go there also, before her father, Venango, returns from his hunts. Why shall I stay on this earth when there are no longer any joy and happiness for me? When, on days of the full moon,' she went on, 'I go to visit the place of her rest, to shed tears there and drops of milk from my breast, I seem to hear her voice calling me. I want to go and rejoin her. All that I ask of you, Aquidnunck, is to place my body in a tree out of reach of the teeth of wolves.'

" 'Has the Evil Spirit taken away your doorsill?' I asked her.

" 'No,' she replied, 'he has taken away from me something more precious.'

---

[12] Roe-deer, according to Crèvecoeur, I, 112.
[13] Sturgeon, according to Crèvecoeur, I, 112. His spelling is close to that of Long's Algonquin "lamek." Cf. Long, p. 247. Earlier in this chapter Crèvecoeur used "Maskinonge" twice to mean "sturgeon."

KESKETOMAH
CHIEF OF THE ONONDAGAS
(*Voyage*, I, 115)

KOOHASSEN
ONEIDA WARRIOR
(*Voyage*, I, 119)

" 'Well, then! why do you want to put out your fire and leave your wigwam? Can one gain the bank from the middle of a rapid? No! He must have courage to go on to the portage. You have been a mother; you will be one again. Why do you want to go away before your sun is set?'

" 'What will Venango say,' she replied, 'when he sees that his first-born is no longer on the earth?'

" 'He will be sorry for you,' I told her. 'In order to ease your pains, he will hide his, as the brave hides the arrow with which he has just been struck. He will dry your tears and relight your fire. It is an evil thought, Tienaderhah, that of wanting to shorten your life. Is not old time still here to shorten it for you every day? You have lost your daughter, but Venango still lives; do you want to kill him also? Call in Courage! Have him sit by your side! Soon he will send for his sister Patience; you will listen to what they tell you. Weep, my daughter! weep! Your tears will soften the anguish of your heart, as the rain calms the fury of the storm. Work, and you will think less; it is thought which holds on to evil and makes it grow. Go to the fire of Onondaga at the next full moon; your ears will listen there to what the chiefs say in order to console you.' That is what passed between Tienaderhah and Aquidnunck. I have spoken."

After a long silence, which the listeners employed in gravely exhaling the smoke from their pipes, Kesketomah, of the village of Onondaga, of the Maskinonge tribe, stood up and spoke.

"Brothers and friends, the greatest of all our misfortunes is the decreasing of our blood and the increasing of that of the whites. And yet today, when we are so feeble, we smoke, we sleep, just as we did when we were numerous and formidable! Where have they come from, these whites? Who guided them across the great salt lake? Why did our fathers, who then lived on its shores, not shut their ears to the beautiful words of those foxes, who have all been false and deceitful, like shadows thrown by the setting sun? Since that time they have multiplied like ants at the return of spring; and like those insects, they need only a little space to live in. Why is that? It is because they know how to cultivate the earth. Brothers and friends, there is the remedy that can still cure all our ailments. But in order for it to be successful, we must all be in agreement, like fingers of the same hand, like oars of the same canoe; otherwise, our projects, our hopes will pass away with the wind that blows.

"Let us hunt in order to retain that precious habit of patience, of perseverance and skill, that makes us formidable in war, and let us cultivate the soil on which we were born. Let us have oxen, cows, pigs, and horses. Let us learn to forge that iron which makes the whites so powerful. Then we shall know how to hold them back. When, as in the past, hunger and need come knocking at our doors, we shall have something to give them that will satisfy them. I remember that Koreyhoosta,[14] the old chief of the Missisages nation, shed tears every time he came back to Hotchelaga; and when he was asked the reason for it, he said, 'Don't you see that the whites live on seeds and we live on flesh? That that flesh is more than thirty moons in growing, and is often scarce? That each of these wonderful little seeds which they put in the earth gives back to them more than a hundred? That the flesh on which we live has four legs on which to run away and we have only two to catch it with? That wherever the whites lay down those seeds, they stay and grow there? That winter, which is for us the time of our painful hunts, is for them a time of rest? That is why they have so many children and live longer than we. I say then to whoever wants to listen: Before the cedars of the village have died of old age, and before the maples of the valley have stopped giving sugar, the race of the sowers of little seeds will have destroyed that of the hunters of flesh, unless the hunters decide to sow seeds too.' These words of Koreyhoosta have already been proved true among the Pequots, the Naticks, the Narragansetts, and so many other nations. Go look at the places where they lived; you will find there not a single one of their descendants, nor the smallest trace of their

[14] In the first chapter of the *Voyage*, p. 25, Crèvecoeur, who claims to be quoting Colonel George Croghan, Indian authority, presents Koreyhoosta's advice and prophecy in much briefer form.

villages, there where formerly all proclaimed liberty and life. The dwellings of the whites have replaced them; today plows dig up the places where rested the bones of their ancestors. It is certain! If you refuse to cultivate the earth, you will meet the same fate.

"Oh! If only I had the wings of the eagle! I would rise up as high as our mountains; then my words, carried by the wind, would resound among all the nations that live under our sun. Oh! that the evidence of truth could penetrate your hearts, as the edge of this tomahawk penetrates the body of my enemy! Then you would never forget what I have yet to tell you. . . . You are lost, brave Oneidas, if you go on wanting to be nothing but hunters. Today's sun is not that of yesterday. You are lost if you do not stifle the voice of ancient tradition in order to open your ears to that of urgent necessity. Brothers and friends, why do you not hear that necessity, when its voice is as loud as thunder. Here is what it tells you through my mouth: 'A rifle is good, a plow better yet; a tomahawk is good, a hatchet with a well-fitted handle better yet; a wigwam is good, a house and a barn better yet.'

"The whites draw near our boundaries and are threatening us, like the distant waves of the lake that come and break on the shores. Already the bees, their forerunners,[15] have arrived among us. Do you want to resist them? If you do, to the products of the hunt add those of the earth; to the milk of your women add that of the cows. Is there under our sun a soil more fertile than ours? No! And the whites know it well. Do we not have red and white cedar, water ash, and black birch in abundance for the building of our canoes? Do not the salmon of Katarakouy come as far as our lakes? With our furs let us buy hatchets and iron, or rather, let us learn how to forge it. Oh! If we had only known about it, this iron on which we have been walking, we would not now be forced to talk like this. We would have sent back the whites under their

---

[15] Crèvecoeur gives a long account (I, 342-44) of this superstition of the Indians, who believed that the coming of the bees signaled the advent of the white man.

sun, which, it is said, goes down when ours comes up. Let us make rules for our trade. Let us keep out of our villages those firewaters that bring madness and death. They are the deadly source from which have come our greatest misfortunes. It is with that poison that the whites have made us foolish and wicked, and with which they have bought so much of our land; it is with this snare, even though so well known, that these foxes from the rising sun have for so many years deceived and seduced the wolves of this great island, and with which they have managed to destroy so many Nishynorbay nations. Let us lay out the boundaries of our country; let us live in peace with them but maintain our rights at the risk of our lives. What is the blood, the life of a warrior, when by losing it he guarantees that of his wife, his children, the independence of his village, of his tribe, of his nation, which is for him as the sun is for the trees and the plants? But I am through. Perhaps among our young warriors there is one who, not approving my words, would like to stop my mouth."

Scarcely had this last word come forth when Koohassen, of the village of Wawassing, of the Mawhingon[16] tribe, letting his mantle fall, pride stamped on his face, his tomahawk in his hand, stood up and spoke.

"Yes, there are a great number of them here! If I have not spoken sooner, it is because I respect old age, and not for lack of good and able thoughts."

Then turning his glowing eyes on the whole group, his chest bare, his head and ears covered with warrior's feathers and his arms with gleaming osselets, he continued thus.

"The powerful Mohawk League, of which our nation was made a member, conquered several seacoast tribes before the whites came, and since then it has more than a hundred times made the people of Hotchelaga and Corlear tremble.[17] And yet those warriors lived well, without digging up the ground

[16] Wolf. Cf. Crèvecoeur, I, 119, and Long, p. 300.
[17] "Hotchelaga" meant the island on which Montreal is now located. Cf. *Voyage*, I, 384. Crèvecoeur also says (I, 385) that the Iroquois, by extension, referred to the Europeans in New York as "Corlear," the name of a famous Dutch trader who retired there and whom the Indians liked.

in Pennsylvania & New York

like women: why should we of today have to do it? Game is not lacking except to the cowardly and lazy. Can a person be brave, firm, carefree, when he has land that grows corn, when he has cows and horses? No! He loves his life too much to risk losing it. And when war comes suddenly, how is a person to do two things at once? Can he at the same time be in the woods wielding his tomahawk and in the fields guiding his plow? No! Those who cultivate the earth spend too much time on the bear skin of their wives. Whoever wishes to strike his enemy with strength and courage must for a long time have turned his back on his wigwam. If we lived like the whites, we would stop being what we are, the children of our God, who has made us hunters and warriors. We would think, we would act like them; and like them we would become liars, cheats, dependents, tied to the soil we cultivate, chained by laws, governed by papers and by lying writings. And then, with their fields, their cows, and their horses, are these whites more happy, do they live longer than we? Do they know how to sleep on the snow, or at the foot of a tree, as we do? No! They have so much to lose that their spirit watches uneasily. Do they know how to scorn life, to suffer, and to die, as we do, without complaints or regrets? No! They are held back by too many bonds. What good anyway is the money for which they work so hard? To make some people rich and some poor, to establish crime, hatred, and jealousy among them. If we become farmers, would we then have to name judges in our villages to torment us, to build prisons with high walls to shut us in, and forge chains to hold us back? Would we then be like our ancestors, bold, proud, brave, forgetting the past, content with the present, caring little for the future? No! Hospitality would go away I don't know where and would never come among us again; for each one would want to grow rich at the expense of the others and would have nothing to give to his neighbor, who would no longer be his friend. Like the whites, we would do everything that we were told to do for money; we would no longer have a will. What is a man who can no longer go here or there, smoke, sleep, or rest? The richest would want to rule the poorest. And then, what would these poor ones do? Would they have to become slaves and work for those who would be all shiny with grease? Would it still be strength, bravery, skill, and patience that determine the reputation of a man? No! It would be money and a full pot. A warrior in whose veins flows the blood of a true Oneida, could he, would he ever want to serve a cowardly rich man because misfortune has knocked at his door? No! No more than the mountain eagle would serve the timid and cowardly fishing-hawk; no more than the proud vulture would serve the fugitive ring-dove. Instead of bending like the reed on the river bank, he would stand up like the mountain oak; or, like the bees, he would go into the great forests to look for freedom and independence. If ever I lose my will and am forced to obey that of another because he is richer than I, I will tomahawk him, I will take off his scalp, after having set fire to his wigwam, because whoever despises me is my enemy. I will go down the rivers of the west and say to the chiefs of the nations of the Mississippi that the Oneidas have become, like the bearded whites, scratchers of the earth and vile workers by day. Yes! Sooner than submit to the orders of a master and become an unhappy hireling, I will go and join my brave ancestors. What is this death of which the cowardly are so afraid? For the hunter, it is the day of rest, the end of all his troubles; for the warrior, eternal peace; for the unhappy, the last boundary to their misery; the trust and comfort of all those who are suffering and in distress; the refuge from which one can brave oppression and tyranny.

"And our wives! And our children! What would become of them with their fields of wheat and corn? What examples of bravery, of patience, would they have before their eyes in this new state? Working with their hands from infancy to mature age, could they ever learn to endure hunger, thirst, misfortune, death? Who would teach them not to fear the teeth of their enemies, to die, like braves, singing their war songs? Look at the nations who have stopped hunting in order to bend down to the ground! What has happened to them now that they have cows and horses and pray to the god of the whites?

Well! The whites and their god despise them and do not take them by the hand. Their number decreases every day. If these men dared to offer me their pipe of friendship, I would say proudly to them, 'Cawen, cawen.'[18]

"Let us continue to be what we have always been, good hunters, brave warriors. I hope that my opinion is that of the greatest number of those who hear me, whose blood has not yet been whitened by the snows of winter nor frozen by the ice of old age. I have spoken."

This discourse, delivered with so much energy, was followed by a very long pause. Then Kesketomah, after having calmly exhaled through his nostrils the smoke of his opoygan, arose for the second time and spoke.

"Brave young man but foolish! in whose memory today is like yesterday, and tomorrow will be like today; on whom moons and events leave no trace in passing, like the arrow which pierces the air or the sparrowhawk that pursues its prey; whose thoughts are like barren flowers; who closes the door to experience, instead of having it sit at your fire—you do not understand that things have changed since the old days, the times about which Koohassen has just spoken, and that it is necessary for us to change also or perish. What would you do if the waters of the lake began to subside? Instead of taking our wigwams elsewhere, as our young men would do, I, being older, would advise that a dike be built in order to hold back the waters and save the village. And so! Young men who are listening, that is what is happening today. The whites are threatening us, overpassing the boundaries which our forefathers prescribed for them. Let us then make a dike here and not elsewhere, before the flood engulfs us, ourselves, our wives, and our children.

"It is because of their number, their wheat, and their corn that they have become strong and proud; it is by these same means that we too may become strong and proud. Let us spare the forests, our first home, our ancient heritage, and cultivate the soil that will increase the number of our people as well as

[18] Chippeway for "no." Cf. Long, p. 246.

our power. Each one can have as much land as he wants, for we do not know that shameful inequality about which Koohassen spoke; judges, chains, prisons are for wicked people, and there are none of those here.

"Let those among us who would be so blinded by their opinions as to prefer that the race of Oneidas disappear from the face of the earth than to see it prosper and multiply by farming, let those, I say, go with the Cayugas, the Tuskaroras, and the Senecas to raise their wigwams in a foreign land, a land which they will not hold very long. On the other hand, let those who are alarmed at the fate of so many nations, formerly as powerful as ours and today extinguished, let them unite in mind and heart behind the opinion of our elders, which is also the opinion of many of our braves, and begin tomorrow to contribute all their means to starting at last that great innovation on which depends our salvation and even our existence! I hope that truth has given light to my words, like sunlight on the surface of the lake. I have answered what the Good Spirit has inspired Koohassen to say. The Good Spirit has also inspired me to say nothing against what anger has placed on his tongue. I have spoken."

Here ended the second day of the Council.

CHAPTER X

A Winter among the Mohawks
or
The Story of Cattaw-Wassy

SEVERAL years ago, while traveling in a bark canoe with two Abenakis of lower Canada, I had the misfortune to be wrecked on the upper bank of the St. Lawrence River just after we had successfully passed over the six-mile-long rapids. The first snows had already fallen. Without hatchet and without means of lighting a fire, forced to eat raw some fish that we had the good luck to catch, we decided to walk towards the south and, in order not to lose ourselves in the forest, to keep the river in sight on our left. Dying of cold, worn out, exhausted, we were on the third day of this painful trip and had just eaten the last pieces of our last fish, when to our great joy we thought we saw signs of smoke in the distance. It was coming from a big village of Christian Mohawks, located at the mouth of the Oswegatchie River, well known then under the same name and today included in the territory of the United States. As soon as we came within shouting distance, my companions squatted down and let out several piercing yells. At these cries of sorrow some Indians from the village came to see who we were, and soon, touched by our misery, they silently led us to their homes, where they placed us separately with three different families. Chance had it that they brought me, as a white, to the home of one who was at the same time the oldest man and the chief of the village and who, consequently, combined the preeminence of his age with his authority as chief. After having taken me by the hand and letting me smoke the great family opoygan, this old man said to me, "Welcome, from wherever you come! Rest your bones on that bearskin; warm yourself, and eat." He spoke a little English and a little French. His family was made up of four women and three men. The next day, after I had told him where I came from and where I wanted to go, he said, "Winter is coming on, as you see; the great river already carries some ice drifts, and our river is frozen over. It is impossible to get to Montreal before spring. Put aside the few clothes you have left and dress yourself as we do; our people will like you better."

Scarcely had I consented by giving him my hand when his women came forward with eagerness and immediately cut off my hair, painted my face, and brought me the clothes I was supposed to put on; they did not even forget to give me a name. After some days of getting used to it, I found myself as well lodged, fed, and clothed as if I had been among my friends in Montreal. How easily one does everything when he is young! Like the others I went fishing both morning and evening, sometimes on the ice, sometimes with a net, depending on the degree of cold or the depth of the snow, and I was not a little proud of being able to help keep the pot full. In addition we had an ample supply of corn and potatoes; for since that tribe had become Christian, they cultivated the earth with more care and foresight. With the inner bark of the birch tree I made myself a big book, on which I wrote with care all the words of their language whose meaning I could understand. This practice seemed to give them as much pleasure as if I had rendered them an important service.

The time was passing lightly away in the midst of these occupations, when, toward the end of January, there arrived a man loaded down with skins and frozen meat. He was one

in Pennsylvania & New York 95

of the sons-in-law of the old Minickwac, and the husband of the woman who had been the most forward in cutting my hair, in painting me, and even in tattooing me. I already knew enough of their language to realize that this newcomer spoke Mohawk almost as badly as I. Surprised at that, I asked the old Minickwac to tell me the reason for it. This is what he told me.

"This man Kittagawmick, of what was formerly the Ouasioto tribe, was made prisoner several years ago by a party of our warriors. After being brought to our village, he was adopted by one of my daughters, whose husband had been drowned while going down the rapids of the great river. He is one of our most skilful hunters, as you can see by the quantity of beaver skins that he has brought back. After he had been here some years, his first wife came down to the land of the Mohawks in order to claim him, something that our oldest people had never heard of. She spoke words here that surprised us all very much; the new wife spoke others in response. That went on all winter. I—I knew not what to think, and Kittagawmick knew not what to do. Our missionaries became involved. Some of our people wanted to send the woman home to her country; some, on the other hand, wanted her to take back her former husband. Finally, in order to do what was right, Henry Nissooassoo, the great chief of the Mohawks, lighted the council fire at Oriskany, to which he invited the chiefs, the elders, and the wise men. I went also. In spite of what the priests and the white men said, this is what was agreed upon after the council had slowly and for a long time smoked several opoygans.

" 'On the day when Kittagawmick was made a prisoner he would have been killed or put in the pot, according to the custom, thus dissolving his marriage with Cattaw-Wassy. But having been brought to the village of Oswegatchie and adopted by Kippokitta, and having since that time been in possession of a new life which he owed to his second wife, the first wife is no longer anything to him.' "

Here is what I learned in 1765. After having grieved for a long time at this decision, Cattaw-Wassy consoled herself by marrying one of the Indians of Oriskany, with whom she lived for a long time. Sir William Johnson,[1] as well as several other white people who admired the courage she had shown in coming alone from her country, a distance of more than two hundred miles, gave her a number of valuable presents. She was the first woman of that great village who had a cow, a horse, and a house, and at whose home one could find milk, butter, bread, meat, and two beds. Where is the man with even a little knowledge who, during colonial times, has not heard of Cattaw-Wassy? With another sort of education she would have been a distinguished woman.[2]

[1] Colonial Superintendent of Indian Affairs.
[2] In the original this story is a note (III, 344-48).

CHAPTER XI

Niagara in Winter

DURING the beautiful days of winter, when the sun reaches the highest point in its meridian and covers Niagara with its rays, the eyes and the imagination of the spectator are offered one of the rarest and, I believe, one of the most magnificent spectacles to be found on earth. The trees, the bushes, the crags and ridges on the banks, and the gigantic rocks in the lake, everything that one sees during summer disappears and is replaced by objects whose forms and appearances are entirely different. It is like a new creation. The vapors from the waterfall, dispersed far and wide by the winds, are condensed by the rigorous cold and attach themselves to all surfaces, covering them with robes of a resplendent whiteness, with crystals and elegant sculpturings, with icicles and verglas, whose numberless and bizarre aggregations are indescribable, like those beautiful dreams that are the issue of health, of youth, and of happiness. Sometimes one is made to believe that he sees Gothic structures, colonnades suspended in aerial perspective, ancient chateaus, ruins, masses—all grouped and carved with a marvelous art and precision.

The surfaces of the promontories, so dismal and somber during summer, are in winter adorned with sparkling plates, and the trees on their summits are formed into transparent obelisks; the rocks in the lake resemble pedestals surmounted by alabaster blocks from which a skilful sculptor might have carved statues, supernatural beings, or perhaps gigantic birds. The debris and crags which surround the basin in a fifteen-thousand-foot circle now seem only a vast amphitheatre of ice, formed by the spray which the cold stops and freezes every second. Here are seen what appear to be stalactites that rear themselves forty feet in the air; there, grooved and truncated columns; yonder, terms, caryatids, busts, all the rich and sumptuous creations that an artistic and fecund imagination can give birth to.

Secular cedars, venerable and moss-covered firs, ancient larches, and mighty pines, all the crystallized trees and bushes that grow among the rocks or on the slopes of the banks, like the candelabra of a spacious sanctuary, enrich still further that scene of hyperborean splendor. Many times, succumbing under the weight of their icy finery, they fall and disappear into the aybss.

The island in the middle, whose width along the edge of the precipice is about nine hundred feet, and whose length is set at a mile—that island so blooming and verdant in summer, like all the surroundings, takes on in winter an altogether different aspect; the trunks, the branches, and the tops of the trees that cover it, the bushes and the mosses, even the soil, everything is changed; the rigors of the season have covered them, embellished them with efflorescences and with congelations as varied in their forms as in their sizes. The trees look like huge pyramids whose silver, sparkling summits contrast wonderfully with the blue of the skies. The richness of the jewel caskets and the glittering brightness of the chandeliers which seem to hang from the extremities of almost all the branches produce on the imagination a magical effect, especially when the heavily laden limbs sway softly at the whim of the breeze. In spite of the regrets that the sight inspires, how impressive is the fall of these wintry ornaments when they are detached by their own weight or the violence of the wind!

in Pennsylvania & New York 99

It is almost impossible to find an object of comparison for that island, so completely resplendent in its glory, light, and transparence. Sometimes it calls to my mind the memory of those beautiful inventions of the Arabian imagination, those enchanted palaces built by the most ingenious fairies; at other times it seems in fancy the abode of some unknown divinity, who, in order to escape the unwelcome worship of man, has chosen as being forever inaccessible the brims of those frightful precipices.

The column of mist, which during the summer is only a mass of transparent, airy vapors, in winter resembles rather a vast whirlpool of winged crystals, of microscopic meteors and sparkling atoms. Light as the air, they obey its whims, now sinking, now rising, and now being dispersed afar in obedience to the force and direction of the winds. Such is the inexhaustible source of all the northern riches that surround the falls.

It is neither from a disorder of the mind nor an illusion of the imagination that these objects borrow their beauty; no, that beauty is the natural effect of the extent, the magnificence, the refulgence of that immense mass of obelisks, pyramids, and accessories at once brilliant, wild, and picturesque, in the center of which fall two sheets of water, whose surface is estimated at 491,400 square feet. How is it possible to describe the profound impression created by the immensity and the variety of so many objects? How may one describe the breadth of those torrents whose forward rush forms two majestic vaults, the height from which they fall, the tumult, the circular and violent movement, as well as the rebounding of the foaming waves that fill up that whole vast enclosure? And how is it possible to express the terror and fright inspired by the ear-splitting roar that rises from that awesome chaos, in the midst of which one often sees trees and blocks of ice churning about.

As one beholds these various and exquisite creations, one can believe that nature here has its storehouse of patterns, matrices, and infinitely varied types, upon which she draws only at this particular time of year in order to exercise upon these crystalline formations all her art in carving and sculpturing and to make of them masterpieces that have the appearance and fascination of works of art.

There, by the Falls of Niagara, the imagination, become a creative faculty, extends itself, rises up and soars over the welter of new objects and decorates them with its most brilliant colors. How that splendid, sparkling scene contrasts with the harshness of the season, the nakedness of the forests, and the somber darkness of the precipitous banks at the bottom of which the torrents of Niagara rush along. For the sharper the cold, the more numerous are the crystallizations and the more resplendent is the huge circle of ice, especially when the sun inundates it with its brilliance.[1]

"When you speak of contrasts," I said to Monsieur E., "we can't forget the one offered by your home and the scene at the Falls. Everything here is calm and tranquil, the abode of peace and repose; three miles to the north everything is, on the other hand, violence, tumult, and noise. Even the night there knows no silence. Here, under this roof and in the nearby fields, nature is laughing, animated; everything grows and matures; the human eye is scarcely able to behold all the profuse fruitfulness. Below us, all that comes from the other lakes and yields to the waters of Erie, is irresistably swept away and ground to atoms in that vast abyss of destruction. Here, everything is the image of order, of life and progress. There, however, all portrays chaos and death. Here, everything breathes tranquillity, ease, and happiness; there, all arouses and incites astonishment, terror, and fright. The poet and the painter will never be able to bring together so eloquently in one scene the two periods of existence: the contrast between birth and death."

[1] This rich tableau—one might believe it to be the work of the imagination of the author if the tales of all the travelers did not attest to the magnificence of the spectacle that he has just offered us—gives a truly sublime idea of the majesty of Nature and the power of the Creator. Who can tell us why such a monument of grandeur entered into the plan of His works? Why was it placed, so to speak, far from the sight of civilized nations, that is, those nations whose religious enlightenment and philosophy have made their admiration and homage more worthy of the Creator? [Crèvecoeur's note. He claims (II, 159) that the description is not his but was read to him by Mr. E.]

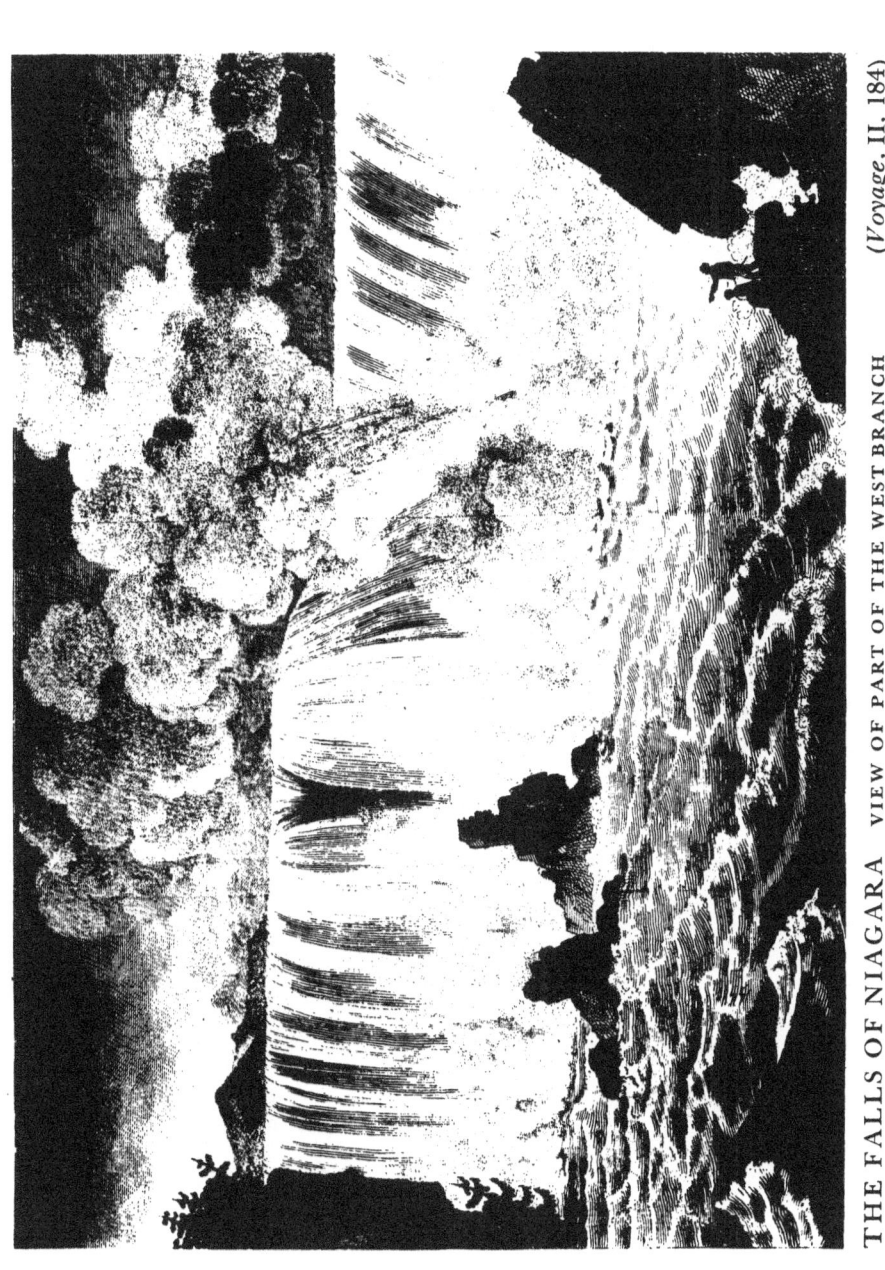

THE FALLS OF NIAGARA VIEW OF PART OF THE WEST BRANCH (*Voyage*, II, 184)

CHAPTER XII

Agouehghon, the Coohassa-Onas of Niagara

THE NEXT day, following the recommendations of Colonel Hunter, we crossed the roadstead of Niagara in his six-oared canoe and, guided by the soldier assigned to carry our dinner, who led us along an extremely wild and picturesque path, we arrived at the wigwam, or rather the hermitage, of the old Agouehghon.

"We have just come from New York, my brother," I said to him, "in order to see the waterfall; but the Officer in charge of the fort, who is our friend and yours, has told us in such an interesting manner of your great wisdom, of your long experience, and of your loneliness, that we desired to shake your hand and spend the day with you before leaving for Lake Erie."

"You are indeed welcome here," he answered us.

After having informed him of my adoption among the Oneidas, as well as of my travels among the nations of the Ohio, I said to him, "Here is some wine that we have brought you, brave and worthy Agouehghon. Let us drink a few glasses of it, in the hope that you will tell us your story. This young European is my friend."

"Give me your hand, Kayo," he replied, "and you also, Cherryhum Sagat. Sit down on that bear skin and let us smoke together; among us that is the symbol of friendship and harmony. As for your wine, wait until we have eaten together. I have been among white people enough to know that it is not poison like their scarat,[1] which burns and destroys; wine, on the contrary, animates and preserves. In the trail of scarat and the other firewaters, there come, like a flood let loose, irritation, anger, fever, madness, and death. Wine invokes only joy, inspires only peace; it is the balm of life and the blood of old men. But before you sit down I want you to see the plots of ground in which I plant my corn, my potatoes, and my tobacco. From there we shall go to the river bank, where you will see how easy it is for me to catch all the fish I need, and often more than that. As for clear drinking water, these little birchbark barrels supply all I want. What more does a man need during his voyage here on earth, when, in addition to all these things, he is as free and independent as I am? As for winter clothes, my little tobacco crop procures for me those which I cannot do without. That is all that nature demands."

"How glad I am," my companion said to me in a low tone, "that we came to see this Indian! How interesting he is! How well he expresses himself! Colonel Hunter did not deceive us."

"Why do you live alone, venerable Agouehghon?" he asked. "Why, in your loneliness, do you not have a companion who would keep your fire going and your pot full, who would light your pipe when you can no longer bend over, who would help you take the fish from your lines, and who would hold the door of your wigwam closed against the harsh winds of winter? Don't you know that old age without a friend is like an old oak without its robe of ivy, like a traveler who has lost his dog?"

"I am going to tell you, my brother," he replied, "how that has happened, and then you will see that the same secret and powerful cause which rules the great destinies of the whites also rules ours. If the ocean storms disturb, sometimes dismast, their vessels and cause shipwrecks, don't we also have storms on our lakes that harass and often swallow up our frail

---

[1] According to Crèvecoeur, II, 396, this is the Chippeway and Mohawk word for "brandy." Long, p. 310, has two spellings for the Chippeway word for "brandy," one of which is "squittywabo."

in Pennsylvania & New York 103

canoes? Haven't you ever heard of the plan that was made a great many moons ago by the chiefs of the nations up above us immediately after the people of Corlear had driven the followers of Ononthyo from Canada?[2] Ashamed of the bondage under which they had been held, as well as of their folly in shedding their blood, sometimes for the quarrel of one group, sometimes for the quarrel of another, they resolved to free themselves of this disgraceful yoke. You know perhaps what happened to our people in the valley of Bushy Run, in spite of their efforts and their courage? Perhaps you have heard of our failure at Detroit. When we saw that for lack of cannon we would not take that fort, we besieged it for two months. I do not know how it happened, but in spite of our vigilance the ships from Lake Erie arrived. We killed a great number of soldiers as they landed, and the rest entered the town. Then we were forced to give up that glorious undertaking. But we had scarcely returned to our villages when those of our warriors who had brought away some Saganash[3] uniforms were stricken with mergum-megat. Like those infectious fogs that neither the winds nor the sun can dissipate, that cruel sickness spread along the banks of our river, entered into every wigwam, and brought terror, desolation, and death. Like the winged thistle seed by the water's edge, become the plaything of the winds, like the trees in the valleys that the floods of spring uproot and carry off, these men, so proud, so strong, and so brave, assailed, beaten down by the power of that murderous poison, disappeared from the face of the earth, and they have left behind them only the sad remembrance of their number and their bravery; and even this remembrance will soon lose itself in the misty distance of the past. Yet a few moons, and the existence of our tribe, which, like the fireflies, sparkled so often in the midst of storms, and the existence of so many others, will be only a forgotten dream. In fact, what is the duration of a warrior, of a family, of a nation, compared with that of this

[2] "Ononthyo" meant "father" and was used by the Indians for the French government in Canada. Cf. *Voyage*, II, 396.
[3] A name given to the English soldiers because of their red uniform.

swift stream before us, which flows on eternally without drying up?

"That deplorable catastrophe is not the only source for the regrets which have filled my heart with bitterness. After the melancholy days of eclipse, the sun, as if to drive away fright from men and console them, reappears as brilliant as the day before; but the children of my youth, who had gone to sleep long before the hour assigned by nature, never reappeared; never again did my eyes behold Nehan, Nehiou, Kayoulah, and Cognawassy. Their mother Agonethya, broken under the weight of her sorrow, like the ice of winter under the feet of the traveler, left me also in order to follow them. Instead of six gay and happy pople my roof no longer sheltered, my fire no longer lighted, anything but the loneliness of a man overcome by his losses. I abandoned it, this fire, as well as hunting and fishing, and I lived with tears and regrets. Like the birds of night I fled the light of day, and like the ferocious marten I inhabited the places most remote from the sight of hunters. Why does the Good Spirit, instead of protecting men, to whom he has refused the fur of the beaver, the quickness of the eagle, and the strength of the moose—why does he permit evil to cover their path with leaves, with traps, and with precipices? If, as someone has said, our breathing is only an emanation of his lifegiving breath, why, when his children suffer and are in distress, is he deaf to their complaints, as the violent northwest wind is to those of the autumn insects when he hurls them by the thousands into the waters of the lake, or as the pitiless laborer is to those of the summer ants when he crushes their dwellings under the feet of his horses? How is one to reconcile the idea of the all-powerful with that of goodness?

"Like the tenacious mercury, that companion of aged oaks, which grows in spite of the lightning with which those trees are often struck, I live on in spite of all the misfortunes with which the arrow of death has so many times struck me, and I even seem to enjoy some moments of calm. But it is only the calm of concentrated sorrow, which too often revives my thoughts, as the night breeze revives the dying echo that is scarcely heard or gives new life to the fire of the sleeping hunter; it is the calm of an evening that comes after a day a hundred times too long because life and the future no longer hold anything for me. O! Why should I want to see tomorrow? And if I do see that tomorrow which is so useless, why should I want to see the day after, still more useless? The moons, those daughters of ancient times, which out of pity sometimes erase from the mind of men the memory of their afflictions, but which have not been able to ease those of the unfortunate Agouehghon—will they, in passing, restore to him the companions, the wife, the children which he has lost? No! As before, they will pursue their eternal paths and will leave him just as they found him, alone, in the midst of these solitary rocks, a prey to his sorrow, reduced to wanting nothing and feeling nothing, except the need of going to rejoin those loved ones in the land of our ancestors: like the old cedar on that promontory, which has so long weathered the winds and the storms, whose sap is dried up and whose shoots are dead, and which the first breeze from the lake will blow over.

"If only the Great Spirit who bestowed life and breath on me had taken me and spared my children! I had breathed enough, and they were just beginning. What remains of this *me* belongs only to the past, and that past is now only the ineffaceable impression of dim but always bitter memories. That is what I have gained from life up to this point.

"Melancholy and sad, old and worn out, such you see me today, but I was once strong and vigorous, brave and daring, chief of a great tribe, and renowned among the Nishynorbay nations. But what is a hunter and a warrior when he begins to bend under the weight of years, when time dries up the marrow in his bones and imprints on his forehead the wrinkles of old age? Descended from the heights of youth and life into the valley of silence, shadows, and death, nevermore will he see the sun of spring, nevermore will his head, bent like the branches of the willow under last winter's burden of snow and ice, be lifted up to new life. His gait, but lately rapid and proud like that of the moose, now resembles the slow and tortuous movement of the snail, and like that reptile he is crushed under the feet of the passers-by. Does he guide his canoe on the water? His feeble hands let the paddle escape in the moment of danger, and soon the current sweeps him from the top of the waterfall into the abyss of destruction and eternal forgetfulness. It is as if he had never been born.

"What is a hunter and warrior whose trembling and decrepitude cause his hands to shake and his steps to falter? Unable to bend his bow, to wield his tomahawk, to keep his pot full, he ends his life like a meteor that, once blazing, is now extinguished, whose traces are only in its smoke; or like a cloud that has discharged its thunder and has become only a humid and airy vapor, the plaything of the breeze and the winds. The respect of those around him, which had inspired his bravery in war, his skill in hunting, and his words in counsel, is replaced by a cold and useless pity, the companion and neighbor of disgust and scorn. And if, like me, he has lost in his children the consolation and support of his old age, a thousand times better would it have been had he never been counted among men. He exists, and that is all; sorrow and dullness attack him; his ears close; he becomes deaf to the voice of friendship as well as to that of nature, which speaks so musically in the song of the birds; fogs, the advance messengers of death, surround him; his eyes grow dim; he is unable to recognize his relatives and neighbors until he has touched their hands; his memory is gradually extinguished, like the rays of the sun when in the evening it immerses itself in the mists of the lake. Hunting and fishing, the passage of the hours and the seasons, the arrival of the fish and the birds, all these no longer mean anything to him; and soon the sad remains of his spirit, of his courage, of his soul, lose themselves in the shadows of death, as the light of the day loses itself in the shades of night.

"In other days, when I was surrounded by my children, I lived only with pleasures and hopes; I enjoyed even more happiness in seeing them as they would some day be than in seeing them as they were. Their departure has crushed my hope, as the hunters crush the grass on which they have camped, as the summer heat crushes the beautiful reeds on the river bank. In those days I dreaded the great arrow of Agan-Matchee-Manitou, which arrives and strikes without being seen or heard; but today, what have I to fear when I have lost everything? What shall I say to you, my brother? What is left to me of life merits the name no more than the rays of the moon, weakened by clouds and reflected from the agitated surface of the lake, merit the name of light.

"However, I feel that this wine is bringing back life and spirit to me, as after a long calm the wind fills the sails of our canoes and dug-outs. Of all the useless riches of the white men, it is this one alone that I envy them. Here! Put your hand on my heart. . . . Feel how it beats? See how my old veins are swelling? how my shrunken eyes are expanding? That is not caused, however, by either anger or pleasure, but by the wine that you gave me to drink. Where, then, does this wine come from? From what is it made? Is it the spirit of the sun or the sap of the tree that makes it? Would it be the product of the white man's industry, or a present from the Great Spirit? If the latter, why should he refuse it to us, when, like the white men, we are the children of his breath? Yes, he gave them odzizia[4] in the days of his goodness, and scarat in the days of his anger, and the whites have made known to us only the one that is a murderous poison."

"They are both useful," Monsieur Herman said to him. "It is only the abuse of them that is hurtful."

"How is the abuse to be distinguished from the use?" asked the old Agouehghon.

"With the help of reason."

"And what if our young people do not want to listen to the voice of reason?"

"There is no remedy, for the man without reason is inferior to the elk and the deer that live in the forests. Why did you not restrain their intemperance when you were chief?"

"What could I do when they knew not how to obey a command?"

[4] The Mohawk word for "wine."

"What did you do then when you wanted them to obey?"

"I commanded them only in war."

"And how did you lead them then?"

"By example and persuasion, that is, by bravery and eloquence. After returning to the village, there remained to me only the voice of exhortation; but as soon as the outbursts of drunkenness and madness began, our young men were deaf to my voice. It is as if I had said to the waters of the flood or the wind of the lake, 'Stop!'

"However, after the ravages of the mergum-megat were past, I stayed some time in the village in order that I might try to gather the remnants of our tribe and go elsewhere to raise our wigwams. My efforts were useless. Our elders were all dead, and the survivors were left without counsel. Some went to join the Oneidas; the others scattered themselves abroad at the mercy of their caprice. Thus disappeared the last members of a tribe which in my youth counted three thousand warriors. No longer able then to find rest in that land of misery, I covered with rocks the bones of our venerable ancestors and withdrew to Sandusky, among the Wyandots. There I lived rather peacefully, although my spirit was disturbed by sorrowful memories, as are the waters of the lake after a tempest. Seven times the snows of winter had swelled the rivers, seven times the ears of corn had grown yellow, when a canoe full of white men, coming from Lake Erie and going to Detroit, was forced by contrary winds to put into port in our bay. Unfortunately they had some scarat aboard with which they traded in the village. Like the devouring fires that our hunters light in the middle of the grassy plains, these waters of madness and war spread in all directions the germ of quarrels and dissensions. One no longer heard anything but sounds of anger, outbursts of violence. Not a wigwam that had young men was spared; their wives, running here and there, could scarcely keep them from selling even their bear skins. 'That,' said I to myself, striking my chest, 'that is the picture of error, stupidity, and ruin; there is the cause of the destruction and annihilation of so many of our nations, of so much havoc and so many bloody scenes; that is how the foxes from beyond the rising sun have been able to delude and overcome the wolves of this great country.' I, as one of the elders, wanted to speak, to plead with them, to restrain those blind young men; but they rejected completely my advice, as well as that of their chiefs. Foreseeing then that the peace and harmony of the village would be troubled for a long time, that hunger would soon come knocking at the door of these drunkards, and feeling my eyesight growing weak, I left for the country of the Genesees, whose sachems, Kayaderossera and Koronkiagoa, I knew. I went back up the Cayuga River as far as the portage of Big Beaver, where I was forced to leave my canoe, since I was alone. Finally, after some days of traveling, I arrived at Shenandoah, where I found the old Poopoko, who took me by the hand, warmed me at his fire, and gave me a shelter. During the beautiful season I was still able to hunt; but as soon as the snows of winter came, my eyes grew dim; I found myself reduced to fishing in the lake on whose shores we lived. One day, surprised by a squall that the weakness of my eyesight kept me from seeing, I was capsized. As for me, I was able to swim to land, but Poopoko's canoe sank to the bottom. Imagine my misery! From the next day on I went out into the woods to strip the bark from the black birch tree, which I had to have, and to bring back some cedar. For some days I worked quite well; but when I came to the seams, my eyes failed me. Then, full of anguish and despair, I said to myself, 'Agouehghon is still alive, and he is no longer good for anything! He lives, and he is no longer a man! He has been the father of four brave boys, and not one of his own blood is near to help him in his old age.' I lay down to sleep, with the burning desire that I might leave for the west. But someone came to console me, to give me help, and the canoe was finished. However, fearing that I would no longer be able to guide it, I built myself a raft of white cedar, from which I kept on fishing, until, threatened by complete blindness, I was forced to give that up.

"I was so humiliated by not being able to put anything in the pot of Poopoko that I made up my mind to come and live among these rocks, whose location I had known of for a long time. After having given my rifle to the son of my host, I came away to the dwelling place of the Cayugas, whose old chief, Nagooar-Missey, brought me among the Onondagas of the lake, from where Ashamut the teller of tales led me to Oswego. And there I embarked in the dug-out of a white man who was going to Niagara. I was quite sure that once my fire was lighted here I could easily catch all the fish I needed, without a canoe or a raft, because every morning the fish from the lake pass here on their way to the foot of the waterfall, where they go to feed on the great variety of debris that the fall brings with it. My hopes have not been deceived. With the aid of these two rocks and the bark that some travelers helped me by leaving, I made myself a shelter against the wind and the rain. I am not lacking for firewood; the job of cutting it and bringing it here is almost the only one that my waning strength undertakes. In order to provide food for the winter, I dry those fish which I catch but do not eat in the summer.

"From time to time I go to Niagara, to Erie, where I am always welcome. Some people say to me, 'Agouehghon, do you need a copper pot? Tell me!' Others say, 'Do you need bedclothes? Tell me! Would you like to have a hatchet with the handle already fitted? You need only say yes.' We smoke together, and after having taken them by the hand, I return here, my heart big and my eyes wet, saying to myself, 'It is possible to find some good people among the whites.'

"Here, as you see, I bother no one and no one bothers me. I can go here or there, remain, smoke, sleep, or fish, according to my whim or my need. I breathe the freshest of air. To my left, I have Ontario, that beautiful azure sea which I can still barely distinguish; to my right, the river that carries to it the agitated waters from the fall, the noise of which, when the wind comes from Erie, is the only thing that is unpleasant. Almost opposite me, I can see Niagara, as well as the vessels that come from all parts of the lake . . . Alas! where are the days of my youth, when these waters were covered only with our canoes, when the tomahawk of war glistened in the hands of our nations like the snows of winter in the sunlight? What has become of them, those nations?

"I sleep much of the time, and that is a great consolation, because time is nothing during sleep. Every morning I go down to the river bank, and I never return empty-handed. Formerly I longed for death as a sick man longs for his cure; today I await it as the tired hunter awaits his sleep of peace after having made a shelter for the night. However, I still receive a few moments of involuntary comfort. For example, I love the sun of our land; it is the only friend I have left. It does not speak to me, it is true, and yet its presence consoles me. I know not why, but for me its splendor takes the place of clothing, of food. Often even, it gives birth within me to something which grows little by little and gives me new life. It seems to me then that if I still had my rifle I could kill geese and foxes. Old fool that I am! Who would go and get them for me, since I no longer have either a canoe or a dog?

"Oh! How good and sweet seems the smoke of my pipe when I inhale it as I lie exposed to the rays of the sun! What I experience then is neither sleep nor drunkenness, but mental wandering, absence, happy forgetfulness of myself. Desiring sometimes to know how much of the thorny passage of time I have spanned, I raise a little stick on a stone slab; then when I reopen my eyes to the light, I quickly learn how long I have ceased to be a victim.

"Nearly all those who come to see the fall take me by the hand and smoke a pipe with me. Like you, some call me Agouehghon; others, brother; still others, Coohassa-Onas, father of the fall. One visitor wants to talk; another leaves me with only the handshake and words of friendship, and that is all I need. During the winter, like an old fox in his lair, a bear in his den, or a squirrel in the hollow of his tree, half of me goes away I know not where and returns only with the spring. My fire keeps me warm, it is true, but it is no longer like a star to me, the father of nature, the friend of old age.

"As for the moons of time, I have lost count of them; they

pass without my being aware of them, like a puff of wind, like the water of the river. Such is the story of the last part of my long life. But what interest can it hold for men who live near the great ocean, in the land of iron and houses, and who have no need of fishing, as I do, to keep their pots full?"

"Have you then forgotten, my brother," I said to him, "the first part of our conversations? I told you that during my youth I had been to the great portage of the Wabash, among the Ouyatanons; to the forks of the Muskingum, among the Delawares? Have you forgotten how you pressed my hand when I told you of my long travels with them, of the quickness with which I threw myself into the water whenever it was necessary to drag the canoe through the rapids, or lent my shoulder to carry it across the big and little portages? Yes, like you I have gone on foot in the snow, slept on leaves at the foot of a tree; like you, I have climbed mountains, descended rapids, and crossed lakes in the wind and rain."

"Your reproaches pierce my heart like an arrow," he replied. "Give me your hand, Kayo . . . I feel it. It is the hand of a man who has known and loves the children of the earth. I am old, and memory, as you know, turns its back on old people. Let us go on; where were we? Talking of time, I believe, which no longer means anything to me."

"I remember it well," I said to him; you were speaking of the moons of which you have lost count. And I, I was going to tell you that I saw with pleasure how much the advantages of your way of life ought to sweeten your loneliness. There is less enjoyment than rest, less pleasure than absence of pain and suffering. The river and your plots of ground abundantly furnish you subsistence. Perhaps you are richer than you think. You need so little! And that little is assured to you. And in order to get it, you need not ask for it, and you depend on nobody. It is nature who offers it to you and who gives it to you. You no longer live except by obeying her laws; your heart no longer beats except to circulate your blood. At Niagara, at Erie, your old age is respected; travelers come to warm themselves at your fire in order to converse with the

in Pennsylvania & New York 113

wisdom of your years. In fact, after that great cataract itself, what is more interesting to find here than a man who, like you, has seventy times seen the sun of spring reclothe the forests in green; who has been witness to so many things and so many different events; whom experience has taught so much; and who, like a rock, has resisted the violence of the flood in which his nation has been engulfed! You live; you exist without pain, and without other infirmities than the weakness of your eyes. You neither think about nor foresee your end, except as the tired hunter dreams about the banks of the stream on which he is going to spend the night.

"We have come in order to commiserate with you, to sympathize with you in your loneliness, and to mix with your tears the sweet tears of compassion. And, in addition, we congratulate you on the advantages of your way of life; on the peace which you enjoy, the treasure of old age; on the consideration that the whites your neighbors have for you; on the happiness, finally, of being free and independent to the last day of your life. Your solitude has nothing of sadness when you know that what you have is sufficient. I know some among the whites who are called rich and who have more to complain of. Like you, they are old, but they are crushed by infirmities unknown to your race. Accustomed to what they call pleasure, they suffer from no longer being able to have it. Languor holds them back; pusillanimity assails them; repentance and remorse, fears for the future and the terrors of superstition, ambition and avarice—a species of pain and suffering of which you are ignorant—pursue and torment them night and day. Often, as they approach the end of their life, they encounter only the forgetfulness, the indifference, or the ingratitude of their relatives; they die a death much more frightful than yours will be, because theirs is not a peaceful leavetaking but a cruel torture."

"I am not complaining, my brother," he said to me; "I know how to suffer, because I am a man; and it is not a thing of today only. I do not know how the whites of your cities die. Is it not necessary that, like us, they give back the breath that has been given to them? You are right. They are too much afraid of being unhappy in what they call the other world, as if it were not enough to have been so in this one; they love money so much, and houses, and the things of earth, that they are bound to leave it with much more regret than we, who go back to that other world just as we left it. Our end then should be much sweeter and more peaceful since death for us is not a chain that breaks but a knot that is untied.

"At Michilimackinac I knew some whites whom I believed to be brave. But, well! they had to have a magician to help them die. It reminds me of a young bearded one, whose name I have forgotten, who, every time some of our people departed for the west, was found in their wigwams. 'What are you doing here?' I asked him one day. 'What am I doing here?' he answered. 'I come to admire the calm and peaceful patience of your sick ones, and the courage with which they die, without regrets or moans. I come in order to learn how to imitate them some day. You are not angry, I hope?' That is what he said to me.

"But when the last rays of my last sun will have ceased to shine on my tree of life and the night breeze will have blown it over, who will cover my sad remains with earth and place them out of reach of the teeth of wolves? Nobody! And I have had five brave sons!"[5]

"Give me your hand," I said to him, "venerable Chippeway, oldest of the old in this country! How many days would one have to travel before meeting another man like you, a Nishynorbay who tells us so many interesting things! You may be sure that I shall never forget them; the highminded spirit which inspired them has also engraved them on my memory. You are a striking proof to what degree the instinct, which comes from nature alone, can raise itself without the help of our education. I have known a great many of your people in my time, but compared with what I have just heard, all that they told me was no more than flimsy feathers blown about at the

---

[5] Earlier in his story the old Agouehghon had claimed four sons. Either his mind is wandering or he had a son who died before the smallpox epidemic.

discretion of the wind. I am happier for having seen you and listened to you than I would have been if, being hungry, I had killed a deer or an elk."

"And I also," said Monsieur Herman. "You may be assured that I shall not quit this part of the country without coming again and leaving you some lasting marks of my remembrance."

"As for your fears with regard to the last moments of your life," I told him, "you may be certain that the people of Niagara and Erie will not forget you. You know the chief there; he is as generous as he is brave and he thinks well of you. You will smoke your last pipes surrounded, cared for, if not by your own people, at least by honest and sympathetic whites who for a long time have had for you the respect which you merit.

"But night is coming on. We came today from the fort; tomorrow we go back there in order to set out for the portage which leads to the fall. Weariness and a desire for sleep overcome the wish to know more of you."

And so our conversation ended. The next day, after having gone with him to the river bank and helped take the fish from his lines, we dined on some of the finest, which he prepared in his own fashion. Finally, after drinking some glasses of wine with him and smoking a long pipe of friendship and good will, we shook his hand and, under the escort of the same soldier, went back down the path we had taken the day before.

CHAPTER XIII

Two Indian Tales

"Now then," said Colonel Hunter on our return, "didn't I predict that you would enjoy your visit with old Agouehghon? I have another excursion to suggest, one a little different from the other. It is a fishing trip which several of our officers are going to take a few miles from here. You will go by water as far as the mouth of the Prideaux River, on the east bank of the lake. During this season the fish there have the most exquisite flavor of any in the lake, and the Indians have taught us how to preserve them by smoking."

Everything contributed to make the trip delightful: the beautiful lake, the favorable wind, the mild temperature, an abundance of fish, and the friendly cheerfulness of the company. When evening came, we decided to return by land in order to avoid the annoying tacking about that would be necessary. Hardly had we traveled two miles through the woods when we saw a fire, around which were gathered a party of fourteen Indians, their pipes in their mouths, their heads bent, and their eyes on the ground.

Since my friend Herman had not seen any Indians except at Onondaga, the officers consented to go nearer. The party was a mixture of young Mohawks and Cayugas, who, like ourselves, had spent the day in fishing and were now amusing themselves by telling stories. Apart from courage in war and skill in hunting, there is nothing which gives one a greater influence among these people than the talent for narrating a tale. The attention that people of Europe give to a sermon, a tragedy, or a scholarly discourse is not comparable to that with which these idle men listen to the speeches of their orators. Some of their stories are gay and others are serious. The former are almost always concerned with making fun of some of our own customs; the latter tell of adventures of the chase, or describe their travels, or relate their military exploits.

After joining the group, I found that the Indian who had just told his story was on my left. Touching with my elbow the man on my right, I said, "Don't you see that it is your turn? Why don't you get up and tell us something?"

"I had rather receive than give," he told me brusquely. "I had rather listen than talk."

"You are not generous, for a Cayuga," I said to him, "or else you are very poor."

"What do you mean 'poor'? Am I not as rich as the others, though less of a prattler; for, like them, I have ears which, during the night, let me know what goes on about me; eyes which, during the day, perceive the game at a great distance; good legs to pursue that game with; and something here (putting his hand on his breast) which makes me proud? Do you hear me?"

"If you are proud," I answered, "in your reply to me, I was not less so when I put the question to you. Do you hear me also?"

But in order to stifle this incipient quarrel, I said to him, "Would you like some wine?"

"I prefer whiskey," he responded. "Do you have any?"

"No." But now, a new speaker having arisen, everyone became quiet and the tale began.

THE COURTSHIP OF MASSOTAWANA

Massotawana, son of Wappanome, of the village of Niskotowasse, of the nation of the Chickasaws, was a warrior and hunter who for a long time had given many proofs of his courage and skill. He had built a beautiful and spacious wigwam, in which his fire burned and his pot hung. He had an abundance of animal skins of all kinds—beaver, buffalo, fox, and bear. In fishing he was as successful as in hunting; in war, as brave as the bravest among us. One day as he mended his canoe on the bank of the river Caspetowagan, he caught sight of Napotelima, daughter of Mico Tatoba,[1] who had come there to draw water. Struck inwardly by something which he had never felt before, he approached her and said, "Would you blow your breath upon my firebrand?"

"Speak to my father," she answered.

And so on the next day he sought out Mico Tatoba at his fire and said to him, "Will you give your daughter Napotelima to me for my wife?"

"Tomorrow," said the old man, "I leave for hunting grounds that are a far distance; do you want to go with me?"

"Yes," answered Massotawana.

And they set out. But the navigation of the rivers was very difficult because of the many rapids and waterfalls. They had to push through the one with poles and avoid the other by carrying their canoe around to calm waters. When they arrived at the hunting grounds, each one set up his own lodge. Massotawana caught a great number of animals—ermines in snares, wolves in pits, beavers under the ice, foxes in traps, and deer on the snow. After smoking the skin and the flesh, he carried it all to the cabin of Mico Tatoba, who said to him, "Ah! I am very glad to see that you are so clever and cunning; tomorrow I leave for the village; do you wish to return with me?"

"Yes," answered Massotawana.

And they set out. But as they descended the river Nistotowa, the canoe scraped the branch of a tree and took on a great deal of water. Massotawana emptied it, carried it to the foot of a tree, and spent a day in repairing it, while Mico Tatoba neither opened his mouth nor lifted his hand to help. The next day, after carrying the canoe back to the river and

---

[1] "Mico," among the southern Indians, meant "chieftain."

replacing in it the bundles of skins, he sought out the older man at his fire and said to him, "All is ready; as soon as you have smoked your pipe, you can embark; there is your paddle." They set out.

When they reached the village, Mico Tatoba said to Massotawana, "I need a four-man canoe; can you make one for me?"

"You will see," replied the other.

And on the next day he dug a ditch to serve for the form; he went to the woods to get some bark from the black birch tree for the lining, some white cedar for the sides, some water oak for the bottom, some vines for the binding, and some gum to cover the whole canoe. And in half a moon the canoe was finished.

"Here," said Massotawana to Mico Tatobe, "here is what you asked me for; see if it is watertight and straight."

"It is dry and well made," answered Mico Tatoba.

"Are you satisfied?" asked the young hunter.

"Not yet. This evening I am going fishing with torches, but while I was gone on our hunting trip, the torches I left were burned up. Can you make some?"

"You will see." And very shortly he brought back six that were four hands long.

"Here are some deer and buffalo hides," Mico Tatoba then said to him. Can you smoke them and dress them cleverly?"

"You will see." And in a few days he returned with the hides dressed. They were soft and flexible.

"Do you know how to fish with torches?" was the old man's next question.

"You will see," answered the young warrior. And they left together, each in his own canoe; and Massotawana harpooned many sturgeons.

When the fishing was done, Mico Tatoba spoke: "Come and warm yourself at my fire." The youth went with him. "Fill your pipe and let us smoke together." And the old man continued, "I see that you are a skillful hunter, patient and tireless; that you know how to repair and build canoes, to fish with a line and fish with torches, both under the ice and on the water, either during the night or during the day. I have heard that you are alert and active in all physical exercises; that you are as brave a warrior as you are a good hunter; that you know how to stand hunger, fatigue, and misfortune without complaining; that you consider death as the road which warriors travel to reach the land where our ancestors dwell; that you are ready to sacrifice your life for the honor of our nation, of our tribe; that you have built your own wigwam where your fire never dies; that you are careful to keep filled the pot of your old father; that you respect old age; that you had rather listen than talk; and finally that you scorn the fire water of the white man. Since all these things are so, you are a man worthy of being a husband and a father. Go and find my daughter Napotelima; repeat to her what I have just said to you; sing her your war song; and if she is willing, let her breathe upon your firebrand. Be happy with her, and may she be happy with you. Never forget what a brave owes to the weakness of women: without them, there would be only bears and wolves to inhabit the earth."

As soon as the narrator had finished his tale, a new speaker arose and announced: "Having only recently returned from Hoppajewot, the Land of Dreams, I am going to tell you how life is carried on there, and what I saw take place. If anyone says to me afterward, 'You dream like a sick man,' or 'You rave like a drunkard,' I shall only say, 'Go and see for yourself.'"

HOPPAJEWOT, THE LAND OF DREAMS

In this land there is neither day nor night; the sun neither rises nor sets; and there is neither hot nor cold, spring nor winter. The people have never seen bows and arrows and tomahawks; and their language has no words that mean *hunter* and *warrior*. Devouring hunger and burning thirst came there once upon a time, according to an ancient tradition, but the chiefs of the land threw them to the bottom of the river, where they remain to this day.

in Pennsylvania & New York 121

Oh! this wonderful land! If one desires to smoke, he can find a pipe anywhere; he has only to lift it to his lips. Anywhere that one wishes he can rest at the foot of a tree. He has only to stretch out his arm and he will encounter the hand of a friend. The earth being always green and the trees covered with leaves, one has need neither of bear skins nor wigwams. If one likes to travel, the current of the rivers takes him wherever he wants to go; he has no need of oars and paddles. Oh! this wonderful land!

"Do you want something to eat?" asks the deer of those who are hungry. "Take my right shoulder, and let me go off into the forest of Ninner Wind[2] where it will soon grow back, and next year I shall return and offer you the left one. But take care not to destroy too much, because if you do, in the end you will not have anything."

"Here," says the beaver, "cut off my beautiful tail; I can do without it until it grows back, since I have just finished building my home. But take care not to be greedy, for it is said: 'Four beavers you will take, but the fifth you will let go in peace.' "[3] Oh! that wonderful land! There one only eats, drinks, smokes, and sleeps.

"Do you want to have a feast?" asks the great fish in the lake. "My job is done; I have just laid ten thousand eggs; cook me in any way you wish. But take care not to be too greedy, for it is said: 'Eighteen fish will you take, but the nineteenth you will let go in peace.' " Oh! that wonderful land! Though the women there never have to anoint themselves with bear grease, they are always beautiful and fresh; they have only to keep the pots boiling and teach the children how to swim.

One day as I was helping at the council fire, an unusual noise was heard, and the great Okemaw[4] who presided there gave orders to investigate. The messenger returned. "The

---

[2] In the Chippeway language "Ninnerwind" meant "all of us." Cf. Long, p. 280.
[3] Cf. Isaac Weld, *Travels through the United States of America* (London, 1801), p. 551, and the last page of Crèvecoeur's story, "Wabemat's Reward," for two other accounts of the Indian custom of leaving every fifth beaver—a custom not observed by the white man.
[4] Chief, both in Chippeway and Algonquin. Cf. Long, p. 242.

sound," he said, comes from some great canoes that draw near our shore. They look like sea birds driven before the winds. Our people are in great wonder and know neither what to think nor to say."

"Are there any men on these boats?"

"Yes," the messenger replied. "They are white people with beards, tired from their long voyage, for they come from the land of Cherryhum.[5] They humbly ask permission to land here in order to rest. What says the great Okemaw?"

"Although they are white and bearded," he answered, "and have come from a land which I did not believe to be inhabited, they are wretched and suffering; let them come ashore and rest here for a few days."

I do not know how long it was after their arrival that these strangers, while walking on the bank of the river, met the great chief of Hoppajewot, from whom they begged a little land on both sides of the place where they were encamped. Surprised at such an unusual request, he said to them, "What do you want it for?"

"To plant some little grains we have brought with us," they answered. "They reproduce a hundredfold, and when one has neither flesh nor fish, one can eat them."

Hardly had the chief given his consent when they set to work scratching the earth and destroying the plant life, to the great astonishment of the people of Hoppajewot, who had never seen anything like it. Some moons later, after their fields of grain had flourished, they again approached the Okemaw, and this time asked for the point of land that formed the entrance to the bay. Finding nothing inconvenient in the request, he granted it. Almost immediately they were seen cutting down the trees with a piece of very sharp metal, digging a hole in the earth, and raising a little mountain of wood, from which, both morning and evening, there issued forth fire and smoke and noise never before heard in the country of Hoppajewot.

[5] Europe or England; an Iroquois word. Cf. Long, p. 254.

in Pennsylvania & New York 123

Then appeared before the Okemaw, Awakesh,[6] the great forest deer, saying, "Woe be unto you, O Chief of the nation! Woe unto your people! And woe unto us and to the other beasts, if you permit these bearded ones to level and burn the forest which the Good Spirit has given us! Soon there will be no longer on the earth either plants or shade; then we will be forced to flee your land. Take care," he continued; "these white people, so soft-spoken and humble, who on first landing called you brother, will drive you away from here when they have become more numerous. Do you not observe how they behave themselves behind their mountain of fire, noise, and smoke?"

These words produced a strong effect on the men in the assembly, and each one present was set to thinking. But while they were thinking, one came to inform them that the bearded men had scattered themselves over the villages and were deceiving the women and children by telling them stories which they said were worth more than the legends of Hoppajewot. The messengers, their indignation aroused by this underhanded conduct, spoke to the great chief, saying: "The peace of families, the harmony within villages no longer exist; the white people have turned the heads of our women; our medicine men have lost their influence. What right have these foreigners from the land of Cherryhum to come here and speak to our people about the god of their country? Does not each country have its own god as it has its own lakes and rivers? And after all, the god of a land on which the hot and radiant sun shines without ceasing, is he not worth more than the god of a place where the sun rises pale and without heat? What is to be done, O, wise and powerful Okemaw?"

"Let the medicine men, both bearded and unbearded, gather here today," he answered, "and we shall see." The two groups did indeed assemble; and following the custom of Hoppajewot, the strangers were permitted to speak first. Among

---

[6] "Awakesh," or "Awaskesh," meant "deer" both in Chippeway and Algonquin. Cf. Long, p. 242.

them were four orators who spoke at such length that the audience had time to smoke two pipes. The first man told of a land where one could go only after death, which astonished the gathering a great deal. That land, he said, lies beyond the sun and knows neither heat nor cold; there the people are happy and content, for need is unknown, and this happiness never ends once it has begun. The second orator explained all that must be done and not done on earth in order to obtain permission to enter into this world of spirits. The third man spoke of a lake of fire, which, though it burns everything thrown into it, does not consume anything, and into which are plunged all those who may not go to the first place. The fourth speaker entertained them with the tale of a court of justice before which appear the spirits of all those who die, and the judgments of which are irrevocable; he assured his audience that if they followed his counsel they would find favor in the eyes of the great judge.

"Those are four good and very long stories," said the Okemaw. "It is now our turn to speak. Beardless medicine men, arise, and tell some of our legends. Begin with the one about the manifestation of the Great Spirit on the mountain of Aratapeskow, when he took two figures of clay and breathed into them the breath of life, the first of which he named Pegick Sagat, meaning First Man, and the second, Sanna Tella, meaning Companion.[7] Speak also of Nassanicomy, who came down from the clouds onto the island of Allisinape[8] and caused to grow there corn, rice, squash, and tobacco, by spitting to the north, to the south, to the east, and to the west."

"Those are only lies and illusions," said the bearded speakers. "We do not want to hear them."

"Since we have listened to you with patience and courtesy," replied the Okemaw, "you should certainly listen to our people with the same patience and the same courtesy. Why do you

[7] For the first of these two names, Crèvecoeur apparently borrowed the Algonquin word "pegick," or "Payjik," meaning "one," and the Iroquois word for man, "sagat." According to Long, "Sannatella" meant "wife" in the Iroquois tongue. Cf. Long, p. 225, p. 254, and p. 256.
[8] Algonquin for "man." Cf. Long, p. 245.

scorn our traditions? Like yours they are venerated for their old age." And he continued, "Why have you cut down the beautiful trees with which the Creator covered the ground I lent you? You merit his indignation and ours, because, like us, these trees are the work of his hands. Why do you keep us away from your mountain with the fire, smoke, and noise of death, we who have received you as brothers? If that is the way men conduct themselves in your country of Cherryhum, your Great Spirit is not so good as ours, for here you have found peace and good faith, and you have brought with your tales division and trouble. Go away, return to your mountain, and let us think and live as our ancestors have lived and thought."

In place of replying civilly, the white men arose, made a great deal of noise, and left the assembly saying things that could not be understood; and from that moment, the two parties swore an implacable hate.

Some time after, having discovered that these same white medicine men, by making use of a water that was fire to the taste, were attempting to insinuate themselves into the village and make the women believe their stories, the great Okemaw had them come a second time before him, and said to them in a loud voice:

"Obstinate bearded ones! You deceive yourselves if you think you can do here what you have done in the land of the Nishynorbays.[9] You will not seduce us with your firewater and your folly, in order to invade our land, as your countrymen have seduced those other unfortunate ones. We are not so blind nor so easily deceived. Drink the waters yourselves; may they succeed in consuming you and destroying you as they have destroyed so many brave nations! Smash those bottles of poison!"

As the Okemaw's order was being carried out, one of the bearded medicine men, with black eyebrows, a ferocious look, and a proud bearing, more hot-headed than the others, dared to lay hold of the great chief, who, while saying coldly to him,

[9] Indians or Red Men, a Chippeway word. Cf. Long, p. 245.

"You have been very badly educated in your country," knocked him down with his powerful arm, and pulled off his hair. But what was his astonishment to see that it was not attached to the skull but was only a wig of borrowed hair!

The Okemaw, as well as all his people, having never seen such a thing before, burst involuntarily into loud laughter. This laughter caused a distraction by which the white medicine man and his companions profited quickly in making their escape, leaving the false hair in the hands of the astonished chief. It was soon apparent that when they reached their companions they spread the alarm among all their habitations and that there was a great movement taking place among them.

Then the Okemaw called for a herd of deer, led by Awakesh, each of whom he ordered to take a flaming torch and set fire to the fields around the white man's mountain. And this they did so speedily that, in spite of the noise, the fire, and the smoke that came from the mountain, everything was burned by daybreak. When the sun rose, the white men were seen going aboard their canoes, carrying everything they had brought with them, and then sailing out of the river with a favorable wind. Since that time one has never heard the bearded white ones spoken of in the land of Hoppajewot. That is my story.

The orator, who had been loudly applauded, was going to start another, when several of the officers, remembering that we had yet some distance to go before reaching Niagara, informed us that it was time to leave.

CHAPTER XIV

Wabemat's Reward
or
Why the First Beaver Was Made

THE following story has been handed down from generation to generation.[1]

Since the beginning of time, the power of desire had lain dormant in the head of Agan Kitchee Manitou, until one day he was struck by the thought of descending to earth in order to see how things were going there.

He at once assumed the shape of a wolf and joined the first pack of wolves he met. Surprised at the arrival of a stranger, the chiefs surrounded and questioned him, and after being assured that he was truly of the ancient breed, admitted him to their group. "I see with pleasure," he told himself as he took part in their hunt, "that these animals still use only the weapons that I gave them. I see also that they are as cunning, agile, and patient as in the beginning, that when the need arises they know how to band together under leaders, either for defense or attack, and that each one is satisfied with that part of the spoils which falls to his lot. Sometimes, it is true, misfortune and want decrease their numbers; but on the other hand more favorable times repair their losses. The fate of the individual concerns me little, for I am interested only in the species; this particular species will be endangered only when destiny brings here a race of men who till the soil, and that time is still far distant."

Five days later, satisfied with his observations, he left the pack of wolves as they were chasing a deer and turned himself into a bear.

"What are you doing in my den?" asked the first bear whose home he entered. "I dug it out, and as you can see, there is room here only for my wife and little ones."

"Don't your friends ever come to see you?"

"I don't know any such people. Get out of here, before I show you that every man is master in his own home."

"You are just as your race has always been, savage and unsociable, and so you can't hurt my feelings," Manitou said as he left and turned himself into a fox.

"Oho!" said the first fox he met. "You have a strange and suspicious look. Don't you smell a little like a bear? Tell us who you are and where you come from, or get ready for a disagreeable reception."

"I am a true fox," Manitou told him. "I come from the land of the rising sun. I am hungry."

"You've landed in the right place, coming here to beg food of those who live only on what they can get by their skill and cunning. Why don't you hunt as we do? Where were you brought up?"

"In the district of Noyawanda, which has game in great abundance."

"That isn't the case here," replied the fox. "What distances we have to travel! What dangers and hardships to overcome! What a life we lead! Continually torn between fear and hunger, between danger and need; forever surrounded by snares and

---

[1] This old legend was translated in 1774, by request of the great war chief Attacul-Culla—The Little Carpenter—in order that it might be sent to Lord William Campbell, at that time governor of South Carolina, whose secretary, Mr. Atkins, permitted me, some years ago, to make a copy. [Crèvecoeur makes this claim in a note, II, 1.]

ambushes! You can judge for yourself if we have food to give you. Go away. Return to your land of the rising sun, to your district of Noyawanda."

"That would suit me fine," Manitou said. "Come with me and I will see that you are well entertained there."

"Perhaps you just want to betray us."

"Do you think that one fox would want to betray another? One would think that you have been living among men."

"We are often among them, it is true, but without their suspecting it, for they are our best providers."

"How is that?" asked Manitou.

"When they make war on each other, which often happens, we eat the carcasses of those that the conquerors don't care to eat."

"What! Do men eat each other?"

"Alas! yes, to our great regret. If they didn't, we should be fat and sleep all year round. Why couldn't that race have been more numerous! How we would eat!"

"Perhaps some day you will have your wish," replied Manitou. And suddenly he became a buffalo on the other side of the Alleghenies.

"What a fine country!" he said to the first buffalo he met. "Look at these prairies that are forever covered with green grass! And these reeds that are always tender! What a wonderful pasture land!"

"All that is true," replied the trans-Alleghenian, "but it doesn't make us the less unhappy."

"And why doesn't it? Aren't you on friendly terms with your comrades?"

"Yes, we enjoy peace and harmony among ourselves. But this Mammoth who bounds down from the top of the mountains and roots up trees with his horns and pursues and devours us without rest—why did Agan Kitchee Manitou create such a terrible animal?"

"Because your people would have multiplied so fast under this beautiful sky that for lack of nourishment they would have starved. Manitou has done what he could to satisfy everybody, but some things are impossible. Some day he will hurl his forked thunder between the two horns of this Mammoth and leave his bones to astonish posterity.[2] Why don't you persuade your comrades to cross the Mississippi with you? On the west bank of that beautiful river they would find prairies that are more than eight days journey across."

"Everybody likes his own country," answered the buffalo. "And this country would have to be bad indeed, or else the power of the Mammoths would have to be very formidable, before my people would decide to leave. Anyway, how do we know this terrible animal wouldn't follow us across the river? But that isn't all: we have still another enemy, no less cruel, who threatens our species with total destruction."

"Who is this second enemy?"

"He is a puny animal with only two feet and no hair. After having satiated himself on our flesh, he lies down to sleep in the shade of some great tree. All his strength and power come from the fact that he knows how to light a fire. What could be the origin of such an unusual gift?"

And Manitou answered, "He was given fire to compensate for his nakedness and weakness; without it what would he do on earth? Besides, he is scarcely more happy than you. But how does he use this fire to harm you?"

"When the summer sun dries up the cane fields and the reeds, he sets fire to them and shuts us up in the middle of an area of huge flames."

"And why don't you run away, since you have four good legs and your enemy has only two?"

"Fright seizes us and we can't move."

"Well, perhaps there is a reason why he does all this." And suddenly Manitou left and became a dog.

"Ah! my friend," he said to the first dog he met, "give me something to eat; I am hungry."

"Ask my master, who sleeps there in the sun," the dog an-

---

[2] This prophecy about the Mammoth was evidently borrowed by Crèvecoeur's Manitou from a Delaware Indian myth first told by Thomas Jefferson in his *Notes on the State of Virginia* (Richmond, Virginia, 1853), p. 43. The *Notes* appeared in Paris first in 1784 and again in 1786.

in Pennsylvania & New York 131

swered. "I who am only his slave, not his friend, have nothing. Very often he doesn't have enough for himself. Then I suffer; I go without. The man with whom I live is an ungrateful brute. Although I am always busy trying to please him, my efforts are often useless. But why should I complain? He doesn't treat his wife any better. I don't believe I would prefer her condition to mine, hard though it is. Why must one free being have two slaves? I want to leave this tyrant and live on my own; for even though I don't speak so easily as he, I think as well, and my thoughts are more reasonable than his. I have done and understood a thousand things that he could not have done or understood. I want to be a wolf; it is said that the wolf and I are descended from the same source. Then I would not have to depend on anybody. I would have a wife and children who would take care of me in my old age, and for the first time in my life I would enjoy freedom."

"You must never carry out that plan. The wolves would scorn you because you have been a slave; they would force you to undergo a harsh apprenticeship. Believe what I tell you, for I have only now left them. Just as the calm is preferable to the tempest, just as rest is preferable to labor, and sleep to delirious wakefulness, so is a soft and reasonable subjection more to be desired than a boundless liberty. Man cannot do without your services, nor you without his help. All masters are not like yours." And Manitou became an otter.

"What a sad figure you cut," he said to the first otter he met. "Poor miserable one! You appear to be overcome with cold—you are shivering in spite of your beautiful fur."

"Yes," she answered him; "the season is severe; the waters are covered with ice. But I must keep alive."

"Are you alone?"

"Yes, almost always. That is my fate. It is very sad, I admit, but I am used to it; and as long as I am able to catch fish, I am satisfied."

"And your little ones?"

"I hide them as well as I can, for I have so many enemies! And among these enemies there is one who always wants my beautiful coat." And as she said that, an arrow flew from far away, piercing her side; and Manitou, in order to converse with the hunter more easily, suddenly turned himself into a man.

"What are you going to do with this otter?" he asked the hunter.

"With its skin I shall cover my bare shoulders, and her flesh will go into my pot."

"Is your pot a big one?"

"Yes, for I have five people to support. Follow me; if you are hungry, I will feed you." And Manitou went with him.

But on entering the hunter's wigwam, what was his surprise to see those five people occupied in dismembering a human corpse! "Is this the flesh you promised me?" he asked.

"Yes, since it is the best that I can give you."

"And why are you eating that man?"

"Because he was my enemy."

"And why was he your enemy?"

"Because he and his people live on the other side of the river Wenowee, and because we have always hated each other and carried on war with each other. They eat us also, when they capture us."

"There is then neither game in the woods, nor fish in the streams?"

"Well, sometimes they get scarce."

"But if it is not necessary, why do you eat your fellow man?"

"Because his flesh is better than that of the buffalo or the elk; because it would be absurd to abandon to the wolves and foxes the carcass of one's enemy. What good would it do to kill him? If I didn't make use of the flesh, I would not deserve a second victory. And then, how proud and happy one is, on thinking that he is gong to feast on the flesh of the hated enemy, satisfying at the same time both hunger and vengeance! How boldly we sing our war songs! How our women, our children, and our neighbors admire us! And it is just as I told you: hunting is not always successful."

"What do you do when it is not?"

"I am in trouble, I suffer; all who live under my roof suffer. And then, when I am gripped by the unbearable restlessness caused by my need, I go far from here, and in order to satisfy that need, I kill the first man or the first woman I meet. Ah! I see indeed that you are not a warrior; you don't know what it is to experience hunger. Go! If ever it pursues and overtakes you, you will see!"

Overcome with horror, Manitou left the cannibal, but not without feeling sorry for having created a man such as he. And as he traveled slowly along, musing over what he had just seen and heard, in order to forget his sad impressions, he turned himself into an opossum.

"Ah! fine! How goes everything, Mother Possum?"

"Quite well. I am able to hide easily because I am small; I have more prudence than courage, since I know how weak I am. By hiding, I escape the persecutions of man, my most cruel enemy. I make up for the boredom of my hiding place by the attentions which I pay my family; the more we are together, the happier we are. You see around me three generations, all thriving. I am a great-grandmother, and they still love me."

"But when the enemy approaches your refuge, how do you escape with all your children?"

"We have pouches under our bellies in which they hide as soon as there is danger."

"Let's see how it works."

She gave the cry of alarm. Instantly the children obeyed. Their pouches full, all the mothers took flight and disappeared. Struck with that happy expedient, Manitou, smiling softly, approved his work.

Becoming a man again, in order to travel more comfortably, he was suddenly overtaken by a terrible storm. The echoes of the woods could scarcely repeat the bursts of thunder. Lightning flared; and the rain, which fell in torrents, began to cover the land. Not knowing what to do, Manitou leaned his back against a tree in which he had seen some squirrels; and then turning himself into a squirrel he climbed among them.

"May health, joy, and nimbleness accompany you," he said to the first squirrel he met. "Although I am a stranger, I come to ask shelter of you."

"Do as we do; attach yourself to the under side of that branch, and curl your beautiful tail up over your back."

"How do you live in this country?"

"Marvelously well. We have beechnuts and walnuts in abundance. During the summer, we play games, we frolic about, we make love, we are gay, happy, and content. As soon as winter approaches, we retire into the hollows of great trees, where we have laid in our stores of food. There, reunited with our families, we await the return of spring in the most perfect peace and harmony."

"Have you no enemies?"

"We are not without them. Man is the most cruel of all, and particularly his cursed children. It is against us that they discharge their first arrows; but our limbs are so supple, our eyes so quick, our judgment so sure, that rarely do they hit us. We are content with our lot, and would not want to change it for that of the buffalo, great giant though he seems to us."

"Your race will, however, have great dangers to run some day."

"What will those dangers be?"

"These beautiful trees will be uprooted; these lovely forests will disappear."

"Who could ever uproot such huge and mighty trees?"

"Bearded men, coming from beyond the rising sun, will some day land on this continent, with sharp iron in their hands; they will multiply like fish in the water. Then all things on earth will change. These men will replace these lovely forests with fields of grain, the bare plains with meadow lands. Strength, wisdom, and happiness will come with them; and as their number increases, that of your people will diminish. The bow and arrow will be replaced by the gun and the death-dealing lead."

"Is that day still far off?"

in Pennsylvania & New York

"Oh, yes! Very far off. You will not see it, because before that time the earth must go more than a thousand times around the sun."

"That is good! Let us live then as we have always lived; too much foresight is foolish."

"You reason well for a climbing squirrel; you are the first happy being I have met since I started my travels."

"Who are you, then? Where do you come from?"

"You would die on the spot if I answered your questions. Be satisfied with knowing that the universe and all its wonders are the work of my shaping hands, the effusion of my fecund goodness, the emanation of my creative power."

"You, a squirrel just like me, are able to tell all these marvelous things! Tell me this then: if you have made the world, why don't you prevent the bearded ones of the rising sun from coming to destroy the beautiful forests which are our heritage?"

"There is a power superior to mine."

"What is that power?"

"Tibarimaw[3] (fate)! She often brings strange things to pass."

"Why don't you reason with her?"

"She is unalterable, inexorable."

And Manitou, having once more become a man, after the storm had ceased traveled slowly on his way still thinking of the happiness of the squirrels. Suddenly, as he was lost in his thoughts, he fell into a pit that had been lightly covered over with moss and brushwood, in the bottom of which he found a panther, two wolves, a fox, and Wabemat,[4] a man from a nearby village.

"You seem to be overcome by something," Manitou said to the man; "are you suffering?"

"Am I suffering! That's all I know; my life up to now has hung by a thread and has been one long succession of mis-

[3] Literally, "to govern." Cf. Long, p. 312. Long's vocabulary includes this word in the Chippeway language. Crèvecoeur inserted "fate" after the Indian word.
[4] This name, also in the Chippeway language, means "I see." Cf. Long, p. 240. Later events in the tale reveal the symbolic use of the name.

fortunes. Why have I been given the power to breathe, when I breathe only to suffer? Daily I undergo the bitter sting of want, and the needs of my family melt my heart. Ah! If I were only a wolf or an eagle! How I would enjoy myself! When I hunt, either my arrow does not reach the mark or a catamount comes to steal my prey. When I go fishing, the fish, who know the hook of the unfortunate Wabemat, nibble at it only to carry it off. The other day I was sleeping under a tree when—would you believe it!—a branch broken off by the wind fell and crushed my leg. Four times my wigwam has been destroyed by fire. My wife is nearly always sick. The eldest of my boys was drowned yesterday in the river, even though he could swim like a fish. During the winter I freeze to death; in the summer the heat stifles me. And now, here I am at the bottom of this hole. A thousand times I have cursed life and all the sorrows it brings. Why is it that the great Manitou, who, they say, lives above the clouds, doesn't come down to earth sometimes? Perhaps the sight of men's condition would touch his heart. Perhaps he doesn't know all the wickedness that they take so much pleasure in doing, nor the harshness of the elements to which, quite naked, they are exposed. Why has he subjected us to consuming hunger, as well as to so many other distresses, when we have no means of satisfying them, no tools except our poor, weak ten fingers? Though still so weak, why are we more wicked than the panther and more ferocious than the wolf, who never eats his own kind? Where do we get that disposition that continually excites us to hate each other, to destroy our neighbors, that fury which drives us to war? Why can't we live in plenty, in the midst of peace and tranquillity?"

But as he spoke, the owner of the pit arrived, and no longer seeing his animals, whom the Animator of life had permitted to escape, he became very angry and was going to beat them to death when Manitou said to him: "Tireless hunter, brave warrior, spare our lives."

"Of what value to me is your life? You have caused me to lose my prey; and now I shall eat you, since I am hungry and stronger than you."

"Don't eat us," replied Manitou. "Before the sun sets I shall provide a very fat buffalo for you, and his skin can serve to cover the nakedness of my unfortunate comrade."

"Let your comrade do his own hunting. I want the whole buffalo or I'll kill you." And he went to fetch a length of vine to help them get out.

"And that is the son of a woman!" Manitou exclaimed to Wabemat.

"But that's the way men around here are toward each other. When they are hungry, which is often the case, they know neither brother nor friend. The weak man is the victim of the strong, the simple of the clever. Would it not be the same everywhere the sun spreads his light?"

"Perhaps," answered Manitou.

"What fate," asked Wabemat, "is there like that of being born without weapons, without clothes, with only two arms, and to be doomed to live in such a climate as this, and to eat only the flesh of animals who have four arms and as much intelligence as we?"

"Ungrateful one!" said Manitou. "Those ten fingers that you scorn are nevertheless quite superior to the tiger's fangs and the wolf's paw. Their flexibility and the exquisite sense of touch of which they are the organs have made them the sceptre of man's power. It is to them that he owes the happiness of having been able to build and use fire; without them he could not have made his weapons, his canoe, his habitation, and his clothes. He has only two arms, it is true, but he is of all beings the most majestic; he alone turns his eyes to the whole of nature; he alone can admire the magnificence of the heavens, the beauties of living things; and he alone is able, by the power of his mind, to raise himself to his incomprehensible Creator.

"The astonishing perfectibility with which the Creator has endowed the intelligence of man, the sublime sentiments He has placed in his heart—that masterpiece of His kindness and His power—are the most precious gift that a father could bestow on his children. And after all, what is man, that being so vain and presumptuous? Nothing but a living atom, generations of which go by on earth like shadows of clouds driven before the wind. And that earth? Only a point in the vastness of the universe, one of the tiniest of millions of globes.

"However," continued Manitou, "being superior to other creatures, who are destined always to remain within the narrow limits of their sphere, although like them subject to the power of chance, one day he will rise to great heights, and that by his own strength. He will master the elements; he will cross the seas, whose storms he will learn to brave; and he will improve the surface of the earth, on which he will create a rich and delightful existence. It will depend only on him to be the worker of his glory and happiness.

"What does it matter if his days are few, if they are full of grief and affliction, the inseparable companions of life? For that inextinguishable spark which causes man to act, to feel, to think, will survive his death and receive in the land of spirits the reward for his sufferings and his virtues, or the punishment for his crimes. If that compensation did not exist, it would be a thousand times better for him if he had never seen the light of the sun, since, endowed with reason and deprived of the consolations of hope, he would be the most unhappy of created beings."

"You have indeed told me some strange things," said Wabemat; "where have you learned all this?"

"In the land from whence I come."

"Where is this land? I have never heard of it. Is one obliged there, as here, to hunt and fish for a living?"

"It will depend on you alone as to whether one day you will find out," replied Manitou, "and that day will be for you one of joy and eternal happiness; want and pain are unknown in that land."

Finally the promised buffalo arrived, and on leaving the pit, Wabemat said to Manitou, "Don't go to the home of this eater of men; come with me."

Manitou followed him. The fire in his dwelling was well lighted, but no pot was boiling—it had been laid to one side. A few roots baked under the cinders were the only food offered the guest.

in Pennsylvania & New York

"Why is your pot empty and your family naked?" Manitou asked.

"Because the Evil Spirit always precedes or follows my steps, and no undertaking succeeds for me. However, I never forget to offer him each day the smoke of my first pipe, as soon as I can distinguish the infant rays of the sun."

"Have you ever seen him, this evil spirit?"

"No, never."

"Then how do you know that he exists?"

"And how could anyone doubt it," answered Wabemat, "when one has forty-two times seen the snows of winter crush our wigwams, as many times the ice of our rivers destroy our canoes, and, while we are occupied with our great hunts, seen the wolves come in bands to carry off our women and children, death-dealing epidemics poison half our villages, tempests level our forests and fire come from above to consume them? Why was it necessary for men to be placed on earth when they were born only to meet misfortune at every turn?"

"What does misfortune look like?" asked Manitou. "Have you ever seen him in your path?"

"Never. I don't know how that could be done; as quick as a squirrel he always hides behind the trees when I go by. But if I ever catch sight of him, I shall kill him, for he is the only enemy I should like to eat: he has made me go hungry so often!"

"Do you mean to say that you are unlike the people of your village, that you do not eat those whom you tomahawk in war?"

"No, I do not eat men."

"And why is that?"

"The fear that you will make fun of me keeps me from knowing what to say."

"Speak boldly; I am not of your country, as you know."

"Well, then, I am going to unburden my thoughts. Here is what my reason tells me every time that, impelled by hunger, I feel myself disposed to imitate my neighbors: 'How could you nourish yourself with a tongue which, like yours, was able to speak? With a heart which, like yours, must have loved a wife and children? How could you consider drinking soup made from the flesh of a man who, if he had been born on the other side of the river, might have been your neighbor, your friend perhaps? A wolf never eats a wolf; a fox would sooner die than eat another fox; and you, a man, you would devour, would digest your fellow man! Ought not your hate and vengeance be satisfied after you have fed the flies by covering the ground with your enemy's blood? If you are hungry, why do you not go into the woods to look for the orikomah, the wotta-tawah, or the wennasimah? Baked under the cinders or boiled as soup, those roots would sustain you and your family.'

"That is what my reason tells me every time my companions start to dismember the body of a slain enemy. They turn my loathing into ridicule; they call me a weak-hearted, feeble Nishynorbay who doesn't know how to enjoy the triumph of victory. And those reproaches, coming from the mouths of my neighbors, serve only to increase my unhappiness."

"But aren't you a warrior?" asked Manitou.

"As good a warrior as the rest. When our enemies cross the river Wenowee to attack the village, I risk my life to defend my family and the honor of the tribe. But when it is necessary to cross to the other side to engage them in battle, that is another thing; I remain here, not wanting to mix in the quarrel, which is of no concern to me. My neighbors turn on me again in ridicule. They come to insult me even under my own roof, where I stay as immovable as that big stone on the river bank."

"Then you have never tasted human flesh, although your hunger has been so great?" Manitou asked.

"No, never. When I am able to trap neither game nor fish, I feed on roots, as you see, and as long as my family thinks they are good, I am content."

"Wabemat, bless the moment when I fell into the pit! Those roots on which you have fed are at last going to bring forth fruit. The day of reward has come. Which do you choose: to wait until death, whose time is uncertain, delivers you from the burden of life, to enjoy the pure, unalterable, eternal happiness of spirits, or will you be satisfied with the fullness of that happiness which can be had on earth, a happiness which will begin immediately?"

"Alas!" replied Wabemat, "what can you do, when like me you are only the son of a woman?"

"Answer," commanded Manitou.

"The happiness of spirits! I have never heard of that. Is that country very far away?"

"Yes, very far."

"Why can't I go there now?"

"That time is not yet come, and the other country is right next to your own."

"Do people there, as here, die of hunger," asked Wabemat, "when they meet with no success at hunting or fishing? Do men of that country make war on each other?"

"People live in peace and abundance there," replied Manitou.

"Ah! what a wonderful place!" The words *peace* and *abundance* made the heart of Wabemat shiver with joy. "Well," he continued, "if you can do whatever you wish, fulfill your promise. I am so tired of my roots and my misery that I am impatient to go there."

"I know an island in the Lake of Tempests (Lake Michigan)," said Manitou, "where I am going to take you, you and all your family. But before hearing my last words, bow down before me!"

"I! . . . bow down before my fellow man!"

"I have only man's appearance."

"Who are you then?"

"Have you never in the stillness of night contemplated the glory of heaven, watched the sparkling stars of a million worlds like this one, worlds which, though invisible to your eyes, revolve in space? Have you never admired the sun radiant in the magnificence of dawn and in the glory of its daily descent into the waters of the lake? As you cast your eyes on the beauties of living nature, do you not sometimes feel an involuntary emotion of respect and admiration? Have you never wondered what the lifegiving principle is that animates all things on the earth, in the air, and under the water; that maintains freshness and eternal youth everywhere; and that out of the worst of rubbish produces new life? Well! Wabemat, I am this life-giving, universal principle. Consider my power and goodness! Without me the order on which the existence of the universe depends, the equilibrium of these great counterbalances, would be immediately disturbed; these suns so luminous would have long since been extinguished, and all matter would have returned into the chaos of nothingness and eternal night from whence I brought it."

Astonished, seized with fear and respect, the trembling Wabemat prostrated himself before the countenance of Agan Kitchee Manitou. Scarcely had his face touched the earth, when the somber clouds that obscured the majesty of the sun dispersed, the winds ceased their whistling; the cry of animals, the buzzing of insects, even the songs of the birds were heard no more, and the primitive silence of nature descended on the earth. And the great Animator of matter continued thus:

"Since you prefer to hasten the moment of your happiness instead of awaiting the great day of reward, it is necessary that you cease being a man. Do you agree to that?"

"What! Stop being what I am! What do you want to make of me?"

"Do you agree, I asked?"

"Let your will be done!"

"In order that you may no longer be misled by your fruitless thoughts, the source of the greater part of your misery, it is necessary that you lose the faculty of speech. Do you consent to that?"

"Not be able to talk! How then shall I converse with my neighbors, with my wife and my children, who are so dear to me?"

"Do you consent, I asked?"

"Yes, since your goodness, the necessary companion to your power, can desire only my happiness."

"That gift," said Manitou, "is going to be replaced by a series of sounds more simple, but as useful as words, as ex-

in Pennsylvania & New York   143

pressive, but less varied, by means of which you and yours can act in concert in all your undertakings. As heretofore, you will know love, conjugal and paternal felicity, as well as sobriety, temperance, and chastity; your children will respect and love and comfort you in old age; the absence of spiritual afflictions will take the place of joy and happiness; you will be able to conceive, direct, and execute with intelligence all the projects necessary to the well-being of your family; and to that end I shall preserve your memory, your foresight, and your judgment.

"You will enjoy the social graces from which peace and tranquillity flow. Misfortune will no longer, as in the past, follow after nor precede your steps; you will love life and enjoy it many days without sickness or infirmity; your appetite, as well as your desires and tastes, will be always simple and moderate; you will hold in horror pillage and war; your pure hands will no longer shed blood; you will have no enemy, and your descendants will never know of such a thing as long as they remain on that island unknown to men.

"You will be a good architect; you will learn the principles of hydraulics; assisted by your family, you will build a spacious dwelling, clean and comfortable, which you will place in the water; you will have sharp weapons for defense, but you will never desire to attack; you will love peace, seclusion, and silence; you will be able to live in the water as well as on land, and for that purpose I shall give you the most beautiful of furs.

"A soft and tranquil light is going to replace the flame of reason, which has only served to dazzle and bewilder you. Led by that new light, which will never flicker, you will be happy without disquietude, wise without sadness, foresighted without empty desires, and thoughtful without restlessness. The chill of death will alone be able to extinguish that light.

"If ever it happens that you regret the loss of your reason, you will be consoled by the realization that you are forever free of its errors, its illusions, its distractions; that no longer will an access of despair enter your heart; that no longer will you know the frightful transports of rage and vengeance, the shameful fits of madness, or the debasing passions of anger and insanity.

"Such is the happiness you will enjoy, Wabemat, the happiness that your privations, your sufferings, and your abstinence from human flesh have so justly merited. What does your heart say? . . . Speak."

"Since you are so powerful, why is it necessary before attaining happiness that I cease being what I am? Have then your eternal decrees ordained that man will never know happiness? You, O Creator, Organizer of matter, Soul and Prop of the universe! Give ear to your goodness, and Wabemat and his race will be happy. Since, before calling man forth from nothingness to life, you must necessarily have foreseen his destiny on earth, why did you not give him . . .?"

But scarcely had that last word been pronounced, when, by a sudden metamorphosis, there appeared the first family of amicks[5] that ever existed on earth.

After having for a long time contemplated this new and final example of his creative intelligence, the masterpiece of his power and goodness, Agan Kitchee Manitou disappeared and has never since manifested himself to his creatures.

And just as Manitou had said, that family of beavers did not delay in constructing a dam to swell the waters of the first stream they found on the Isle of Tempests, to which they were suddenly transported, and on that dam a spacious dwelling, clean and comfortable, where, after so many misfortunes and troubles, they at last found peace and plenty. For that island, unknown to men, was covered with a great number of alder trees, birches, and willows. The family sometimes shed tears, it is true—but only tears of joy, of happiness, and of gratitude —when, gathered on the bank of the stream, they listened to the father's stories of other days, of the wars, the famines, and the misery. For by a special dispensation, which was to end with the first generation, the great Manitou desired to permit the

---

[5] The Algonquin and Chippeway word for "beavers." Cf. Long, p. 241.

first of the beavers to retain the memory of his former condition as a man.

The old beaver Wabemat, after seeing many snows, finally died in the arms of his children. And, following the decree of Manitou, his descendants were continually happy, until at last that happiness they had enjoyed so long increased their numbers to such an extent that some of the families were compelled to leave and start new colonies on the shores of the great Lake of Tempests, whence they gradually spread throughout all the northern part of the continent. Then man, enemy of all that lives, declared war on them so that he might cover his nakedness with their beautiful furs, but with some regard for their divine origin. And that regard persists even today, for when the hunters encounter a settlement of beavers, they always permit a certain number of them to escape.

CHAPTER XV

*The Use Made of Salt in America
and
The Mountain Pasture Lands*

THE custom of giving salt to animals from time to time, a custom known from Nova Scotia to the Mississippi, is as old as the establishment of the American colonies. The need, or rather, the desire of eating salt seems irresistible. By using this bait the colonists take to pasture those horses and cattle that are necessary at home and bring them back from the woods; by means of it they tame those that have been away for a long time and make them love, follow, and finally obey all their commands.

In the midst of the forests, in the heart of the mountains, salt makes up for the lack of fences by regularly enticing the animals back to the inhabited places. Not only does it preserve their health but it cheers them up when they are sad or dejected. No matter how far away they may be, as soon as this strong desire, or rather this hunger, seizes them, guided by the infallibility of their instinct they are able to find again the habitation from whence they came, and the road they take is always the shortest. This is so true that a great many of the roads which today traverse and bind together the different districts of the county in which I live[1] were originally (that is to say, forty years ago) only paths made by the animals which then filled the forests.

The need for salt is common among the animals of European origin as well as among the wild beasts of our forests. Shortly after the first settlers arrived, they discovered a number of salt licks to which the deer and the bear, the moose and the elk, often came to lick the surface. They noticed also that in satisfying this common need the animals forgot their natural antipathy, as is often the case among the different species of fish and crocodiles that frequent the transparent waters of the lakes of eastern Florida.[2] Because of the sagacity of the animals several sources have been discovered which today supply all the salt needed by the inhabitants of the new trans-Allegheny states.

The appetite for salt is not limited to the quadrupeds; innumerable flocks of wood pigeons come twice each year to overrun our fields and fill up our forests in their flight from the interior of the continent to the shores of the sea, where they go to satisfy their hunger. One may judge the power of the attraction which causes them to undertake a journey of more than a thousand miles!

Although our animals, which live almost the entire year at liberty, are rarely ill, they are sometimes subject to infirmities and to what we call dullness. Then it is necessary to give them salt a little more often, and to mix with it some crushed sulphur and antimony. My preservative panacea, especially for my horses, is asafoetida, which, after long experience, I find to be very salutary for them. I obtained this remedy from the owner of the great ironworks of Ringwood,[3] who uses a large number of animals.

In order to realize how necessary it is to feed salt to animals, one must observe how their dispositions change when

[1] Crèvecoeur claimed (II, 249) that this piece was read to him by "the patriarch of Orangeburg, South Carolina."
[2] Cf. the *Voyage*, II, 424, for a quotation from Bartram about the "natural antipathy" of the fish of east Florida.
[3] Here, Crèvecoeur seems to forget that he is supposed to be quoting a man from South Carolina, for the Ringwood Ironworks to which he refers was in New York, not far from his old home in Orange County.

they have been deprived of it for a long time; it is astonishing. I have seen cattle, ordinarily gentle and peaceable, which no enclosure could hold; like bulls, they bellowed, leaped fences and ditches, apparently having lost all idea of obedience or submission. And—most remarkable!—their milk no longer produced butter, no matter how much it was churned.

As for the horses, they often stop in the middle of their work with a troubled expression, disturbed, and look at their driver with fixed eyes. It is impossible not to understand what they want. The sheep, weaker and more timid, bleat in a plaintive tone, refuse to go to the fields, and lose their fleece. Nothing is more pitiful to see than a herd which has been without salt for a long time.

The swine is the only animal insensible to that attraction. However, at the time of his fattening it is necessary to season his food with it; otherwise he becomes weary of what is given him, eats little, and as a result, fattens slowly.

Saturday is ordinarily the day for salting. No matter how far in the woods the animals may be, they rarely fail to appear on that day. Some colonists throw handfuls of salt from place to place on the grassy spots; others put it on flat stones. The best way is to use squared tree trunks with small holes bored on the upper side a foot or two apart and filled with salt. But the trees or the stones must be put in a roomy place, because at the time of the first excitement of the desire, the stronger animals are liable to injure the weaker ones. So acute is the craving that in spite of the instinct which indicates to each member of a large herd the degree of his strength, and consequently the distance at which he ought to keep himself from his superiors, the youngest, being the quickest, dare sometimes to get to the salt first. Then it is that the right of the strongest, the law that rules over small events as well as big ones, exerts itself in all its force. As for the salting of the sheep, that must always be done in a separate place for fear that after the large animals have been driven away the salt which remains may not be enough for the sheep. Happy and contented, these little animals spend entire hours at the salting places before wanting to go to the fields.

Salt, especially in the summer, seems to be necessary to all breathing things. One day, having noticed that my bees were stopping frequently at places on which brine had once been spread, I placed a few grains of salt in front of their hives. What was my astonishment when I saw that they tasted it several times, and even carried it away with them! I would never have believed, previous to that observation, that makers of honey would have tasted with pleasure anything so different from the stamen of flowers.

In order fully to know the shades of character that result from the use or from the need of salt, one must have lived as long as I surrounded by a great number of animals of all ages, as their master and their friend, and isolated in the middle of the woods; they are then in their natural state and it is easy to study them. It is impossible for me to tell how amusing and instructive it is to see them daily, to live with, and, so to speak, converse with them, to command them, and finally to arouse in them love and fear. The slavery, the solitude, the harshness with which they are treated in Europe make them so stupid and debased that they no longer are the same interesting creatures, they no longer have the same intelligence. They have lost their original character and that perfectibility which is so striking here. One must see them running free in our fields, freer yet in our forests, where they spend a part of their lives. It is there that experience develops their faculties, and that, in several instances, their instinct has seemed to me to raise itself to the level of reason.

Just as we, beings endowed with reason, have passions, so do they; that is to say, they have appetites that excite them, desires, and intercourse among themselves, especially in a large herd. Consequently, differences in character result. Like men, they know spite, jealousy, the pleasure of domination. The strongest feel their superiority and abuse it; the weakest are crafty, timid, and fearful. The former are arrogant and imperious; the latter are slow, astute, and continually on their guard. Without careful supervision, or the use of pens in the barn yard, the weak would die of hunger. The horses, more generous and more susceptible to reason, are much less liable to encroach upon the property of their neighbors; moreover, since each horse knows his own name, it is easy to put on their bridles while speaking to them.

Six dogs accompanied me in my nomadic life.[4] A person would doubt my veracity if I dared tell to what degree of perfection this new mode of existence had elevated their understanding. Taking turns, two of them mounted guard every night with one of my servants. Whenever my children went into the woods, my dogs never failed to go with them, for fear that they might lose their way. A deer that we had wounded escaped us and died about seventeen miles from our camp; the dogs followed it, came to inform us of its death, and led us to the place where it had fallen. Is not an animal so perfect and so useful a more respectable being than a wicked man? Is not the gift of an intelligence so sure and so infallible a more striking proof of the kindness and power of the Creator than is that of reason, which has so often occasioned evil on the earth by the horrible abuse that has been made of it?

Salt is absolutely necessary in handling the animals. What does the colonist do who for lack of enclosed pasturage has during the day confided his draft horses and oxen to the vast extent of the neighboring woods? Guided by their tracks, he listens carefully until he hears the sound of the leader's bell. As soon as he sees the animals, he calls to them while holding out his hand. Aroused by the thought of salt, they obey his voice, approach, and follow him home, where, while they lick the salt trough, some are harnessed and others are put under the yoke. And when, some years later, this same colonist has been able to obtain fences for his fields, how, among a large number of cattle and breeding animals, can he catch those

[4] In the preceding chapter of the *Voyage* (II, Chap. XIII), the narrator has related how during the Revolution he wandered in the mountains with his family, servants, and animals. Here again Crèvecoeur apparently forgets that he has attributed this chapter to someone else.

in Pennsylvania & New York 151

he needs? for often it takes only one, either wilder or more suspicious than the others, to give the alarm and set them all in flight. Will he be forced to call his family to help him? Not by any means. Fortified by a handful of salt or an ear of corn, he goes into his field, stands still, and calls them. All hasten to press forward and surround him. Then he extends his bait towards the one he needs and grasps him softly while he eats. And what will perhaps appear extraordinary to you, even the children are often entrusted with this operation.

It happens sometimes, however, that taught by experience the older horses and oxen are not to be duped, especially when they see the yoke or the bridle. Then it is necessary to speak like a master who commands and not like a friend who entreats. If that does not suffice, leather shackles are put on the legs of the most obstinate. It is to the use of salt, then, that we owe both the happiness of not knowing the murrain, and the means of keeping the animals near us without fences, and of mastering their wills. The following details will prove all that in a manner still more striking.

THE MOUNTAINS

At the time this colony was established, that is to say about the year 1745, our predecessors, on buying from the colonial government or from the Indians the cultivatible land of the province that I live in,[5] acquired also the chain of mountains in the northern part in order to make a reserve, which was to remain undivided always. There, during the heat of summer, their animals could find shade, coolness, drinking water, and abundant pasturage. The inhabitants of each district of this county then constructed, at the common expense, several little houses on the banks of the streams, in the neighborhood of which could be found enough alluvial ground for a field that was to be cleared and fenced in. Since that time the rights on these reserves have been extended to a great number of

[5] That is, northwestern South Carolina.

families; but that chain of mountains, which is sixty-four miles long and thirty miles wide, offers enough to feed, during the six months of summer, more than 20,000 head of animals. Every year each of these associations hires a keeper, to whom, besides provisions and the privilege of cultivating the field, they give a quarter of a piastre for each animal, not for keeping an eye on them, which would be impossible, but to give them salt once a week.

The dispositions of these men, who at the same time pursue both the civilized and the savage life, make of them a very peculiar class. Although they have not enough industry to undertake a lucrative profession or cultivate the earth, they know how to trap the wolves, the panthers, and the mountain cats, the destruction of which the government encourages by offering large bounties. Would you believe it? These men are almost all Europeans.

The sudden passage from an extremely populous country to a vast desert; from a state of dependence and constraint to a boundless liberty; from penury to the ease of living almost without working; from the cramped space of villages to the immensity of the forests—all these changes, added to the salutary air and the sojourn in the woods, which appears to be so natural to man, produces on the spirit of the new inhabitants, especially during the first year, a sort of exultation that I cannot describe.

Such are the men that are commonly employed among us to keep the animals and give them salt while they are in the forest. Some weeks before conducting our herds to the reserve, one finds it necessary to deprive them of their salt and to place a bell on the neck of the strongest and most intelligent animal in the group. Soon, accustomed to this sound, they can distinguish it from all the others that they encounter daily in the forest. After that the bell carrier becomes the leader of the file for the entire season.

The day of departure being fixed (it is generally in the month of April), the colonist, on horseback, offers some salt to the leader, taking care to withdraw himself in proportion

in Pennsylvania & New York 153

as the animal approaches, continuing that maneuver until he has arrived at a considerable distance from his habitation; then the herd follows him without difficulty. Arrived at the cabin in the woods, he lets them run wild, after having given each a handful of salt.

During the first few days they seldom stray away from the cabin. The abundance of pasture and the timidity resulting from inexperience keep them in the neighborhood, until finally, emboldened by habit and by familiarity with their surroundings, they plunge into the valleys and gorges, often to great distances. They lack nothing: shade, coolness, extremely nutritive plants, young shoots, clear and limpid waters. If they are given salt every eight or ten days, they are happy and quickly grow fat.

In the autumn they are led back to the plantation by means of the same bait, and rarely is any animal lost during the long trip home. One keeper can salt as many as 1,500 of them if they are divided into several groups. No matter how numerous they may be, each of them invariably follows the file-leader, without ever mixing with other groups. These wandering herds, peaceful and happy, encounter each other without spite or jealousy, without doing harm or wanting to do harm. As to the casualties resulting from wolves and panthers, they become extremely rare; the strong protect the weak with a courage and intelligence worthy of admiration. The gratuity of ten piastres a head that the government offers arouses competition among keepers and hunters, who have almost entirely purged the mountains of Tugaloo[6] of these carnivorous animals.

Eight or ten days before the time fixed for the return of my animals, I never fail to go and spend some time in the woods. Besides the pleasure of seeing my herd healthy, fat, glistening, I love to wander alone in these vast and profound solitudes, the sanctuary of nature, which fire and the destructive tools of man have not yet profaned. I love to contemplate the surface of this globe in its primitive state, so uncouth to vulgar eyes but so interesting and instructive to the careful ob-

[6] In the northwesternmost part of South Carolina.

server. I love to pass suddenly from the glare of light into a region somber and obscure; from the observation of works of art and industry to that of this new order of things; from a cultivated country into the forests, majestic and imposing not only because of their almost limitless extent but also because of the number, the size, and the magnificent carriage of the trees. I love to gaze at these eminences, even to the summits of which the vegetation extends its empire. The sojourn in the mountains has for me a charm impossible to analyze. Never do I stray into these venerable retreats without being involuntarily moved, seized with respect and admiration. My ordinary gaiety is replaced by a kind of soft and dreamy melancholy that I do not experience in the cultivated fields. Moreover it is a welcome diversion for me to spend a few days exempt from the cares and labors that are exacted by a numerous family and the inspection of a large farm.

During the night, a bear skin stretched out beside that of my keeper serves as a bed. That man, now become my companion, recounts the story of his former troubles, of the days when privations, misfortunes, and misery seemed attached to his steps. To the account of these calamities he joins the details of the circumstances, of the accidents, which have led him from the overpopulated towns of the Old World into the forests of America in order to become there, if not an opulent farmer, at least a free and independent being, obtaining the necessaries of life without excessive hardship and without being exposed to the disquietudes caused by foresight. I share his simple and frugal life. Knowing how to make artificial flies, we amuse ourselves by deceiving the finest of fish (salmon trout), which abound in the streams and tumbling creeks that water all the valleys.

When that exercise bores me, I climb the neighboring hills which are most accessible and most covered with cedars, the emblems of vegetal immortality, or with chestnut-oaks, no less ancient, whose roots, as if they were endowed with a peculiar intelligence, cross great distances on the naked rocks in order to get to the earth and moisture with which the slits and crev-

in Pennsylvania & New York 155

ices are filled. From these hills I gaze out upon the valleys, the sides of which rise up around me shaded by venerable hemlocks covered with long mosses, a symbol of old age and decreptitude; by pines of a prodigious height; by ancient oaks whose vast branches and thick shade have stifled all that would grow around them.

Of all the moments I spend in the woods, those I enjoy most come just before the dawn, when everything is calm and serene. It is then that I dare to lift up my thoughts to the eternal principle of all things, the Guardian of that universe of which I am only an atom, and to address to Him my humble prayers.

How imposing and solemn is the silence, the mysterious obscurity of the forests, during that struggle between the shades of night and the dawning day! It is the silence of a temple, the august divinity of which, through pity for my weakness, is hidden from my eyes, but whose magnificent works announce His power and goodness, since all that is around me breathes life and being.

But the morning twilight gradually increases. The stars disappear, the eye begins to distinguish objects, the horizon lights up, colors can be recognized, the dawn appears. Then the morning breeze, held captive during the gloom of night, arrives and resounds through the branches and sharp leaves of the pines and cedars. It is the hymn of nature, which is saluting its father and its king at the moment when his first rays gild the face of the mountains and plunge into the valleys. This is the time when all forms of life are aroused to wakefulness and express their joy and pleasure in a universal concert.

Another object of my solitary rambles is the contemplation of the cascades, the rapids, and the falls whose sounds approach or retreat at the will of the winds which diffuse them or at the caprice of the echoes which repeat them. What variety in their appearance! What extravagance in the accessories which accompany them! For the elegance and the combination of the forms of nature are inexhaustible: some streams hurl themselves with a heavy roaring sound across the windings of the rocks, the black color of which offers a striking contrast to the whiteness of the foaming torrent; others, after having for a long time struggled against and surmounted a thousand obstacles, pour out into pools of water that are silvery and smooth, in the midst of which one can at times distinguish isolated points decked with greenness. Often one encounters a torrent roaring in the depths of a ravine, where thick, overhanging trees hide its tumultuous waters. One divines them, one hears them, one follows without seeing them until the time when, bruised and exhausted, they finally come to rest in the bed of a little river, sometimes navigable for several miles.

Several of these rivers enclose islands whose vegetation, coolness, and beauty contrast marvelously with the barrenness, the ruggedness, and the harshness of the banks. I know some which are eight or ten acres in size on which one could raise a garden or cultivate the rarest fruit, for during the summer the sun's rays have a great power on them. Some are covered with weeping elms, with water ashes, with white and veined maples whose delicate and inimitably varied colors offer to the eyes one of the most beautiful tableaus of autumn; others have thorny oaks, sassafras, platans, and all the varieties of willows and alders. I remember one of these little islands, situated at the foot of a very long cascade which came down the side of a mountain. On seeing it, one could not help but believe that the hands of good taste had made it and planted it with vegetation. This background, like a beautiful green tapestry, was adorned with flowers, without odor it is true, but with vivid colors, and embellished by tall cedars, in the middle of which could be seen those beautiful bushes known by the name of purple kalmias. A European whom chance had conducted into these mountains, struck as I was by the beauty and fertility of this almost inaccessible place, bought it and built there a handsome cabin. Although still young and apparently well educated, rarely is he seen away from his retreat. In the summer he cultivates his vegetables and his corn; in the winter he hunts. Nowhere except in his little garden have I seen such beautiful melons; his vines are beginning to yield; the two branches of the river which surround his island provide him with fish; the hides of wild beasts and the bounties from the government furnish his clothes. Like Robinson Crusoe he is self sufficing and never idle.

"As young as you are, why do you live here alone?" I asked him one day. "Why do you prefer this gloomy retreat to all the other parts of Carolina?"

"Men are tigers," he answered me with an agitated countenance. "I have seen human nature under its most hideous colors. I have seen virtue proscribed and crime triumphant. Perhaps even that period is not yet past![7] After having lost my friends and my fortune in the middle of the convulsive storms of a disorganized society, I am no longer able to find rest except in these solitary mountains. I hope that your government, so affable and just, will not remove me from this little island which furnishes my sustenance."

Among the great variety and multitude of trees which fill our forests, the oaks especially attract my attention. Nothing, in fact, is more striking than these giants of the earth, whose existence antedates by several centuries the discovery of the continent. Their colossal grandeur, the length of their branches, their longevity, everything about them is imposing, everything, even to the scars left by lightning, which, like immortal beings, they have resisted. And often when their weakened vigor can no longer give life to the utmost branches, nature, in order to render their old age and decadence more venerable, causes to grow on them these enormous garlands of moss which float about at the whim of the breezes. I have seen some of them more than thirty feet long.

One of the most interesting circumstances of these annual excursions is the taming of the wild character that my young colts have acquired in the woods. It is difficult to depict their fright at the first sight of men. Uneasy and shy, they follow their mothers only at a great distance, and often even refuse to obey their whinnies. It is useless to call them; these strangers do not yet know the voice which one day will command them and inspire them with confidence. However, after sev-

[7] This was written in 1796. [Crèvecoeur's note.]

eral attempts, they finally dare to follow their mothers. That is the time to give salt to the older animals. I know not how nor by what magic they are able to communicate to the foals the pleasure which they experience, or rather the happiness which they enjoy. If the colts are not insensible to these first invitations, it is a favorable sign. But it is necessary to be as still as a post; for the slightest movement of the hand will make them take flight, and it will be necessary to put off the attempt until the next day. Gradually encouraged by new whinnies, emboldened by repetition, they take a step and then stop, the hind legs bent like springs ready to uncoil. They start a second time, and stop again. Finally, after an interval more or less long, spent in fear and dread, suddenly seeming to desire what they do not yet understand, they advance trembling and stop once again, until, reassured by the stillness of the hand which offers the salt, as well as by the presence and the invitations of their mothers, who are eating, they stretch out their necks and heads, their eyes protruding bright and inflamed; they extend their tongues and gradually approach the salt. It is then that one sees the expression of enjoyment and pleasure. How they relish this new food! How the saliva drips from their mouths! From this moment their wild, shy natures becomes softened, and the sight of man less frightful to them.

Such are their first steps toward civilization. That operation once ended (it often requires several days), the herd is led back to the plantation by the same methods used in guiding it to the mountains. After their arrival they are feasted on the promised allowance of salt, and the next day turned into pasture. Such are the resources that the mountains of Tugaloo offer us, and such are the means by which we lead our animals to the reserve, keep them there, and bring them home. What would we do without salt?

APPENDIX

The Contents of the Voyage

A SUMMARY BY CHAPTERS

VOLUME ONE

I. Colonel Croghan's information about Indians, especially the Mohawks. (Probably not from Colonel Croghan but written by Crèvecoeur himself from his own knowledge and from books, especially Carver's *Travels*. See the Introduction to the present volume.)

II. Benjamin Franklin's speech at Franklin College in Pennsylvania on the subject of Indian mounds and fortifications along the Ohio River. (Not Franklin's speech really, although it has been translated and accredited to him by the Duyckincks in their *Cyclopedia of American Literature*. The material is taken from Imlay's *Topographical History of North America*. See the Introduction.)

*III. Departure of the two travelers from Shippenburg; their visits with certain pioneers; their arrival near Lewisburg. [Chap. IV]

*IV. Their visit with Mr. Nadowisky, a surgeon from Poland and a farmer in Luzerne County, Pennsylvania. [Chap. V]

V. Their visit with Mr. J. V., near Lake Otsego, a frontiersman member of the New York Legislature; departure for Fort Stanwix.

*VI. Arrival at Onondaga, where the great council of the Mohawks is to take place. [Chap. VIII]

*VII. The opening of the council; the second day of the council; speeches concerning the plight of several unfortunate Indians; the debate between Koohassen and Kesketomah. [Chap. IX]

VIII. The third day of the council; adoptions; Kanajoharry's consolation of the unfortunate Indians.

IX. Address by one of the travelers at the council, who pleads for the adoption of agriculture by the Indians; Kanajoharry's answer.

X. Trip from Fort Stanwix to Lake Otsego; visit with Mr. Wilson.

*XI. Visit with Mr. Seagrove. [Chap. VII]

XII. Second visit with Mr. J. V.; his description of the wife he is seeking.

XIII. Mr. J. V.'s autobiography.

XIV. Monsieur Herman's description of an old Gothic castle in Germany.

*XV. A boat trip up the Hudson. [Chap. I]

*XVI. Visit with Colonel Woodhull. [Chap. II]

*XVII. Inspection of the ironworks of New York state. [Chap. III]

VOLUME TWO

*I. An Indian legend: How the first beaver was made. [Chap. XIV]

II. Visit with Mr. *** of Bedford County, Pennsylvania.

*III. Lost on a bee hunt. [Chap. VI]

IV. Departure for Niagara Falls; boat trip across Lake Ontario.

*V. Visit with the old Indian Agouehghon. [Chap. XII]

*VI. A fishing trip; two Indian tales: The courtship of Massotawana; The land of Hoppajewot. [Chap. XIII]

VII. Visit with Mr. E. in his home near Niagara Falls; a walk to the Falls.

VIII. Mr. E.'s autobiography.

*IX. A description of Niagara Falls in winter. [Chap. XI]

* The asterisks indicate the chapters that are included, at least in part, in the translation. Their location in the present volume is indicated in brackets at the end of the chapter description.

Appendix 161

X. Mr. E.'s account of old Agouehghon's trip to the scenes of his childhood.

XI. Mr. E.'s information about the Falls.

XII. Mr. E.'s account of the travels of two Russians among the Indians of the interior of America.

XIII. A trip into Virginia; a South Carolinian tells of his experiences during the Revolution, when he wandered in the Alleghenies with his family and servants.

*XIV. The South Carolinian tells of the use of salt in America and describes the mountain pasturelands. [Chap. XV]

XV. The adventurous life of Juan of Bragansa, a natural son of Juan V of Portugal.

XVI. Monsieur Herman's boat trip to New Haven; conversation between two passengers about the new government of the United States.

XVII. Monsieur Herman's visits with several important people of Connecticut; a Yale graduation exercise; the commencement address.

VOLUME THREE

I. The biography of Don Juan of Bragansa, known as Father Geronimo, the father of the Juan of Volume Two, Chapter XV.

II. Visit with Mr. Vining, Senator of Delaware; visit with Mr. Hazen, former aide-de-camp of Colonel Bouquet.

III. Mr. Hazen's account of his trip in the southern parts of what is now the United States. (Apparently Crèvecoeur's one-chapter reworking of *The Travels of William Bartram*. See the Introduction.)

IV. Mr. Hazen's account of the expedition of Colonel Bouquet into the Ohio Country in 1764. (Crèvecoeur's unacknowledged reworking of William Smith's *Historical Account of Bouquet's Expedition against the Ohio Indians in 1764*. See the Introduction.)

V. General Butler's antiromantic letter on the American Indians; the lament of Panima for his absent friend.

VI. Visit in the Mohawk River country; visit with a frontier family near New Geneva.

VII. Details on the settlement of the Lake Seneca and Lake Cayuga area.

VIII. Senator B.'s information on the Indian mounds of Georgia and Florida. (Crèvecoeur's reworking of materials taken from Bartram's *Travels*. See the Introduction.)

IX. Details concerning the founding of numerous societies, colleges, and hospitals in the United States.

X. Visit with Mr. G., on the banks of the Passaick River; information on the progress of industry in the United States.

XI. Mr. G.'s information on the history and industry of New York; Monsieur Herman's farewell and departure.

Index

Abenakis, 93.
acacia, 2.
Adair, James, xxxvi.
Adams, Percy G.: "The Historical Value of Crèvecoeur's *Voyage dans la haute Pensylvanie et dans New York*," xxiiin; "Crèvecoeur—Realist or Romanticist?" xxxn; "Crèvecoeur and Franklin," xxxviiin; "The Real Author of *William Byrd's Natural History of Virginia*," 10n.
adoption: custom of, 80; of Kittagawmick by the Mohawks, 95; of the narrator by the Oneidas, 101.
Adquakanunck (village), 84.
Africa: slaves from, 65-66.
Agouehghon: visited by travelers, 101-15; praises wine, 101-102, 107; conversation of with travelers, 101-102, 112-15; on evils of brandy, 102, 108-109; melancholy autobiography of, 102-12; family of, 104; contrasts Indians and whites, 114; travelers part with, 115; Colonel Hunter comments on, 116.
Albany, New York, xxi, 10, 46.
alders, 156.
Algonquin, 79n, 81n, 84n, 121n, 123n, 124n, 144n.
Aliquippa River, 54, 62.
allagriches: served to travelers, 61.
Allegheny Mountains, 49, 58, 63.
Allen, Ethan, xxix.
Allisinape: mythical island of, xxxi, 124.
Allison, John: invites travelers to lunch, flour mill of, 16; second visit with, 16.
America, xiii, xv, xvi, xviii, xxii, xxviii, xxx, xxxvi, xxxviii, xli, xliii, 40, 57.

American Farmer, the, xiv, xxii, xxxv, xxxvi, xlii.
American Philosophical Society: De-Witt and Crèvecoeur members of, xxviin; Franklin's paper on Gulf Stream read to, xxxvii.
American Revolution (*see also* War of Independence), xiii, xv, xxiii, xxvi, 26n, 28, 30.
Andrew, the Hebridean, xxx.
animal life: Crèvecoeur's notes on, xli.
animals: instinct and sagacity of, 52, 58-59, 149-50; of North America compared with those of Europe, 149.
Anthony's Nose, 4.
Antigua, 25.
antiquities (*see* Indians).
apple trees, 60.
Aquidnunck: speaks to council, 84-85.
Aratapeskow, mountain of, 124.
asafoetida: panacea for animals, 147.
ash (es), water, xli, 87, 156.
Ashamut, teller of tales, 110.
Atkins, Mr., Secretary of Governor William Campbell, 127n.
Attacul-Culla: said to have ordered "Wabemat's Reward" translated, 127n.
Awakesh (deer): warns Okemaw, 123; burns white men's fields, 126.

B***, Senator (*see* Brown, Senator).
Bahamas, xli, 23.
bald eagle: and fish hawk, 9-10.
Barbé-Marbois, François, Marquis de: at Indian council, xxxiv; friend of Crèvecoeur, xxxiv, 10n; on fight between fish hawk and bald eagle, 10n.
—*Our Revolutionary Forefathers, the Letters of François, Marquis de Barbé-Marbois*, xxxivn.

Bartram, William, xviii, xxxvi, xl; confused with John Bartram by Crèvecoeur, xxxix*n*, xli.
—*The Travels of William Bartram*, xxxvi*n*, xxxviii, xxxix*n*, 147*n*.
Baskind Ridge, New York, xxvi.
bear, cries of, 83.
beaver (*see also* Wabemat): Crèvecoeur's story of the first, xxxi, 127-45; tears of, 83; offers tail to people of Hoppajewot, 121; custom of leaving one of every five, 121, 145.
Bedford, Pennsylvania, 61.
Bedford County, Pennsylvania, xxix, 49, 63.
bee hunt, xxxii, 49.
bees: superstition about, 87.
Bellvale (*see* ironworks).
Bengal, 32.
Bermuda, xli.
Bethlehem, New York, 16.
Big Bay, 2.
Big Beaver: portage of, 109.
birch, black, 87, 119.
birch bark: book made of, 94.
Blake, Warren Barton: Introduction to Everyman *Letters of an American Farmer*, xvi; opinion of *Voyage*, xvii.
Blooming Green, New York, 16.
bog cranberry, 23.
Bolama island, 66.
Boston, Massachusetts, xvi, xviii.
botany: Crèvecoeur's interest in, xvi.
Bouquet, Colonel (General) William (*see also* Smith, William): expedition to Ohio country, xxxvii, xxxviii; Frederick Hazen supposed aide-de-camp to, xxxvii, xxxviii.
Bourdin, H. L. (editor of Crèvecoeur), xvii*n*.
Brazil, 57.
Brickell, Dr. John, 10*n*.
Bridle Road, 33, 34.
Brissot de Warville, J. P., xviii, xxiv.
British Isles, xv.
Brown, Senator John: not author of Senator B***'s paper in the *Voyage*, xxxviii.
Buffon, Georges Louis Leclerc, Comte de: friend of Crèvecoeur, xv, xxix; bachelor farmer studies, 69.
Bushy Run: Indian defeat at, 103.
Butler, General (Zebulon): used by Crèvecoeur, xxxv, xxxix.
Buttermilk Fall, 10.

Caen, Normandy, xiv.
Campbell, Thomas, xxviii.
Campbell, Lord William, Governor of South Carolina, 127*n*.
Canada, xiv, 47, 82*n*, 93, 103.
candles: chinese, 12; of vegetable wax, 24.
cannibalism, evils of, xxi, 57, 71, 73, 132-33, 136, 139-40.
Canton, China, 1.
Cape Frederickhook, 3.
Carlisle, Pennsylvania, xx, 47.
Carver, Jonathan, xviii.
—*Travels through the Interior Parts of North America*, xxxvi, xxxvii, xxxix, xl.
Caspetowagan River, 118.
Cattaw-Wassy: marriage with Kittagawmick dissolved, 95; second marriage, 95-96; fame of, 96.
cawen (Chippeway for *no*), 91.
Cayuga (s), 92, 116; folly of in selling lands, 73-74, 76; Agouehghon among, 110; band of and Mohawks telling stories, 116.
Cayuga River, 109.
cedar(s), xli, 4, 6, 7, 87, 98, 109, 119, 154, 155.
Charlevoix, Pierre de, xviii, xxxvi.
Charlottenburg (*see* ironworks).
Chastellux, François-Jean, Marquis de, xviii, xxiv, xxxvi, 10*n*.
—*Voyages dans l'Amérique septentrionale, dans les années 1780, 1781 et 1782*, xxxvi, 12*n*.
Chedabooktoo: travelers dine with, 74; speaks to council, 76-78.
cherry cider, 22.
cherry mead, 22.
cherry trees, 2, 60.
Cherry Valley, 64.
cherry wine, 22.
Cherryhum (*Europe*), 122, 123, 125.
Cherryhum Sagat (*European*), 73, 101.
chestnut-oaks, 154.
China, 1, 47.
Chippeway, 70, 79*n*, 91*n*, 114, 121*n*, 123*n*, 125*n*, 135*n*, 144*n*.
Chiquisquaque Creek, 31.
Choctaw Indians, xxxix.
Clermont, New York, xxi.
Clinton, Governor George, xxi.
coffee, 22.
Colden, Cadwallader: *The History of the Five Indian Nations*, xxxiii*n*.
colts: taming wild, 157-58.
Columbia County, New York, 13.
commerce (*see Voyage*).
Congress: astonishment of at expense of Washington's secret services, 28; encouragement of to hemp cultivation, 47.
Connecticut, xv, xix, xxii, 13, 30, 31, 33, 43, 46.
Constitution: on duties of militia, 24.
consul: Crèvecoeur as, xv, xvi, xxix.

Index

Coohassa-Onas (*father of the Fall*), 101, 111.
Cook, Captain, 57.
Copenhagen, 39.
Corlear, the trader, xli; name for people of New York, 88, 103.
corn: used in making allagriches, 61; mythical origin of, 124.
Cornplanter: debate of with Red Jacket, xxxiii-xxxiv.
Cornwall, district of, 21.
cotton, 22, 24.
council fire: lighted, 74; Indians around, 75-91.
cranberry bushes, xli.
Crèvecoeur, Guillaume Alexandre de (Crèvecoeur's son), xv, xxvii*n*.
Crèvecoeur, Michel-Guillaume Jean de (James Hector Saint John) (*see also* American Farmer, the): reputation of, xiii, xv-xvii, xxiii, xxix, xxx, xliv; as historian, xiii, xxiii-xxviii; as man of literature, xiii, xxviii-xxxv; the old compared with the new, xiii, xxiii-xxiv, xxv, xxviii-xxxi, xxxiv-xxxv, xlii, xliii; as traveler, xiv-xvi, xxvi; as soldier, xiv, xxvi; as colonist and farmer, xiv-xv; scholarly comments on, xiv*n*, xvi-xvii, xxiii, xxiv-xxv, xxvii*n*, xxx*n*, xxxviii*n*, xxxix*n*; as consul, xv-xvi; as author, xv-xvi; his friends, xv, xxii*n*, xxix, 18; his models for *Voyage*, xviii, xxii; as travel writer, xviii-xxiii; lack of method of, xix, xxi-xxii; as romanticist, xxii, xxx-xxxi; as observer, xxiv, xxviii; as authority on swamp lands, xxvi; and Niagara Falls, xxvi-xxvii; his knowledge of surveying, xxvii-xxviii; as narrator, xxviii, xxxii, xliii; his natural history, xxviii, xxix, xl, xli; faults of as writer, xxviii, xliii; his style, xxxix-xxxv; "authorities" of, xxxv-xli; plagiarisms of, xxxvi-xlii.
—*Eighteenth-Century Travels in Pennsylvania & New York*, xiii, xliv: *Le Voyage dans la haute Pensylvanie et dans l'état de New York* (see *Voyage*); *Letters from an American Farmer*, xiii, xv, xvi, xvii, xxiii, xxiv, xxviii, xxx, xxxiv, xliii, xliv; *Sketches of Eighteenth Century America*, xiii, xvii, xix*n*, xxiii, xxv, xxvi*n*, xxix, xxxiv, xlii, xliv; *Lettres d'un cultivateur américain* (1784), xvi, xvii, xxxiv; *Lettres d'un cultivateur américain* (1787), xvi, xvii, xviii, xxvii*n*, xxxiv*n*, xxxvi; "What is an American?" xxiii; "Thoughts of an American Farmer on Various Rural Sub-

Crèvecoeur, M.-G. Jean de (*continued*): jects," xxiii; "Ant-Hill Town," xxix; "The Wyoming Massacre," xxix; "The American Belisarius," xxix.
Crèvecoeur, Robert de (grandson of Crèvecoeur): *Saint John de Crèvecoeur, sa vie et ses ouvrages*, xiv*n*.
crocodiles: natural antipathy of, 147.
Croghan, Colonel George: used by Crèvecoeur, xxxv-xxxvii, xxxix; Crèvecoeur's notes on, xli; Koreyhoosta's prophecy given also by, 86*n*.
current wine, 62.
Cuxhaven, Germany, 35.

Davis, Thomas & Lockyer (publishers), xv.
De Lancey (Loyalist family), xv.
Dean, Captain: tells of voyage to China, 1; discusses Tappan Sea, 2; discusses Hudson River passage through mountains, 3; on beauties of nature, 5; prophecies of about homes along Hudson, 6; on echoes of Hudson, 7-9; on West Point, 12, 14.
Delaware, xix, xxi, xxvi, xxxviii.
Delawares, 112, 130*n*.
democracy, American: Crèvecoeur's idealization of, xix.
Detroit, 108; Indian defeat at, 103.
DeWitt, Simon, Surveyor-General of New York: visit with, xxi, xxvii; in American Philosophical Society, xxvii*n*; his map of the New York-Pennsylvania boundary, xxviii.
Director General of the post: establishes mail line across Cherry Valley, 68.
Dismal Swamp, xxvi.
Dneiper River, 39.
dogs: marvelous intelligence of, 150.
Doolittle, W., Mr.: visited by travelers, 31-34; as schoolteacher in Connecticut, 32; tells history of his farm, 32; M. Herman's reflections on, 33-34.
doorsill: superstition about, 79, 84.
Dow, Charles Mason: *Anthology and Bibliography of Niagara Falls*, xxvii.
"drowned lands," xxvi.
Duchess County, New York, 13.
Dutch East Indies, 71, 72.
dyeing, 22, 24.

E., Mr. (*see also* Ellsworth), xxvii, xl, 100; supposed author of description of Niagara, 100*n*.
East: Crèvecoeur most familiar with, xxii.
Ebeling, Doctor (Lutheran minister), 39-40.

echoes of Hudson River, 7-9, 11, 14.
Elbe River, 35.
Ellsworth, Mr. (see also E., Mr.), xxvii.
elm(s), weeping, xli, 156.
Emerson, O. F.: "Notes on Gilbert Imlay, Early American Writer," xxiin.
England, xiv, xv, 122n.
Erie, Lake, 100, 101, 103, 108, 110.
Erie, New York, 112.
Erskine, Mr.: owner of ironworks at Ringwood, 29; his study of ironworks of Europe, 29; his statistics and products, 129-30.
Europe, xv, xxi, xxvi, 3, 66, 70, 122n.
Evans, Oliver, xli.
Evil Spirit (see also Manitou, Agan Matchee), 76, 78, 79, 80, 83, 84, 139.
evil versus good: bachelor farmer on, 66-69; Crèvecoeur on, 66n; Yoyogheny on, 80-81; Siasconset on, 83-84; Aquidnunck on, 85.
Exchange in Philadelphia: maple sugar on, 47.

Fairchild, H. N.: The Noble Savage, A Study in Romantic Naturalism, xviin.
Fairfield, Connecticut, 32, 33, 36.
Falls of St. Anthony, xl.
Fay, Bernard: quoted, xvin.
—L'Esprit révolutionnaire en France et aux Etats-Unis à la fin du xviiie siècle, xvin.
firebrand: blowing on (courtship custom), 78, 120.
fireflies: Crèvecoeur's description of borrowed, xliin.
firewaters, 88, 125.
firs, 97.
fish: custom of leaving every nineteenth, 121; natural antipathy of, 147.
fish(ing) hawk: and bald eagle, 9-10.
Fishing Creek, 35.
Fishkill County, New York, 13, 15.
flax, 24
Florida territory, xxxviii, xxxixn, 147n.
flour (wheat) mills: at Buttermilk Fall, of John Allison, 16; of J. Thorn, 16-17.
flutes: travelers play on for Indians, 74.
Forbes family: its hospitality, 61-63.
forests: evils of decimating, 123, 125, 134.
Fort Niagara, xxi.
Fort Schuyler: Indian Council at, xxxiii.
Fort Stanwix: Indian council at, xx, xxxiii.

France, xiv, xv, xvi, xvii, xviii, xx, xxii, xxxvii.
Franklin, Benjamin (see also Adams), xviii; correspondent of Crèvecoeur, xxix; paper by in Imlay's Description, xxxv; "authority" used in Voyage, xxxv, xxxvii, xxxviii.
Franklin and Marshall College: Franklin's supposed speech at, xxxvii-xxxviii.
frontier: Crèvecoeur's analysis of, xxiii, xxiv, xxv, xxvi, xxviii, xxx, xliii, 32-34, 35-48.

Gabriel, Ralph Henry (editor of Crèvecoeur), xviin.
geldings: of Colonel Woodhull, 19.
Genesees, 109.
Georgia, xxxvii.
German Flats, New York, 40.
Germany, xliii; Mr. Erskine's visit to, 29.
Gibbon, Edward, xiii.
ginseng, 47.
Good Spirit (see also Manitou, Agan Kitchee; and Great Spirit), 76, 82, 83, 92, 104, 123.
Goshen, New York, xxiv, 18n, 23.
Gothic castle: Crèvecoeur's description of, xliii.
Gott, Percy V. D.: authority for Schunnemunk Mountain, 18n.
Great Kanawha River, 3.
Great Lakes, xv, xxiv, xl.
Great Lakes region (see also Middle West and Mississippi territory), xv.
Great Spirit (see also Manitou, Agan Kitchee; and Good Spirit), 105, 124, 125.
Grimm, Jakob, xxviii.
Gulf Stream, xxxvii.
gum: for covering canoe, 119.

Hackensack River, 29.
Hall, James (see McKenney).
Hartford, Connecticut, xxi.
Haverstraw Bay, 4.
Hazard, Lucy L., xxvi.
Hazen, Frederick: supposed aide-decamp of Bouquet, xxxv, xxxvii, xxxviii, xxix; supposed trip to South, xxxviii, xxxixn.
Hazlitt, William, xxviii, xliv.
Heart, Major Jonathan: used by Imlay, xxxv; used by Crèvecoeur, xxxv.
hemlock, 4, 7.
Herman, M.: his naïveté, xx; as confidant, xx; in New England, xxi; sails for Europe, xxi; at Niagara, xxvi; visits Simon DeWitt, xxvii;

Index   167

Herman, M. (*continued*):
contrasted with narrator, xxxii; with
Mr. E., xl; curiosity of, 16; reflections
of on pioneer life, 34; courage of
tested, 35; observes origin of society,
36-37; comments on Mr. Nadowisky's
happiness, 47-48; loses flint and steel,
50-51; anger of at companion, 52;
delirium and torments of when lost,
54; resolution of to kill self, 55; and
narrator saved by herd of cows, 58-
60; remorse of, 59; and narrator with
Forbes family, 60-63; a primitivist,
72-73; and companion play on flutes
for Indians, 74.
Hessian Fly, 16.
Highlands, the, 3.
Hooper, Sir Robert, xxvi-xxvii.
Hoppajewot (Indian Utopia), xxxi,
xxxii, 120-26; wonderful life in, 120-
21; visited by whites, 122-26; people
of astonished at visitors' customs, 122;
people of listen to white medicine
men, 124; people of drive away
white men, 126.
Hotchelaga (*Montreal*), people of, 88.
Houdetot, Elizabeth Françoise Sophie,
Comtesse d': friend of Crèvecoeur,
xv, xxix.
Hudson River, xxi, xxx, 1-15, 26n.
Hume, David, xiii.
Hunter, Colonel, 101, 102, 103, 116.
Hutchins, Thomas: used by Imlay,
xxxv.

Imlay, Gilbert, xviii, xxiin, xxxv,
xxxvi, xxxviiin, xl.
—*Description of the Western Territory
of North America*, xxii.
Indian council (*see also* Indians): at
Onondaga, xx, xxxiii, xxxvii, xli; at
Fort Stanwix, xx, xxxiii; at Fort
Schuyler, xxxiii.
Indian tales: analysis and influence of,
116-17.
Indians (*see also* Indian council):
Crèvecoeur on, xiii, xxxi, xxxii,
xxxiv, xxxv, xxxvi-xl; tales of and
legends of, xiii, xxxi, xxxii, xxxvii;
analysis of by Rice, xviin; travelers
who wrote about, xviii, xxxvi; unhappy at Onondaga, xxix; material
on in *Voyage*, xxx, xxxi, xxxvi-xl; a
winter among the, xxxi; debates between, xxxii-xxxiv; Lafayette speaks
to, xxxiv; metaphorical language of,
xxxiv-xxxv; of Georgia and Florida,
xxxvii; antiquities of, xxxvii, xxxviii,
xli; theory of sexual impotence of,
xxxix-xl; Crèvecoeur's notes on, xli.

Indies, 3.
indigo, 21, 22.
industry (*see Voyage*).
ironworks, xxiv, xxx; at Sterling, 26-
29, 30; at Ringwood, 29-30, 147; at
Charlottenburg, 30; at Bellvale, 30.
Iroquois, xxxvii, 88n.

Jamaica, xxiv, xxv, 23, 25, 64, 65.
Jefferson, Thomas, xviii; correspondent
of Crèvecoeur, xxix; refutation of
Buffon by, xl.
—*Notes on the State of Virginia*: used
in "Wabemat's Reward," xxxii, 130n;
used at least twice in *Voyage*, xl.
Jenner, Samuel, 10n.
Johnson, Sir William, xli, 96.
Josselyn, John, xviii.
Juniata River, xx.
Juniata Valley, xxi.

Kahawabash: despondent at loss of
family, 81-83.
Kalm, Pehr, xxiv.
Kanadoghary (*see also* Kanajoharry):
at Philadelphia conference, xxxiiin.
Kanajoharry (*see also* Kanadoghary):
at Onondaga council, xxxiiin.
Katarakouy, salmon of, 87.
Kayaderossera (Genesee sachem), 109.
Kayo (*friend*), 73, 101, 112.
keeper of forest reserve: nature of, 152;
duties of, 153; melancholy story of,
154, 157; misanthropy of, 157.
Kentucky, xxxviii, 47.
Keskeminetas (grandfather of
Wequash), 78.
Kesketomah: debate with Koohassen,
xxxiii, xxxiv, xxxv, 75, 76; host to
travelers, 73; first speech at council,
85-88; response to Koohassen, 91-92.
Kippokitta: adopts Kittagawmick as
husband, 94-95.
Kittagawmick: adopted by Mohawk
woman, 95.
Koohassen: debate with Kesketomah,
xxxiii, xxxiv, 33, 91.
Koreyhoosta: Kesketomah quotes, 86.
Koronkioga (Genesee sachem), 109.

Labrador tea, 22.
Lackawack (village), 79.
Lafayette, Marie Joseph Paul Yves
Roch Gilbert du Motier, Marquis de,
xxix; speech to Indians, xxxiv.
Lahontan, Louis Armand de Lom
d'Arce, Baron de, xviii, xxxvi.
Lamb, Charles, xxviii.
Land of Dreams (*see* Hoppajewot).
landscape poets, xviii, xxxi.

larches, 98.
La Rochefoucauld-Liancourt, François-Alexandre-Frédéric, Duc de, xxix.
laws: aid manufacturing and trade, 3, 33.
Lawson, John, xviii, xxxvi, 10n.
—*A New Voyage to Carolina*, xxxvin.
leaves: displacement of, 50.
Long, John: Crèvecoeur's use of, xl.
—*Travels of an Indian Interpreter and Trader*, xln, 70n, 73n, 77n, 79n, 88n, 91n, 102n, 121n, 123n, 124n, 135n, 144n.
Long Island, 20.
Loyalist, xv, xxiii, xxvii.
Lyons, E. Wilson: *The Man Who Sold Louisiana*, xxxivn.
Luzerne County, Pennsylvania, xxiv, 36.

McKenney, Thomas L., and James Hall: *History of the Indian Tribes of North America*, xxxivn.
Madison, James, xxxix.
Magazine of American History, xxvii.
Magdeburg, Germany, 35.
Magellan: lands discovered by, 71.
mammoth: Manitou explains reason for, 129-30; Manitou's prophecy about borrowed from Jefferson, 130n.
Manitou, Agan Kitchee (*see also* Good Spirit *and* Great Spirit), xxxi, 82, 83, 92, 104, 105; descends to earth, 127; as wolf, 127-28; as bear, 128; as fox, 128; as buffalo, 129; as dog, 130-31; as otter, 131-32; as man, 132, 133, 135-45; as squirrel, 133-35; prophecy of about coming of man, 134-35; on his function, 135, 141-42, 144; on nature and destiny of man, 137-38; in Wabemat's home, 138; offers Wabemat new life as beaver, 142; explains destiny and nature of beaver, 142-44.
Manitou, Agan Matchee (*see also* Evil Spirit), xxxiv, 77, 79, 80, 81, 83, 84, 107.
maple sugar, 22, 25, 47.
maple syrup, 22, 25.
maple trees, xli, 25, 156.
maple vinegar, 22, 25.
Maskinonge (tribe), 76, 85.
maskinonge (fish), xxxv, 79.
Massotawana (Chickasaw warrior): falls in love with Napotelima, 110; his ordeals to win her, 118-19; Mico Tatoba's speech to, 119-20.
Matamusket, 78.
manufacturing (*see Voyage*).
Mawhingon (tribe), 88.
Meegeeses (tribe), 79.
melting pot, xxiii.

mergum-megat (*smallpox*), 82, 103, 108.
Meshoppen, Pennsylvania, ferry at, 35.
Michilimackinac, 114.
Mico Tatoba: father of Napotelima, 118; tests Massotawana, 118-19; admonishes Massotawana, 119-20.
Middle West (*see also* Great Lakes region *and* Mississippi territory), xl.
Minickwac (chief of Christian Mohawks), 94-95.
Missisages (Indian nation), 86.
Mississippi: nations of the, 90.
Mississippi River, xviii, xl, 130.
Mississippi territory (*see also* Middle West *and* Great Lakes region), xxxviii.
Missouri River, xviii.
Mitchell, Julia Post: opinion of concerning the *Voyage*, xvii.
—*St. John de Crèvecoeur*, xivn.
Mohawk Indians, xxxi, 40, 73n, 95, 102n, 116; band of and Cayugas telling stories, 116.
Mohawk League, 88.
Mohawk River, xx, xxi.
Mohawks, Christian, 93.
Mondajewot (dead husband of Muskanehong), 79.
Montcalm de Saint-Veran, Louis Joseph, Marquis de, xiv.
Montesquieu, Charles de Secondat, Baron de la Brède et de, xiii.
Montreal, 70, 88n, 94.
Moore, J. B.: praise of Crèvecoeur, xxiii.
—"Rehabilitation of Crèvecoeur," xxiiin.
Moors: and slavery, 66.
Moreau de Saint Méry, Médéric Louis Elie, xxiv.
Morgan, Lewis H.: *League of the Ho-do-no-sau-nee*, xxxiiin.
moss, 155, 157.
Mount Ararat, Pennsylvania, 37.
Mount Vernon, 27.
Mulhausen, Reverend: aids and advises Mr. Nadowisky, 40-45; his analysis of frontier life, 41-45; on trees, 43-44; on laws, 44; on education, 44-45.
Muncie Creek, 33, 34.
Murderer's Creek, 16.
Muskanehong: complaints of at death of husband, 79-81.
Muskingum, forks of, 112.

Nadowisky, Mr., xxiv, xxv, xxix; his hospitality, 38; his ambition, 38; his history, 39-40, 45-48; as doctor, 39-40; marries daughter of Reverend Mulhausen, 40; his orchard, 46; his barn, 46.

Nagooar-Missey (Cayuga chief), 110.
Nantucket, xxviii.
Naponset, 81.
Napotelima: loved and won by Massotawana, 118-20.
Narragansetts, 86.
Narrows, the, 2.
Nashville, Tennessee, xxxviii.
Nassanicomy: brings useful plants to man, 124.
Nassau, 22.
Naticks, 86.
nature: state of versus civilization, 70-73.
"nature de salon" (*see* landscape poets).
Nepinah, rapid of, 79.
New England, xxi, xliii.
New England system of laying out districts: adopted by New York, xxviii.
New Guinea, 72.
New Haven, Connecticut, xxi, xxiv, xxx.
New Jersey, xv-xvi, xix, xxi, xxvi, 2, 13, 17, 29, 30, 43.
New Windsor, New York, 1, 15.
New World, xiii, xiv, xx, 75.
New York, bay of, 29.
New York City, xv, xvi, xviii, xxi, 2, 3, 10, 39, 46, 101.
New York State, xv, xix, xx, xxi, xxii, xxiv, xxvi, xxvii, xxviii, xli, 29, 64, 67.
New Zealand, 71, 72.
Nezalonga (dead wife of Kahawabash), 82.
Niagara, Fort of, 110, 112, 126.
Niagara Falls, xiii, xxi, xxvi-xxvii, xxx, xxxi, xl, 83, 97, 100.
Niagara River, xxvii, 101.
Ninnerwind, forest of, xxxi, 121.
Nishynorbay (*Indian*), 88, 105, 125, 140.
Niskotowasse (Chickasaw village), 117.
Nissooassoo, Henry (great chief of Mohawks), 95.
Noble Savage, xviii, xxxi, xxxvi.
Nobscusset (dead son of Siasconset), 83.
North America (*see* America).
North Carolina, xxvi.
Northern Powers: divide Poland, 39.
Northumberland County, Pennsylvania, xx, 33, 47.
notes: of Crèvecoeur to the *Voyage* described, xli.
Noyawanda, district of: a Utopia, 128-29.

oak(s), xli, 7, 43, 46, 119, 155, 157.
Ockwacok, 78.
odzizia (*wine*), 107.
O'Hara, James (Indian agent), xxxix.
O'Harrah, Adrien: Indian tale ascribed to, xxxvii, xxxix.

Ohio country: Bouquet's expedition into, xxxvii; antiquities of, xxxviii; protection of, 24; narrator's travels in, 101.
Ohio River, xv, xviii.
Okemaw (*Chief*): orders investigation of strangers, 121; welcomes white men, 122; gives permission to whites to plant seeds, 122; warned by Awakesh, 123; orders council with whites, 123; whites refuse to hear his medicine men, 124; indignation of, 124-25; drives off whites and obliterates their traces, 126.
Onas, land of (*Pennsylvania*), 73.
Oneida, Lake, xxi.
Oneida Nation, xxxiii*n*, 70, 87, 90, 92, 101, 108.
Onondaga (village), xx, xxi, xxix, xxx, xxxii, xxxiii, xxxvii, xli, 64, 116; travelers arrive at, 70; council at, 75-92.
Onondagas: Agouehghon among, 110.
Ononthyo (*Canadian government*), 103.
Ontario (narrator's dog), 56-57.
Ontario, Lake, xxi, xl, 68, 110.
opoygan: travelers smoke, 70, 73; Kesketomah smokes, 91.
Orange County, New York, xv, xxx, 17.
Orangeburg, South Carolina, 147*n*.
orators: from Cherryhum speak to people of Hoppajewot, 124.
Orikomah (a root), 140.
Oriskany: council fire at, 95.
Oriskany River, xxi.
Orsa, Poland, 38.
Ossewingo (village), 74, 76.
Oswegatchie (village), 95.
Oswegatchie River, 93.
Oswego, xxi; Agouehghon at, 110.
Otsego, Lake, xxi, xxx.
Otsego County, New York, xx, 46.
Ousiato (tribe), xxx.
Outagamy (tribe), 81.
Ouyatanons, 112.

Pakatakan (Indian family), 82.
Parrington, V. L.: praise of Crèvecoeur, xxiii*n*, xxiv-xxv.
—*Main Currents in American Thought*, xxv*n*.
Passaic River, xxi, xxx.
Paxson, Frederick L., xxviii.
peach brandy, 22.
peach trees, 2.
Pegick Sagat (*First Man*), 124.
Penn, William, 61.
Pennsylvania, xix, xx, xxi, xxii, xxiv, xxviii, xxix, xli, 17, 31, 32, 33, 62, 64, 73*n*.
Pennsylvania Archives, xxxiii*n*.

170

Pentagoet (village), 81.
Pepin, Lake, xl.
Pequots, 86.
Philadelphia (see also Exchange in), xviii, xxxiiin, xxxviii.
Philippopolis, Pennsylvania, xx, 37.
pine(s), 4, 7, 43, 46, 98, 155.
Poland, xxiv; Mr. Nadowisky from, 39; dismemberment of, 39, 40; life in contrasted to life in New York, 41.
Pontiac, xli.
Pooploskill (waterfall), 11.
Poopoko: welcomes Agouehghon, 109.
Potash, 47.
Potomac River, 3.
Poughkeepsie, New York, 1.
Prideaux River, 116.
punch, 23.
purple kalmias, 156.

Quakers: and maple sugar, 47.
Queen Charlotte (river), 67.

·Red Jacket: his debate with Cornplanter, xxxiii-xxxiv.
reserves: in mountains for animals, 151-58; supervised by keeper, 152.
Rice, Howard C.: his opinion of the *Voyage*, xvii.
—*Le Cultivateur américain*, xivn, xviin.
rice, 61n; mythical origin of, 124.
Ringwood (see ironworks).
Robinson Crusoe: keeper of reserve compared to, 157.
Romans, Bernard: used by Crèvecoeur, xxxv, xxxix.
Romanticism, xviii, xxx, xxxi.
Rush, Benjamin: used by Imlay, xxxv.
Russia, 39.
Russians: supposed trip of two, xl.

Saganash (*English soldiers*), 103.
St. Anthony (see Falls of).
St. George, Nassau, 22.
Saint-Lambert, Jean François de, xv, xxix, xxxi.
St. Lawrence River, xviii, xxxi, 93.
St. Pierre River, xl.
salmon, 62, 74, 87, 154.
salt: feeding of to animals, xxx, xlii, 146-53, 158; mixed with sulphur and antimony, 147; effect of lack of on horses, sheep, and swine, 148; method of feeding, 148-49; need of by bees, 149, 150-51; fed by keeper of reserve, 153.
salt lick farms, 37.
salt licks, xli, 147.
Sandusky (Indian village), 108.
Sanna Tella (*Companion*), 124.

Index

Saratoga: capitulation at, 14.
Sato, Shosuke, xxviii.
S. B.: marries Jesse Woodhull, 21-22.
scale of being: plan of nature, 72.
scarat (*brandy*), 101; evil influence of on Indians, 108-109.
Schenectady, New York, xxi.
Schoharie, New York, xx, 46.
Schunnemunk Mountain, 24.
Schunnemunk Valley, xxiv, 20, 25; home of Jesse Woodhull, 18; Crèvecoeur's spelling "Skonomonk," 18n.
Scotland: Mr. Erskine's visit to, 29.
sea bass, 9.
Seagrove, Mr., xxv.
Senecas, 92.
sentimentality, xviii, xxxi.
sesame oil, 22.
shad, 47.
Shenendoah (Indian village), 109.
Shenendoah River, 3.
Sherrill, Charles H.: *French Memories of Eighteenth Century America*, xvin.
Shickshinny Creek, 33, 34.
Shippenburg, Pennsylvania, xx, xxi.
Siasconset: speaks to council, 81-84.
Siategan (Chippeway chief), 70, 73.
Sierre Leone River, 66.
Six Nations, xxxiii.
"Skanandoé": Crèvecoeur reports Oneida Nation met at, xxxiiin.
Skenenton (tribe), 84.
Skonomonk (see Schunnemunk Valley).
slavery: bachelor farmer on, 65-66.
Smith, Dr. William: Crèvecoeur's use of, xxxviii, xl.
—*Historical Account of Bouquet's Expedition Against the Ohio Indians in 1764*, xxxviii.
soap, 24-25.
South, the, xxii, xxxviii, xxxixn.
South Carolina, 147n, 153n, 157.
Southey, Robert, xxviii.
Spiller, Robert E., ed., *The Literary History of the United States*, xviin.
squash: mythical origin of, 124.
Staten Island, 2.
Sterling, Lord, xxvi.
Sterling Ironworks (see ironworks).
sturgeon, 14, 119.
sugar, 21, 47.
sugar maples (see maple trees).
Surinam, 21.
surveying: Crèvecoeur authority on, xxvii-xxviii.
Susquehanna River, xx, xxiv, xxv, xxx, 33, 35n, 36, 46, 47.
Sussex County, New York, 17.
Swank, James M.: *History of the Manufacture of Iron in All Ages*, 26n.

Index

Sweden: iron of better than that of New York, 28; Mr. Erskine's visit to, 29; visit with colonist from, 36.
sycamore, 2.
symbolic names in *Voyage*, xxxi, 79n, 121n, 124n, 135n.

Tappan Sea, 2.
Temiskaming (dead wife of Wequash), 77-78.
Tempests, Isle of, 144.
Tempests, Lake of (*Lake Michigan*), 141, 145.
Tennessee River, 3.
tewtag (fish), xxxv, 79.
Thorn, J.: his flour mill, 16-17; his statistics on making and cost of flour, 17.
Thunder-Berg, 4.
Tibarimaw (*fate*): superior to Manitou, 135.
Tienaderhah: despair at loss of child, 84-85.
Tienah (dead son of Siasconset), 83.
Tigheny (dead daughter of Tienaderhah), 84-85.
Tioga (dead son of Siasconset), 83.
Tioga County, New York, xx, 46.
Tippet, Mehitable (Crèvecoeur's wife), xv.
tobacco: as offering to Matchee Manitou, 80; mythical origin of, 124.
Tocksikanehiow l'Anier: travelers dine with, 74.
torches: Massotawana fishes with, 119.
Toronto, 83.
Townsend, Peter: owner of Sterling Ironworks, 26; his hospitality, 26; his furnace, 26-27; his statistics and products, 26-28; his forge, 27; on George Washington, 27-28; his meadow, 28-29.
travel books: about America, xviii, xxii.
Treat, Payson, xxviii.
Tugaloo (in South Carolina), 153, 158.
tulip, 2.
Tully "County," New York, xxi.
turkeys, wild, 53.
Turgot, Anne Robert Jacques, Baron de l'Aulne, xxix.
Turner, Frederick J., xxvi; Crèvecoeur's foreshadowing of, xxv.
Tuskaroras, 92.
Tyler, Moses Coit: opinion of Crèvecoeur, xxx.

Ulster County, New York, xv, 17.
United States, xxiv, xxxviii.
Utopia, xxx, xxxi.

Venango (husband of Tienaderhah), 84-85.
Verplanck's Point, 4.
Vining (supposed senator from Delaware), xxxviii.
Virginia, xix, xxi, xxvi.
Voltaire, François Marie Arouet de, xiii.
Voyage: in German, xiin; as history, xiii, xxiii-xxviii; as literature, xiii, xxviii-xxxv; neglect of, xiii, xvi, xvii; compared with Crèvecoeur's other books, xiii-xiv, xxix-xxxi; Crèvecoeur's most pretentious book, xiii-xiv, xvii; as travel book, xviii-xxii; models for, xviii, xxii; arbitrary organization of, xix-xx, xxi, xxii, xliii; not best title, xix-xx; romantic subject matter of, xxii; omissions from in *Eighteenth-Century Travels in Pennsylvania & New York*, xxvi-xxvii, xxxi, xliii-xliv; romanticism in, xxx-xxxi; realism in, xxx; optimism in, xxx; Indian material in, xxxi-xxxv, xxxvi-xl, 70-96, 101-45; on evils of cannibalism (*see* cannibalism); on evil influence of whites on Indians, xxxi, 88-90, 107-109, 120-26; humor in, xxxii; character depiction in, xxxii-xxxiv; style of, xxxiv-xxxv; figures of speech in, xxxiv-xxxv; plagiarisms in, xxxv-xli; essays in attributed to other writers, xxxv-xl; borrowings from Carver, xxxvii, xxxix, xl; borrowings from Franklin, xxxvii; borrowings from Imlay, xxxviii; borrowings from William Smith, xxxviii; borrowings from Bartram, xxxix, xl; borrowings from Long, xl; borrowings from Jefferson, xl; problems of making selections from, xliii-xliv; faults of, xliii; on commerce, manufacturing, and industry, 3; on brevity of time, 23, 33, 42; on primitivism versus progress, 70-73.

Wabash River, 112.
Wabemat: rescued from pit by Manitou, 135-37; his misery, 135-36; takes Manitou to his dwelling, 138; abhors cannibalism, 139-40; abhors war, 140; blessed by Manitou, 140; accepts Manitou's offer and becomes first beaver, 142-45.
"Wabemat's Reward": supposed author of, xxxix; tells of custom of leaving every fifth beaver, 121n, 145.
Wappanome (father of Massotawana), 117.

Index

War of Independence (*see also* American Revolution), 13.
Washington, George, xviii, xxxviii; his map of Hudson River passageway, 12; his supervision of his estate, 27-28; his secret services during Revolution, 28.
Wawassing (village), 88.
Weld, Isaac: *Travels through the United States of America*, 121n.
wennasimah (a root), 140.
Wenowee (mythical river), 132, 140.
Wequash: despondent at death of wife, 76-78.
West, 22.
West Point: cannon for retreat at, 12; fortifications at, 12, 14; chain across river at, 12, 14, 26n.
whiskey: Cayuga prefers to wine, 117.
Whitestown, New York, xxi.
wig: of white man pulled off by Okemaw, 126.
Wilkes-Barre, Pennsylvania, 32.
Williams, Stanley T. (ed. of Crèvecoeur), xviin.
Wilmington, Delaware, xxi.
Wilson, Mr., 64, 69.
wine: Agouehghon's praise of, 101-102, 107; travelers drink with Agoueh-

wine (*continued*): ghon, 101, 115; narrator offers to Cayuga, 117.
Wollstonecraft, Mary (Godwin): friend of Crèvecoeur, xxiin, xxix.
—*Letters from Sweden, Norway, and Denmark*, xxiin.
Woodhull, Colonel Jesse: friend of Crèvecoeur, xxiv; third-generation farmer, xxvi; travelers visit, xxx, 18-25; his estate, 18; his method of farming, 18; his experiments with heifers, 18; his geldings, 18, 19; his plans for his children, 19; account of clearing and developing his estate, 20-21; his father's help, 20-21; his wife, 21-22; his professor brother at Yale, 22; repairs own plow, 23; his duties as citizen, 23; on brevity of seasons, 23-24; colonel of militia, 23, 24; duties of wife of, 24; his maple orchard, 25.
wool, 24.
wotta-tawah (a root), 140.
Wyandots, 108.
Wyolusing River, 37.

Yoyogheny: speaks to council, 78-81.
Yoywassy (Ottawa sachem), 70, 73.

www.ingramcontent.com/pod-product-compliance
Lightning Source LLC
Chambersburg PA
CBHW022059160426
43198CB00008B/285